Guide to

Export-Import
Basics

SECOND EDITION

The world business organization

A number of contributors collaborated in an active and helpful way to prepare the second edition of this publication. We would like to express our appreciation in particular to:

- *Jonas Astrup*
- *Stefano Bertasi*
- *Ayesha Hassan*
- *Guillermo Jiménez*
- *Emmanuel Jolivet*
- *Ron Katz*
- *Viviane Schiavi*
- *Corinne Truong*
- *Christiaan van der Valk*

First edition *by Guillermo Jiménez* published in May 1997.
Second edition published in March 2003 by

ICC PUBLISHING S.A.
An affiliate of ICC: the world business organization
38, Cours Albert 1er
75008 Paris - France

This edition is published by arrangement with ICC Publishing S.A.

ICC Publishing, Inc.
156 Fifth Avenue
New York, New York 10010
www.iccbooksusa.com

ICC Publication No. 641
ISBN 92 842 1309 6

Foreword

By Maria Livanos Cattaui
Secretary General, ICC

When *Guide to Export-Import Basics* first appeared in 1997, it struck a chord among readers who were pleased to find, in a single volume, an overview of the world of trade – from preparing the sales contract to the arranging of transport and the settling of international disputes. The text, both compact and highly practical, was welcomed by traders and practitioners worldwide.

But the world has moved on since 1997, and it was necessary that a new edition of this book reflect the changes that have taken place. These include, among others, an increasing globalization of markets, a marked increase in the use of electronic documents, and a series of new rules and contracts that take into account the commercial realities of the 21st century.

This revised second edition of *Guide to Export-Import Basics* admirably explains these developments. Written by a team of experts from the International Chamber of Commerce (ICC), the organization responsible for drafting many of the rules that govern international trade, this revised text covers, among other items, *Incoterms 2000*; *ISP98*, the new rules on standby letters of credit; the *eUCP,* an electronic supplement to the ICC rules on documentary credits; and the amendments to international model contracts, such as the *ICC Model Distributorship Contract*. The authors of this book were instrumental in bringing these important new ICC documents to completion.

Since its inception in 1919, ICC's mission has been to facilitate world trade. Whether by the creation of contractual rules – such as Incoterms and UCP 500 – or by advocating the business point of view before governments and international organizations, ICC has fulfilled that mission consistently through the years. The publication of this second edition of *Guide to Export-Import Basics* is yet another of the practical "tools for trade" that ICC provides to the world business community.

February 2003

A note on terminology

In general, the terms EXPORTER and IMPORTER will be used to denote the SELLER and BUYER. However, it should be remembered that especially when intermediaries or brokers are involved, the seller may very well not be the original supplier, nor the buyer the ultimate importer.

The reader should be familiar with at least the following basic terms that may be used to refer to either the exporter or importer in different stages of the export transaction.

Contract of sale

Exporter – SELLER

Importer – BUYER

Transport

Exporter – SHIPPER; CONSIGNOR

Importer – RECEIVER; CONSIGNEE

Transport service providers: CARRIER, SHIPPING LINE, FREIGHT FORWARDER

Letter of Credit

Exporter – BENEFICIARY

Importer – OPENER; APPLICANT; ACCOUNT PARTY

Banks involved –

Importer's bank: ISSUING BANK (and also, in some cases, ADVISING BANK, CONFIRMING BANK, PAYING BANK)

Exporter's bank: PAYING BANK, ADVISING BANK, and/or CONFIRMING BANK

Bill of exchange

Exporter – DRAWER

Importer – DRAWEE

Payment obligations

Exporter – CREDITOR; PAYEE

Importer – DEBTOR; PAYER

Table of contents

CHAPTER ONE

Beginnings: an Introduction to Export–Import Practice

"A pocket full of currants, c.i.f. London...."
T.S. Eliot, The Waste Land

The basics: Professional exporters and importers increase profits and reduce risks by relying on time–tested practices and techniques. In particular, the export trade requires a mastery of the relevant contracts and documents. Thus, traders should understand how to construct an effective and complete contract of sale, since this "master" contract will in turn determine the other documents to be procured, such as the transport document (e.g., bill of lading), insurance policy, and payment–related documents (e.g., documentary credit).

1.1 Scope of book

This book is intended as a concise introduction to export–import practice, with a focus on the legal, finance, and transport aspects of international trade in goods. We will concentrate primarily on the export sale of *goods*, as opposed to the sale of services or other intangibles, such as intellectual property (i.e., patents, licences, trademarks), or financial products (i.e., stocks, bonds). A solid understanding of the international sale of goods will provide traders with the conceptual framework necessary to understand more complex international transactions, such as those involving services, intellectual property or financial products.

1.2 Why export and import? The benefits of international trade

a. EXPORTING

In practice, small firms may begin exporting simply through the receipt of unsolicited orders from abroad, rather than as a result of any formal management decision or export strategy. As the volume of export orders grows, management begins to pay attention to export, and may set up an *export department*. In some cases, small trade ventures have been precursors of mighty export empires. Toyota's exports to Europe in the 1950s started at the initiative of a Danish auto dealer who travelled to Japan and bought a few trial cars.

Sometimes exporting begins after a firm has had a successful showing at a foreign trade show, and starts to receive a volume of export orders. Whatever the initial impetus, it makes sense for companies to invest in export whenever they believe it will maximize their long–term revenues or competitiveness. In the past, many companies exported only after domestic markets had become saturated or when it came to their knowledge that extremely high profit margins could be earned from sales to particular foreign markets. However, in today's increasingly integrated global markets, many companies adopt an export programme as a necessary part of competitive strategy, i.e., "export or die". If a company's competitors are exporting, it may need to do so as well to avoid being placed at a disadvantage.

One of the main sources of competitive advantage today lies in a company's ability to learn faster than competitors. Export activities, in particular, enhance a company's status as a "learning" organization. The contact with international customers and foreign marketing and distribution techniques can teach the firm lessons which may prove useful even in the firm's home market. Economies of scale can be achieved with export training, because once personnel have been trained for international trade with one country, that knowledge can be applied to trade with future markets.

Another attraction of exporting is that selling in more than one country diversifies risk, because the firm is no longer wholly dependant on sales from any single market. Exporting also tends to diminish the impact of a domestic deceleration in sales, because the life cycle in foreign export markets tends to lag behind that of the domestic market. When sales are slow in the domestic market, they are often still strong in the export markets. Transitions can then be made more easily to new products.

Since governments consider strong exports to be essential for a healthy economy, most countries provide a variety of public support services for exporting firms. This support ranges from publications and expert advice to subsidised export credit insurance and low–cost loans. Local chambers of commerce often provide assistance in terms of training and counsel. Small companies that have not fully investigated possibilities for government support may be unaware of low–cost consulting and finance that would greatly increase their chances of success.

b. IMPORTING

On the import side, a variety of brokers, sales representatives, agents, whole–sale buyers, re–sellers and distributors are occupied with bringing products into the domestic market. Importers are often marketing professionals who work exclusively in the domestic market. Frequently, the only international aspect of their business is the supply contract.

In small or rapidly developing markets, there may be competition amongst domestic merchants to sign on as agents or distributors for manufacturers of prestigious foreign brands. Some very large companies have grown by expanding upon foreign representative status, eventually becoming manu-facturers in their own right under licence. Thus, Turkey's largest company, Koç Holding A.S., grew in the 1920s and 1930s as an importer of Ford and General Electric products, then became a manufacturer in its own right in the 1940s and 1950s.

One of the advantages of importing is that it provides a relatively low–cost entry into international trade. It is possible to begin to broker import trade transactions even with the most minimal of office facilities. Some very successful import traders started out with nothing more than a table–top and a telephone. Other importers have started up when they discovered attractive, low–cost products while travelling in foreign countries, and realized that these products had great market potential in their home country.

1.3   The need for a professional approach

A professional approach to exporting and importing provides the surest way for companies to manage the risks inherent in international transactions. Ideally, each of the parties involved in an international sale would understand the entire process and its component sub–processes. The exporter and importer, bankers, carriers, insurers, inspectors and customs officials, would understand each others' roles. They would further understand the use of each of the legal, banking and transport documents upon which the transaction is grounded.

In reality, however, one often finds that overall understanding of the export process is not widespread. Traders are often expert, for example, in calculating costs and opportunities, but they may not understand transport logistics, preferring to delegate this to freight forwarders. A trade banker will understand perfectly the documentary credit mechanism, but may not fathom the legal implications of the underlying contract. Likewise, the lawyer may prove ignorant as regards marine insurance; and so on. No one can be expert on everything, but some familiarity with the basics of the entire transaction will help alert traders to those areas where they need to consult specialist colleagues, such as trade bankers, lawyers, insurers or customs agents.

1.4 The risks of exporting and importing

Intelligent risk management is at the heart of international trade. While risk is an element of all commercial transactions, international trade multiplies and adds risks to those encountered in domestic trade:

a. TRANSPORT–RELATED RISKS

International transportation tends to involve greater distances, with cargo often changing hands or undergoing prolonged storage, so that there is a greater risk of damage, loss or theft, than in domestic trade. Consequently, exporters and importers must understand their legal rights against carriers. If the goods have been damaged through the carrier's fault or negligence, the carrier's liability may depend on the contractual provisions and shipping information contained in the *bill of lading* (a document which evidences the terms of the contract of carriage; examined at length in Chapter 9). Similarly, the importer needs to understand the extent of coverage provided by the insurance policy, because she may need to claim under its provisions if the goods are damaged during transport.

b. CREDIT RISK OR NON–PAYMENT RISK

Since it is often difficult for exporters to verify the creditworthiness and reputation of foreign buyers, there is an increased risk of non–payment, late payment, or outright fraud. Consequently, wary exporters frequently insist on payment by *irrevocable documentary credit*, (examined in detail in Chapter 6), or make use of other security devices (see Chapter 8).

c. QUALITY OF GOODS RISK

Importers may find it difficult to physically check the quality of the goods before shipment, and thus it may happen that they do not receive goods of the quality they had expected. One way of avoiding this is for the importer to insist on provision of an *inspection certificate*.

d. EXCHANGE RATE RISK

If a price has been set in a particular currency in an international contract, subsequent exchange rate fluctuations (between the contract currency and the accounting currencies of the parties) will inevitably benefit one party at the cost of the other. The easiest solution for a party wishing to avoid uncertainty is simply to stipulate contractual prices in one's own currency (note that this simple method does not truly *avoid* currency risk, because the trader still runs the risk that her own currency will weaken between the time of contract and the time of payment). Quoting prices in one's own currency is useful for small firms because it standardizes the currency of payment, which can facilitate accounting and cash–flow projections. However, in many cases it is commercially necessary to make quotes in various foreign currencies. In such cases, exporters will seek to protect themselves from exchange rate fluctuations, such as by purchasing foreign exchange *forward* or *option* contracts, sometimes referred to as *hedge* contracts.

e. UNFORESEEN EVENTS

A strike, natural disaster or war may render delivery impossible. Unexpected events may also dramatically alter the cost of transport, by raising the price of shipping fuel or by closing off the most economical routes. Well–drafted contractual *force majeure* provisions can help protect the parties; these are dealt with further in Chapter 4.

f. LEGAL RISKS

Foreign laws or regulations may change or be applied differently than in the past, impeding or frustrating the transaction. A customs licence may suddenly prove impossible to obtain. Moreover, whenever a contract is subject to the jurisdiction of foreign courts under foreign law, there arises the risk that it may prove impossible for the other party to obtain speedy justice in the event of a dispute. This is one reason why exporters and importers alike often seek to impose *choice of law* and *choice of forum* clauses, which stipulate that disputes will be settled under their own national law and courts. One way out of the resultant negotiating impasse is to contractually stipulate that dispute resolution will be by *international commercial arbitration*, such as that supervised by the *ICC International Court of Arbitration* (see chapter 3).

g. INVESTMENT RISKS

The normal commercial risks involved in marketing any product become magnified in the export context because of the additional investments required by an export programme. For example, a market which has been steadily growing for several years may suddenly decline (e.g., due to exchange rate instability), before an exporter can amortize investments in local distribution. Companies should begin by seriously considering whether or not to export at all. Some firms are not quite ready to export, and some may never be able to compete internationally and should concentrate on domestic niches. To launch a proper export effort requires the commitment of resources which can be irretrievably lost in the event of failure. This author is aware of companies that have gone bankrupt after investing heavily and over–optimistically in export operations which subsequently foundered.

1.5   The role of standard documents and systems

International trade is flourishing today because traders have learned to manage and overcome the risks listed above. Export–import risk management is based on documentary systems and customs which translate the rights, costs and responsibilities of the export process into documentary equivalents. Thus, the export process is actually twofold, involving :
1)   the real shipment of physical goods, and
2)   the complementary documentary exchanges.

This documentary system developed centuries ago through transactions referred to as "documentary sales" under the classic "shipment" trade terms, FOB and CIF[1]. Documentary sales have been considered by courts of law to be transactions in *documents* to the same extent that they are transactions in *goods*. It is just as important for the exporter to provide the correct documents as it is for him to provide the correct goods.

The key documents in this scheme can be quickly enumerated:
1)   the contract of sale,
2)   bill of lading (or other transport document),
3)   payment–related documents (particularly the documentary credit and bill of exchange or bank draft), and
4)   insurance document (policy, certificate or note).

A good deal of this book is devoted to a discussion of the relationship between these documents. Other important documents include the inspection or quality certificate and certificate of origin. Inspection and understanding of the above documents must be as painstaking as that related to the goods.

While there are advantages to this documentary system, there are also inherent risks. Paper documents are particularly susceptible to forgery, alteration or simple misrepresentation. In some cases, an importer may find that the documents presented are apparently conforming, but that the goods delivered contain defects. The unfortunate importer may be unable to stop or avoid payment, despite the exporter's breach of contract. Importers seek to protect themselves from these risks by carefully checking the identity of their counterparties, and in cases of doubt, by calling for verification, such as that provided by an inspection certificate.

On the exporter's side, the documentary system has a drawback in that the fulfilment of physical delivery does not excuse documentary failures. Thus, it is possible for an exporter to substantially perform a contract and yet find himself unable to receive prompt or complete payment, as a result of a failure to comply with a documentary formality. This is particularly a problem for small exporters who have requested payment by documentary credit, but then find that their own faulty record–keeping makes it impossible for them to present conforming documents in time. What was intended to be an irrevocable credit now becomes a credit conditional upon the importer's willingness to waive objections to the documentary discrepancies. The all–too–common result is delayed payment or other payment difficulties.

The only solution, for exporters and importers alike, is to make sure before entering into an international contract of sale that they thoroughly understand the documentary obligations that will be required of them.

Case Example

In a case in which goods were sold on terms "c.i.f. Hong Kong shipment from continental port not later than 31st October", the goods were actually shipped after that date, but the bill of lading was forged to indicate shipment on time. The buyers discovered the forgery only after having accepted physical delivery of the goods and did not make any objection to the quality of the goods delivered. The court observed:

"[T]here is a right to reject documents, and a right to reject goods, and the two things are quite distinct. A c.i.f. contract puts a number of obligations upon the seller, some of which are in relation to the goods and some of which are in relation to the documents. So far as the goods are concerned, he must put on board at the port of shipment goods in conformity with the contract description, but he must also send forward documents, and those documents must comply with the contract."

- Kwei Tek Chao v. British Traders & Shippers Ltd (1954) 2 QB 459

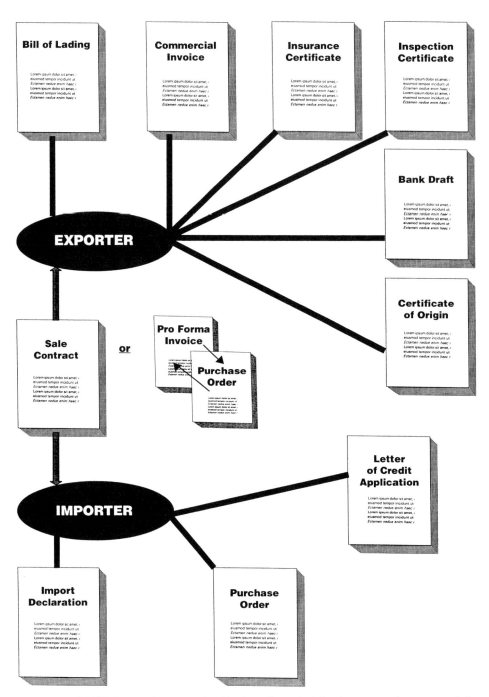

THE PAPER CHASE: Don't go into international business if you don't like documents – the export trade is a documentary game. A typical CIF treansaction may call for 10 or more important documents.

Documentary safeguards, such as those provided by the documentary credit or inspection certificate, can only do part of the overall job of countering international trade risk. Other important services, such as credit investigations, export credit insurance, and factoring, can help complete the risk–reduction plan. Moreover, traders should in general adopt verification procedures for all proposed international transactions – international fraud is a reality and all trade professionals should be aware of the need to verify credentials and deal only with established and well–known partners.

1.6   Cultural and language differences

Misunderstandings in international transactions can arise because the parties come from different cultures and express themselves with differing vocabularies.

Example

An Australian importer of clothing recounts the following story: He had ordered a custom shipment of 5,000 rugby shirts from a foreign supplier. The importer requested a sample shirt to test for cotton content in the fabric. He cut off one of the sleeves of the shirt at the elbow, extracted a few fibres, and tested them. Satisfied, he returned the shirt with the notation: "OK – send shipment as agreed." Several months later he received an irate call from a major clothing distributor, to whom the shipment had been sent directly. The client had received 5,000 rugby shirts – each missing one sleeve!

Not only do cultural and business practices differ across national borders, there are also differing tax systems, regulations, accounting methods, currency controls and customs systems. The same legal term, such as "agent", may have different legal connotations in different jurisdictions. Technical and product standards may differ, as well as consumer tastes. Providing after–sales service to remote markets may be prohibitively expensive, with the result that foreign products can acquire a bad reputation. Also, translating marketing brochures and technical manuals into foreign languages can be unexpectedly time–consuming and costly, especially when the documents must be frequently revised or updated.

1.7 Solutions: examples of risk management for export–import

Well–established professional practices enable traders to manage the above–described risks:

■ *The risk of misunderstanding, e.g., risk of disagreements over payment terms or quality conditions; risk of having to undertake a legal action in a foreign, biased forum.* SOLUTIONS

   – substantial credit checking of counterparties; demanding references
   – negotiating firmly for minimum legal protection, or refusing deal
   – use of well–drafted contracts and general terms and conditions, including provisions for choice of law/forum, arbitration
   – specifying *Incoterms 2000*
   – well–researched and well–prepared contract negotiations

■ *The exporter's risk of non–payment.*
   SOLUTIONS
   – use of suitable payment securities, such as the documentary credit under UCP 500
   – alternative: using open account terms backed by a standby credit or demand guarantee

■ *The importer's risk that goods of inadequate quality will be shipped.*
   SOLUTION
   – requirement of inspection certificates made out by recognized authorities

■ *The risk that the other party will not go ahead with performance as promised.*
   SOLUTION
   – partial advance payment, e.g., bank guarantees, standby credits; also, use of performance bonds

■ *The risk that the goods will be damaged in transit, or lost, or that part of the shipment will be stolen.* SOLUTIONS

   – sufficient insurance coverage against all likely contingencies, and attention to stipulations in the bill of lading
   – proper review of conditions in the contract of carriage
   – proper packaging and shipment instructions

■ *The exporter's risk that an apparently good customer will manage to receive the goods and then seek to avoid paying; the importer's risk of outright fraud.*
   SOLUTIONS
   – thorough credit investigations of prospective partners
   – membership in and/or utilization of ICC Commercial Crime Services.

1.8 Typical export transactions

International transactions can take an endless variety of forms. The most common categories are summarized below.

1.8.1 The case of a documentary sale

> Note: At the risk of some over–simplification, we will now sketch the broad outlines of a "typical" export transaction: a shipment of consumer goods on CIF Incoterms 2000 in conjunction with payment by confirmed, irrevocable documentary credit[2]. This type of transaction will be the focus of much of this book and will be explored in greater detail in Chapters 2 through 9.

a. THE CONTRACT OF SALE: OFFER AND ACCEPTANCE – PRO FORMA INVOICE – GENERAL CONDITIONS OF SALE

Commonly, the *exporter* makes known his range of goods and prices at trade shows or through the direct–mail circulation of catalogues and brochures. Thereafter, he receives an inquiry from an importer, requesting a price quote for a certain amount of goods of a specified quality. The importer's inquiry may arrive on a pre–printed form which is commonly referred to as an RFQ (Request for Quote) or RFP (Request for Proposal). At this point, the exporter may issue some kind of contractual *offer*, including a price quote. A common technique is for the exporter to send a *pro forma invoice*, a document which specifies the basic terms and conditions of sale, including the price, delivery and payment terms. Since the pro forma invoice is meant to mirror precisely the commercial invoice which will be sent to the importer when the transactions is completed, the likelihood of disputes is reduced – the importer can see in the pro forma invoice exactly what she will pay for if she goes through with the deal, in particular as regards transport or insurance costs. Again, remember that there is no universal, standard procedure. In some cases the exporter will first send a simple price quotation and only use a pro forma invoice later, after having acknowledged and accepted receipt of the importer's purchase order.

In law, a contract is formed when the seller's offer receives the buyer's unequivocal *acceptance*. The acceptance required to form the contract can be supplied by the buyer's *purchase order*, indicating assent to the prices and conditions contained in the pro forma invoice (or other sale offer).

EXPORT DOCUMENTS – PRO FORMA INVOICE

Copyright ©1996 UNZ & CO.

SHIPPER/EXPORTER	
Glotz Industries 1492 Columbus Blvd. Fort Wayne, IN 12345-6789	

PRO FORMA INVOICE NO.	DATE
TO-06	July/4/...

COUNTRY OF ORIGIN
USA

CONSIGNEE
Widgets by Otto Rudiger Paschold Strasse Baden-Baden, Germany

TERMS
Sale: CIP Hamburg
Payment: Irrevocable L/C calling for
"received for shipment" ocean B/Ls

EXPORT REFERENCES
Currency: U.S. Dollars

Marine Cargo Insurance at 110% CIP value
all risks plus war risk plus strike
and civil commotion risk coverage

NOTIFY
Zoll Clearance 6 Haberkamp Strasse Stuttgart, Germany

FORWARDING AGENT
A. N. Deringer 29320 Goddard Rd. Romulus, MI 48174

EST. SHIPPING DATE
Within 45 days of receipt of order and L/C

VALIDITY
Thirty days from July 4/...

Terms of sale and terms of payment for this offer are governed by Incoterms 1990 (ICC 460), UCP 500 for letters of credit, and URC 522 for documentary collections.

PKGS.	QUANTITY			DESCRIPTION OF MERCHANDISE	UNIT PRICE	TOTAL VALUE
	6000 ea			Blue widgets (HS# 123456)	$ 4.00	$ 24000.00
				TOTAL EXW FORT WAYNE, IN		$ 24000.00

Approximate gross weight 19,300 kg.
Packing: one 20 foot container

MISC. CHARGES (Packing, Insurance, etc.)	
Total Carriage	$ 1900.00
Forwarding	$ 100.00
Marine Cargo Insurance	$ 151.20

CIP HAMBURG	INVOICE TOTAL	$ 26151.20

CERTIFICATIONS

We certify that this proforma invoice is true and correct, and that the origin of these goods is the United States of America.

AUTHORIZED SIGNATURE

Concluding an export contract

EXPORTER

1.
Exporters market their products to potential importers. This results in enquiries from prospective customers.

IMPORTER

2.
The importer's enquiry is generally considered an invitation to negotiate.

3.
The exporter may make a precise sales offer; these are commonly presented in the form of a Pro Forma Invoice.

Negotiation

4.
If the importer's purchase order precisely reflects the terms of the offer, it may constitute an acceptance, concluding a contract. Otherwise, new terms may be treated by the Exporter as a counter-offer.

New negotiations

5.
When the exporter is satisfied that the importers purchase order is acceptable, he may wish to confirm this with an acknowledgement of order.

Contract

The exporter's sales quotation or pro forma invoice often consists of two parts. On the front page or face side of the document, the seller will provide price, quality and shipping information. On the reverse side, or in an attachment, the seller will provide legal provisions, often referred to as *general conditions of sale*, which set forth a detailed legal framework in support of the brief recitals contained in the price quotation.

This exchange of pro forma invoice and purchase order is just one way to form a contract. It is also possible (and frequently preferable) to draft a specific *contract of sale* for a particular transaction, to be signed by both parties. A good example is the ICC model contract discussed in detail in chapter 4. In practice, the actual form of international sales contracts varies immensely, ranging from lengthy and precise documents to terse exchanges of telexes, email or fax communications.

b. THE PAYMENT AND DELIVERY TERMS: DOCUMENTARY CREDITS – *INCOTERMS 2000**
When the exporter does not know the importer or is unable to obtain sufficient credit information about them, the exporter may wish to insist on payment by a confirmed, irrevocable *documentary credit* (commonly referred to as a "letter of credit"), a payment mode which offers certain security features for the exporter. In our case, the exporter quotes a CIF Incoterms 2000 price, which means that the price includes freight to destination, plus insurance. *Incoterms 2000* are a set of 13 standard "trade terms" (such as FOB, CIF or EXW), developed by ICC. Incoterms define various cost and risk obligations of the parties and are dealt with in detail in chapter 4. CIF stands for "cost, insurance and freight", and was developed in the context of the maritime shipment of general cargo. ICC has also developed a series of terms that are specifically suitable for other kinds of shipments, particularly those involving containerized cargo (see Chapter 4).

c. TRANSPORT: THE FREIGHT FORWARDER – THE BILL OF LADING
The exporter commonly prepares his shipment with the assistance of a *freight forwarder*, who books space for the cargo and may in addition take care of customs formalities. Under CIF Incoterms 2000, the exporter must respect an Incoterms requirement to obtain insurance coverage for 110% of the value of the goods (the extra 10% is meant to cover the minimum profit anticipated by the importer; it is possible to request greater coverage). The exporter must also provide the importer with a marine bill of lading, sometimes called a

---

* Incoterms™ 2000 (ICC Publication 560) is an ICC registered trademark. For more information, please visit www.iccwbo.org/index_incoterms.asp

"*shipped*" bill of lading. A marine bill of lading indicates that the goods have been loaded on board a seagoing vessel.

The exporter must also be aware under CIF Incoterms 2000 that he is responsible for export customs formalities, such as obtaining an export license. Import formalities and duties, conversely, are for the importer's account. An experienced export trader understands that there are often disputes about unloading or discharging costs under CIF, so he may choose to specify in the pro forma invoice or contract of sale that all unloading charges are for the importer, in which case this arrangement should also be made clear in the exporter's instructions to his freight forwarder. When the goods are delivered to the carrier, the exporter, as shipper, receives from the carrier the *bill of lading*. This central document acts as a receipt indicating that the goods were received in apparent good order and quantity, and also stipulates the contractual rights of the holder of the bill of lading against the carrier.

d. ISSUANCE OF THE DOCUMENTARY CREDIT

In our example the contract specifies payment by *letter of credit* or *documentary credit* (they mean the same thing). In the bank's terminology, the importer is referred to as the applicant or the account party. The exporter is referred to as the *beneficiary* of the documentary credit. The letter of credit contains the terms and conditions under which the bank will pay. Generally, this includes a listing of documents which the beneficiary (exporter) must furnish, such as the commercial invoice, insurance certificate, packing list, inspection certificate, bill of lading, etc.

e. CONFIRMATION OF THE CREDIT

Let us assume in this example that the beneficiary has stipulated that the credit be *confirmed*. By this, the exporter requires the importer to obtain from another bank (usually one located in the exporter's country) a confirmation of the credit, which means that the confirming bank adds its own irrevocable undertaking to pay under the terms and conditions of the credit. This may be considered advantageous by the exporter who prefers to work with a relatively close and reliable paymaster, such as his own bank. Let us assume that the confirming bank agrees to confirm the credit. NOTE: not *all* credits are confirmed; confirmation is an additional bank service performed for a fee, and therefore makes sense whenever the exporter does not wish to take the risk that the issuing bank may become unable to pay under the credit. Of course, the exporter may simply be more comfortable dealing with a known bank, and that is also a sufficient reason for requesting a confirmed credit.

f. SHIPMENT OF THE GOODS AND PRESENTATION OF DOCUMENTS FOR PAYMENT

The exporter prepares the shipment and instructs the freight forwarder to obtain the necessary transport document. After shipment of the goods, the exporter goes to the confirming bank and presents the various documents required under the credit. The confirming bank takes up the documents, examines them, and if it finds them *conforming* to the conditions of the credit, gives or promises to give value to the exporter under the credit. There are different ways that the exporter can get paid, depending on the type of credit. He can be paid immediately ("sight" credit) or at a later time ("deferred payment" credit), or a draft payable in the future can be discounted for a partial, immediate payment ("acceptance" or "negotiation" credit). Documentary credits are explored in detail in Chapter 6.

The confirming bank will transmit the documents to the issuing bank, which, if it finds they are conforming, will in due time reimburse the confirming bank for the funds it has paid out under the credit, and will then turn the documents over to the importer and debit her account for the amount of the credit. The importer will use the transport documents to obtain delivery of the goods from the carrier. This is assuming that everything works out as planned. However, it should be kept in mind that shipping documents frequently contain errors when they are first presented to the bank for payment, and correction and/or waiver of these discrepancies may take time and in some cases even delay or impede payment.

g. DISPUTES ARISING OUT OF THE TRANSACTION

But now let us say that there is a dispute. The market price for the contract goods has fallen very rapidly and the importer wants to escape the contract, the fulfilment of which would be ruinous for them. An unscrupulous or uninformed importer might instruct the issuing bank to "stop payment", claiming the goods were not up to contract quality. Such an importer might claim that an insufficient quantity of goods was delivered, that the insurance coverage was insufficient, or that the carrier damaged some of the goods. However, if the beneficiary is able to present conforming documents, the bank must normally pay or accept drafts against the documents. The only exception is for cases involving manifest fraud.

Payment under a letter of credit is not necessarily the end of the story. If it is true that the goods are not of contract quality, then the importer may seek legal redress against the exporter, even though the exporter may have already received payment under the credit. The availability of such a remedy will depend on the law applicable to the transaction, which will in turn depend on provisions in the contract of sale. For example, the parties may have specified that all disputes will be settled under the *ICC Rules of Arbitration*, in which case arbitration will become the mandatory form of dispute resolution. Commonly, the exporter's general terms and conditions will include *choice of law* and *choice of forum* clauses, which specify that disputes will be settled under the commercial law, and in the courts, of the exporter's country (see Chapters 2 and 4).

If the dispute involves interpretation of the provisions of the ICC rules on documentary credits (UCP), it may also be settled by a less expensive procedure called DOCDEX (described in greater detail in Chapter 6), under which the parties (or one of them) contacts the ICC Centre for Expertise and requests a decision by a panel of ICC experts. The DOCDEX decision process can then start and it generally lasts for 30–60 days. There is a fee for this service, but it is less expensive than arbitration or court action. One possible drawback: a DOCDEX decision is not binding on the parties, unless they agree to make it so. (See the DOCDEX rules under "Business Topics/Banking" on the ICC website, www.iccwbo.org).

h. LIABILITY OF CARRIERS AND COVERAGE OF INSURANCE

If the goods are damaged or short–delivered, the ability of the importer to recover from the insurance company will depend on whether or not the damage arises from a cause or circumstance excluded from coverage under the insurance policy. If the damage or loss is a result of the carrier's acts, the importer or her insurer may be able to recover damages from the carrier, but this will depend on the exclusions and limitations on liability contained in the carrier's bill of lading, as well as on the law applicable to the bill.

1.8.2 Common variants on the basic export sale

a. ONGOING CONTRACTS – INSTALMENT, SUPPLY, OUTPUT OR "LINE" CONTRACTS

The example of an international sales transaction above was based on the assumption of a "one–off" or "spot" transaction: the one–time sale of a particular cargo under a single contract. A different kind of contractual relationship arises when the contract is designed to have a significant duration, as when an importer agrees to purchase the entire output of a particular exporter's factory over a period of years. In these kinds of contracts, it is very important that flexibility be built into the arrangement; for example, by allowing price adaptation according to a particular formula. Particular financing arrangements, such as those of the *revolving credit*, may be called for; these are examined in Chapter 6.

b. "STRING" CONTRACTS

In these situations, the "exporter" or "importer" is really only one in a chain of sellers and re–sellers. Transferable and back–to–back credits, dealt with in Chapter 6, are common payment methods in this context.

c. DIFFERENT PAYMENT MECHANISM

Although documentary credits are a very common payment mode in international trade, their expense and complexity are such that they are most advisable in situations of imperfect trust or knowledge between the parties, or when otherwise called for by governmental restrictions. In other situations, such as when both parties are well established and creditworthy, *open account* terms are more common – the exporter simply invoices the importer after shipment, granting her a certain credit period. As we will see in Chapters 6 and 8, this kind of arrangement can be risky for the exporter. Another type of payment mode, the *documentary collection*, provides the exporter more protection than open account, though not as much as an irrevocable documentary credit. In a collection process, the exporter forwards shipping documents and a draft, for example, to a bank in the importer's country. To obtain the documents which will allow access to the goods, the importer must pay or accept to pay the draft. With collections, the exporter is at least assured that the importer cannot physically obtain the merchandise without paying or agreeing to pay.

In an increasingly popular payment variant, the exporter agrees to grant the importer favourable open account terms, but only on the condition that the importer issue a *standby credit* or bank guarantee as a payment security. In the contract, the credit or guarantee functions much like a cash deposit, available for the exporter. If the importer fails to pay the invoice, all the exporter has to do is present a copy of the invoice (or other document stipulated under the credit or guarantee) in order to be assured of payment. Clearly, the importer is exposed to the risk that the exporter will claim the standby credit in bad faith. These types of payment mechanisms, including the ICC rules on *International Standby Practices* (ISP98), are reviewed at length in Chapter 6.

1.8.3 Other types of international transactions/agreements

a. AGENCY AND DISTRIBUTORSHIP RELATIONSHIPS

Agency and distributor-ship are two very common modes of export distribution in which the exporter reaches the foreign consumer through the assistance or representation of a foreign intermediary. In the case of agency, the foreign agent merely markets the exporter's products, leaving the contract of sale to be concluded directly between the exporter and the foreign customer. The agent's income is usually derived from a percentage commission on the sales made in his territory. In the case of distributorship, the distributor buys the exporter's products and then re–sells them in the distributorship territory. The distributor's earnings come from the difference between the price at which he buys from the exporter and the re–sale price to the domestic customer.

Both of these types of arrangements are therefore complementary to international contracts of sale. Agency and distributorship will be explored in detail in Chapter 5, with particular reference to the model contracts developed by ICC.

b. INTERNATIONAL TENDERS

In the tendering process an employer or customer issues a public invitation for *bids* (contractual offers) on a particular project. The purpose is to stimulate competition between the various bidders and enable the customer to select the lowest price offered. Common examples of customers using the tendering process are large governmental entities or major corporations. The public tendering process not only provides a mechanism for eliciting competitive prices, it reduces the likelihood of granting contracts on the basis of corruption or inside connections. Although the project which is at the heart of a tendering process may generate a series of "typical" export transactions, we will not examine international tendering processes in themselves at any length. Nonetheless, Chapter 8 on bank guarantees is relevant to international tenders because of the widespread use of tender guarantees, bid guarantees, and other *demand or surety guarantees* in the tendering process and the subsequent project–implementation period.

A related area is that of *project finance*, which covers the array of sophisticated financial devices underlying major construction or infrastructure projects, such as the building of power plants, airports or highways. There is a wide variety of approaches encountered today in project finance, but one increasingly common feature is that lenders are willing to rely to some extent on the revenues generated by the project itself to repay the loan. Although, as noted above, the use of guarantees and bonds is relevant in this context, project finance is not otherwise treated in any detail in this text. It should be noted, nonetheless, that the great complexity of legal questions which can be generated by such projects, with the attendant possibility *of conflict of law* confusion, frequently militates for the selection of *international commercial arbitration*, covered in Chapter 5, as the most appropriate dispute resolution scheme.

c. CROSS–BORDER FINANCE LEASING

Finance leasing is a form of financing for the acquisition of equipment or supplies which enables the importer, in this case referred to as the lessee, to obtain the desired goods without taking on a direct loan. The lessee takes possession of the goods, uses them, pays a monthly instalment on the lease, and at the end of the lease period may acquire full ownership of the goods with the final payment. Under many tax systems, leasing is attractive because the lease payments can be deducted. In a cross–border context, one of the primary legal concerns is the status of the lessor in the event that the lessee becomes insolvent before the end of the lease period. Can the lessor recover the goods, or will they first be subject to the liens of the lessee's other creditors – such as, for example, those of the local tax collector? The answer will depend in particular on the national insolvency law. Finance leasing is a highly specialized field and will not be dealt with in detail in this text. However, note the relevance to finance leasing of our discussion in Chapter 4 on *retention of title*, a contractual device by which the exporter asserts his property rights in the goods until the purchase price has been paid in full.

d. INTERNATIONAL FRANCHISING

Franchising is a form of shared investment in the expansion and replication of successful business systems. Typically, the owner of the successful business format or system, the *franchisor*, grants against payment the right to exploit the system to a local investor, the *franchisee*. Franchising has proven itself to be particularly useful in an international context, because it allows the franchisor to grow rapidly in foreign markets with a minimum of direct capital investment. In the international context, it is useful to distinguish two types of franchise agreement:

- *Direct (unit) franchise contract* – A direct agreement between the domestic franchisor and the franchisee who operates the foreign franchise.
- *Master franchise contract* – An agreement between the domestic franchisor and a foreign master franchisee. The master franchisee is granted the right to exploit a franchise for the purposes of concluding franchise contracts with franchisees in the territory. A master franchise structure is particularly suitable for international trade because it allows for flexibility and local supervision.

Franchising contracts can be extremely complex and in some jurisdictions must conform with local laws for the protection of franchisees. The *ICC Model International Franchising Contract* will be discussed in Chapter 5.

e. INTERNATIONAL LICENSING AND TRANSFER OF TECHNOLOGY

Many high–technology or engineering firms have found that they can generate substantial revenues in foreign markets by *licensing* the right to use their patents, trademarks, copyrights, trade secrets and or technical processes. As with franchising, licensing provides the exporter with a way of penetrating foreign markets with little or no direct investment. From the importer's side, many companies find that as licencees, or purchasers of licences, they may acquire and profitably exploit in their home markets new processes or products.

f. COUNTERTRADE

In countertrade transactions an element of barter or an ancillary purchase obligation is attached to the underlying export transaction. Although countertrade transactions adopt myriad forms, it is not uncommon for them to involve governmental entities of developing economies. Typically, the exporter will insist that as part of a particular transaction the importer additionally agree to a purchase of a separate group of goods, which, for example, may be relatively unattractive from a commercial point of view but which the exporting country wishes to convert into ready cash. Countertrade, which is said to account for a considerable portion of world trade (from 5% to 30% according to certain studies), is frowned upon by international trade organizations because it tends to distort international markets.

1.9 International organizations and chambers of commerce

1.9.1 Chambers of commerce

Local, regional and national chambers of commerce often contain international departments for assisting importers and exporters. Many chambers organize seminars and provide information on trade and trade–related procedures. Commonly, large or well–funded chambers will also organize trade missions, primarily oriented to assist new exporters find agents and distributors in foreign markets. The first "chambre de commerce" was established in 1599 in Marseille. The concept caught on and expanded in the 18th and 19th centuries, with chambers opening in New York (1768), Calcutta (1834) and Paris (1873). Today, virtually every major city in the world has an active chamber of commerce.

1.9.2 ICC, supplier of tools and standards for international trade

The International Chamber of Commerce (ICC) – the world business organization based in Paris, is of fundamental importance in international trade. Although ICC's activities are diverse, of primary interest to the exporter and importer is ICC's role as a developer of international commercial, legal and banking standards. Thus, ICC developed the rules that govern global documentary credit (letter of credit) practice – the UCP. On the legal side, ICC's International Court of Arbitration is probably the world's foremost private commercial dispute–resolution forum. ICC Incoterms, standard trade terms such as FOB and CIF, define the legal content of price quotes in international transactions.

Objectives – ICC serves world business by promoting trade and investment and open markets for goods and services, as well as the free flow of capital. It defends the private enterprise system and encourages self–regulation by business. Founded in 1919, ICC is a non–governmental organization of thousands of companies and business associations in more than 140 countries. Approximately 70 ICC national committees throughout the world present ICC views to their governments and alert Paris headquarters to national business concerns.

Membership and revenues – ICC is financed partially through revenues received from dues paid by its 7000 member companies and trade associations to ICC national committees. A further important share of ICC's revenues is derived from the administrative fees earned by the ICC Court of International Arbitration. Additional income is generated by the marketing of ICC rules and codes, as well as other books (ICC Publishing) and seminars.

Special status – ICC has Class 1 (top–level) consultative status with the *United Nations* (UN), where it puts forward the views of business in industrialized and developing countries. It also maintains close working relations with the *World Trade Organization* (WTO), the *Organization for Economic Co–operation and Development* (OECD), the *European Commission*, and other intergovernmental and non–governmental bodies. ICC permanent representatives at the UN in New York and Geneva monitor developments affecting business within the UN and its specialized agencies. ICC ensures that business concerns are brought to the attention of governments, through statements from its international headquarters in Paris, and via the representations of ICC national committees throughout the world.

Business self–regulation – ICC also draws up voluntary codes for business which set ethical standards. Its *Business Charter for Sustainable Development* contains 16 principles governing every aspect of a company's activities in relation to the environment from product design to customer advice. ICC's Marketing and Advertising Codes cover ethical conduct as regards direct marketing, advertising, sales promotion, marketing research, environmental advertising and sponsorship. In 1996, ICC issued rules against corruption, bribery and unethical business practices in international trade, which were revised in 1999.

ICC commissions and working parties – *forums for international business policy* – Specialist ICC commissions meet regularly to review issues affecting world business. They cover a wide range of sectors, among them banking, competition, the environment and energy, financial services, insurance, intellectual property, marketing, transportation, taxation, and trade and investment policy. These policy commissions are, in effect, international committees of top–level traders, lawyers, carriers, bankers and other professionals. When a particular commission decides to undertake a project, it creates a sub–committee, known as a *task force*, to accomplish the given task.

Many of ICC's key instruments are products of these high–level task forces. For example, the revision of the Incoterms or UCP is initially entrusted to a small working party operating as a drafting team. Revised drafts are then circulated broadly and internationally through ICC national committees, with the resulting comments channelled back to the working party. Final drafts, once approved by the working party and commission, are submitted for adoption by the ICC Executive Board. Although the broad international consultation entailed by this procedure is quite time–consuming, it ensures that official ICC products carry a certain authority as representing the true consensus viewpoint of the world business community.

ICC Commercial Crime Services – This is the umbrella organization of three ICC units dealing with different aspects of crime affecting business. They are the:
- *Commercial Crime Bureau*, set up to combat the increase in commercial frauds worldwide;
- *International Maritime Bureau*, which deals with all types of maritime crime, including fraud, cargo theft, and piracy; and
- *Counterfeiting Intelligence Bureau*, which helps companies to prevent the faking of their products.

The **World Chambers Federation (WCF)** is ICC's specialized division for its chamber of commerce members worldwide. WCF has taken over from the International Bureau of Chambers of Commerce (IBCC). Through its extensive global support network, WCF enables chambers from all over the world to exchange experiences and improve their performance in areas such as finance, management, and the development and promotion of services. WCF runs the *World Chambers Network* (WCN) – a global internet platform fostering a comprehensive exchange of business information between chambers and their member companies throughout the world. WCF also manages the *ATA Carnet System* and its guarantee chain for temporary duty–free imports. Currently, 58 countries use the ATA Carnet for the temporary admission of commercial samples, professional equipment and goods destined for international trade fairs and similar events.

ICC Publishing offers international business people more than 80 practical reference works. New guides, sets of rules, model contracts and handbooks are added to the list every year. ICC publications may be ordered directly from ICC Publishing in New York, from ICC national committees, or from the bookstore's website www.iccbooksusa.com.

1.9.3 International organizations

There are a variety of other international organizations involved in the field of international trade. International organizations are commonly divided into two categories: *intergovernmental organizations* (IGOs), which are the creation of nation states and are staffed with international civil servants, and non–governmental organizations (NGOs), which may be associations or federations representing business, sectoral, professional or consumer interests. Several of the key international organizations are listed below.

a. INTER–GOVERNMENTAL ORGANIZATIONS (IGOS)
See the end of this book for addresses and contact information.

The United Nations Commission on International Trade Law (UNCITRAL) (Vienna) – The United Nations' international private law body is UNCITRAL. UNCITRAL works primarily on instruments intended to become a part of international or national law, such as treaties, conventions, model and uniform laws. UNCITRAL has approved an international convention for independent bank guarantees and a model law for electronic data interchange. Perhaps UNCITRAL's key contribution to international trade has been the Vienna Convention on the International Sale of Goods, the drafting of which was concluded in 1980 and which entered into force in 1988. UNCITRAL Rules for international commercial arbitration provide an alternative to other arbitral and litigation systems.

Their website is at www.uncitral.org.

Institute for the Unification of Private Trade Law (Unidroit) (Rome) – This international organization was set up under the League of Nations and continued an independent existence after the founding of the United Nations. In recent years, Unidroit has been active in studying the international private law relating to leasing, agency, franchising and inspection contracts, with a view to proposing international legal conventions where necessary.

Their website can be found at www.unidroit.org.

World Customs Organization (WCO)(Brussels) – Officially known as the Customs Cooperation Council, the WCO is the competent global inter–governmental organization on customs matters. Its membership is composed of national customs administrations, who work together to advance the efficiency of the customs process.

Website information is at www.wcoomd.org.

The International Trade Centre (ITC) UNCTAD/WTO (Geneva) is the central agency of the United Nations' system for export assistance for developing nations. ITC conducts a very wide range of training programmes for exporters and importers as well as local chamber of commerce trainers. The ITC also publishes a full range of export guides focusing on specific areas of trade, such as packaging, marketing or promotion.

The ITC website is at www.intracen.org.

b. NON–GOVERNMENTAL ORGANIZATIONS (NGOS)

International Air Transport Association (IATA) (Montreal and Geneva) – The trade organization for the world's airlines, IATA has had an important role in simplifying and standardizing air transport documents, such as air waybills.

More information is available at their website, www.iata.org.

International Federation of Freight Forwarder's Associations (FIATA) (Zurich) – A world organization which promotes standards and quality in international freight forwarding. Certain FIATA standard documents, such as the FIATA Bill of Lading, have become important references in international trade. FIATA's customs clearance manual is an important professional reference tool in transport circles.

More information is available at www.fiata.com.

International Maritime Committee (CMI – for Comité Maritime International) (Brussels) – An organization founded in 1897 to promote the unification of maritime and commercial law, maritime customs, usages and practices. Between 1910 and 1971, the CMI's work gave birth to 18 "Brussels" conventions and protocols on maritime law, including those key pieces of international regulation of bills of lading generally referred to as the Hague and Hague–Visby Rules.
Their website is at www.comitemaritime.org.

International Road Transport Union (IRU) (Geneva) – An international federation representing commercial operators of road vehicles, the IRU notably administers the TIR customs system which allows lorries or trucks sealed by customs officials to cross intervening national borders without having to undergo full customs formalities.
The IRU website is at www.iru.org.

1.10 The multilateral framework for world trade: the General Agreement on Tariffs and Trade (GATT) and the World Trade Organization (WTO)

a. THE GATT AND FREE TRADE

After World War II there was a strong international consensus in favour of creating an international trade organization to oversee the progressive liberalization of international markets. From 1947 until 1995, the supposedly "interim" GATT functioned very effectively as the co–ordinator of the multilateral trade system. As a result of the GATT, tariffs, which had averaged 40% in the industrialized countries in the late 1940s, dropped to about 5% by the early 1990s. World exports grew from USD 61 billion in 1950 to USD 4090 billion in 1994. At the conclusion of the Uruguay Round in 1994, the WTO was established as the successor to the GATT. The Uruguay Round, which lasted from 1986 through 1993, was the most ambitious and comprehensive trade liberalization round ever negotiated. Its content is summarized in the ICC publication *The GATT Negotiations: a business guide to the results of the Uruguay Round* (ICC Publication 533).

b. THE WORLD TRADE ORGANIZATION (WTO)(GENEVA)

WTO replaces the GATT, and has quite a different character. While the GATT was primarily a set of rules, administered by an interim body, the WTO is a permanent institution with its own secretariat. Although the GATT's scope of application was limited to trade in goods, the WTO also covers trade in services and trade–related aspects of intellectual property. Of great practical significance is the fact that settlement of disputes under the WTO mechanism is much faster and more automatic than under the GATT system, so that trade blockages are more rapidly and efficiently overcome.

The long–standing principles enshrined in the original GATT have not disappeared under the WTO – rather, they have simply been subsumed under the new structure. Thus, the original GATT (from 1947) lives on as the so–called "GATT 1994", an amended and updated version of GATT 1947, which forms an integral part of the WTO agreement.
The WTO's website is www.wto.org.

NOTES

(1) Also spelled f.o.b. or c.i.f., see Chapter 4 on *Incoterms 2000.*

(2) This Incoterm is chosen simply as example; for a full discussion of the different Incoterms, see Chapter 4.

CHAPTER TWO

The Export–Import Legal Framework

The basics: International trade transactions are composed of an inter–locking series of contracts involving exporters, importers, agents/distributors, banks, insurers, transporters and brokers, and inspection agencies. Ideally, these contracts will interact harmoniously. All too often, however, important details are left un–negotiated, or terms in one contract (e.g., the transport or insurance contract) are allowed to conflict with terms in another (e.g., the sale contract), leading to unwanted and even disastrous consequences.

Properly drafted contracts are the first step in managing the risks of inter-national commerce. Since the contract of sale plays the role of "master" contract, it is particularly important that it be drafted carefully and completely. Trade professionals should in addition have a good understanding of the legal principles generally applicable to international transactions.

Traders are well–advised to rely on expert legal counsel, and in any event should go through a checklist of basic legal questions before signing a contract or concluding a deal. In particular, the parties should be clear as to which law and dispute–settlement procedure will apply to the contract. As an alternative to formal court procedures as the means of resolving disputes, traders may wish to stipulate that disputes will be submitted to settlement proceedings, such as alternative dispute resolution (or ADR Rules – as an example, see infra ICC ADR Rules) or commercial arbitration, such as that administered according to the *ICC Rules of Arbitration*.

The key legal difference between international transactions and domestic ones is that in the international context one is faced with the question of applicable national law. A court requested to decide a particular case will first have to decide whether or not the case has been brought in the appropriate forum, and if so, which law to apply.

During negotiations, exporters may wish to refer to model contracts (such as the ICC Model Contracts for international sale, agency, distributorship, franchising or occasional intermediary). Even when the model contracts are not used directly, they may be useful for preparation of contract negotiations – one can compare the standard model provisions with the provisions in the contract offered by the counterparty.

2.1   Introduction to legal concepts and terminology

Note: Because national systems of law may differ on significant points relating to commercial matters, the many general statements on legal subjects made in this book should always be understood as mere generalizations. There may be exceptions in particular jurisdictions, and the general contractual principles stated herein may not apply under all systems of law.

2.1.1   Different Legal Systems

National legal systems around the world fall into a few great legal "families", with the most influential of these being known as the civil law and common law systems. The civil law system (also known as the Romano–Germanic Civil Law) is applied in France, Germany and throughout Continental Europe, as well as in Japan and much of South America. The defining characteristic of civil law systems is the reliance on a comprehensive code. Civil law traces its history back to Roman law, and in particular the Corpus Juris Civilis (also known as the Justinian Code). Modern civil law remains greatly influenced by two national codes, the French Civil Code of 1804 (often referred to as the Code Napoleon) and German Civil Code of 1896.

The common law system (also known as the Anglo–American Common Law) derives from medieval English legal practice. Common law is applied in countries with some historical link to England – e.g., the US, Canada, Australia, New Zealand, Nigeria. The distinguishing characteristic of the common law is its reliance on prior court decisions known as precedents. While judges in civil law systems may generally take notice of precedents, judges in common law systems are more likely to be strictly bound by the previous rulings. In civil law systems one can say that the law is encapsulated in codes or statutes and the judge's job lies in applying the relevant code to a particular case. In common law systems the judge is bound by previous decisions, but must create new law when novel situations arise. Another distinction lies in the scope of activity of the judge: in civil law systems the judge may have a greater investigative role, while common law judges are more neutral, waiting for lawyers to bring forward evidence for consideration.

Another prominent legal system is that of Islamic law (also known as Shari'a), which is applied in countries in which Islam is the principal religion, such as Saudi Arabia, Jordan, Syria, Iran, Iraq, Afghanistan, Egypt, Indonesia, Pakistan, Algeria, Tunisia, Morocco and several others. Shari'a derives principally from the Koran and the teachings of the Prophet Muhammad and early Islamic scholars. As contrasted with the civil and common law systems, Shari'a places greater emphasis on religion as the source of guiding legal principles.

It is important for international traders to be aware of the existence of different families of law. The differences between legal systems can sometimes help explain actual differences in business practices. Thus, for example, business people around the world – particularly those from civil law jurisdictions – may profess shock at the length of contracts produced by American lawyers. This relative long–windedness can be explained in part by the freedom of contract allowed under the common law, and in part by the uniquely litigious nature of the American marketplace. Traders doing business in Islamic countries are well advised to understand concepts in Shari'a such as that of "riba", a legal doctrine which may be interpreted as prohibiting the charging of interest on business loans. However, one should be wary of over–generalizing as regards legal systems. Even between two common law systems such as those of the US and UK, there are important differences. Thus, for example, the US practice in certain types of cases of using "contingency fees", under which an attorney receives a percentage of the amount he recovers, is not allowed in the UK.[1]

2.1.2 The value of a precise, written contract

International traders are not always fully aware of the value of having negotiated a precise, detailed, written contract. Some traders prefer to do business without recourse to lawyers or formal written contracts at all. For them, their word – and perhaps a brief fax or telex confirmation – is enough contract. Indeed, in certain commercial sectors and in certain countries, informal means of contracting may be customary. However, traders should be conscious of the dangers of contracts based on a "handshake" or a "gentlemen's agreement".

International trade lawyers can attest – through the cases they plead – to the risks of casual optimism. When a dispute arises, reference to the contract is the first recourse of the parties. If the contract is silent or is unclear with respect to the element in dispute, the parties may have to enter into litigation or arbitration. International contracts, especially, should provide clear and detailed stipulations regarding documentary obligations, such as, for example, the obligation to open a confirmed letter of credit or tender a negotiable bill of lading.

Traders are notorious for signing contracts without reading them, then waking to the danger when faced with a loss. Consequently, the contracting process should involve more than signing a long standard document produced by the other side or by one's own export department. Traders should not be hasty to assume that they have no negotiating power. Even if the other side is clearly in control of the negotiations, it may still be possible to obtain an important contractual concession. A failure to insist on minimum contractual precautions, regardless of the counterparty's negotiating posture, amounts to recklessness.

Contract negotiation should not be seen as mere haggling, or a test of wills between the parties. Contracts should not be thought of as weapons to be wielded in the event of disputes. Rather, contracts should be looked at as the written record of an information–exchange process by which the vast majority of foreseeable disputes can be completely avoided.

Case Example

What was that I just signed? MCC Marble Ceramic v. Ceramica
An American dealer of ceramic tiles visited a trade fair in Bologna, Italy, where he negotiated an agreement to purchase tiles from an Italian manufacturer. An oral agreement was reached on the issues of price, quality, quantity, delivery and payment. The Italian manufacturer then requested the American dealer to sign a standard form contract, which was written in Italian. Although the American dealer did not read or speak Italian, he did not hesitate to sign the contract. Later, when a dispute arose, the Italian manufacturer sought to impose the conditions of the form contract. In US courts, the Italian manufacturer obtained a ruling that barred the American from introducing evidence of their supposed oral agreement, but this ruling was later reversed on appeal.[2]

Comment: Do not be so hasty to conclude an agreement that you skip over minimum contractual formalities (such as reading the contract before you sign it).

The export "symphony": harmonizing the contracts

Contract of sale

The Contract of Sale is the "conductor" of the export symphony - all related documents should accord with it.

Insurance contract

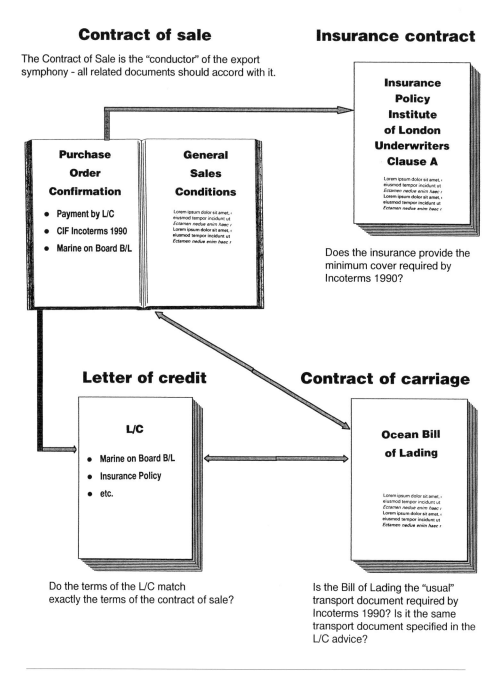

Purchase Order Confirmation

- Payment by L/C
- CIF Incoterms 1990
- Marine on Board B/L

General Sales Conditions

Lorem ipsum dolor sit amet, eiusmod tempor incidunt ut Ectamen nedue enim haec r Lorem ipsum dolor sit amet, eiusmod tempor incidunt ut Ectamen nedue enim haec r

Insurance Policy Institute of London Underwriters Clause A

Lorem ipsum dolor sit amet, eiusmod tempor incidunt ut Ectamen nedue enim haec r Lorem ipsum dolor sit amet, eiusmod tempor incidunt ut Ectamen nedue enim haec r

Does the insurance provide the minimum cover required by Incoterms 1990?

Letter of credit

L/C

- Marine on Board B/L
- Insurance Policy
- etc.

Do the terms of the L/C match exactly the terms of the contract of sale?

Contract of carriage

Ocean Bill of Lading

Lorem ipsum dolor sit amet, eiusmod tempor incidunt ut Ectamen nedue enim haec r Lorem ipsum dolor sit amet, eiusmod tempor incidunt ut Ectamen nedue enim haec r

Is the Bill of Lading the "usual" transport document required by Incoterms 1990? Is it the same transport document specified in the L/C advice?

2.1.3 Written vs. oral contracts

Traders may be uncertain as to whether or not they have any legal recourse for a dispute when there is no written contract underlying a given transaction or part of a transaction, although there may be a verbal agreement or other informal understanding. It may indeed be possible to enforce an oral agreement, even if there is no writing evidencing the agreement, but this will depend on the national law governing the contract (in some countries, all commercial agreements must be evidenced in writing), and on the existence of other contractual clauses (some contracts contain clauses specifying that any modifications to the contract must be in writing).

One potentially relevant consideration will be whether the parties have an established course of dealing (a habitual or standard way of doing business established in past transactions) or whether there is a custom of trade (a standard practice in the particular industry). In any event, any allegation of the existence of an oral promise or contract would have to be proven somehow, such as by acts of the parties consistent with the terms of the alleged oral contract or condition.

2.1.4 The key contracts related to export transactions

a. CONTRACT OF SALE

The central export–import contract is the contract of sale: the parties to this contract are the seller (exporter) and the buyer (importer). A broker or agent may act for seller or buyer in this basic framework. In a contract of sale, the parties generally specify at least the price, quantity, products, delivery and payment terms. If the parties do not specify one of the essential terms, the question arises whether there is a way of "filling the gap", and the answer will depend on the circumstances of the case and the applicable law. In some sectors, standard form sale contracts are prevalent.

If there is no formal written contract of sale, it is quite common for the contract to be formed by an exchange of telexes or faxes comprising, for example, the buyer's enquiry (the invitation to negotiate), the seller's pro forma invoice (the offer), and the buyer's sales order or confirmation (the acceptance of the offer). This exchange of offer and acceptance generally constitutes a legally valid contract.

The contract of sale is the "master" contract ruling the export transaction, because the series of contractual arrangements which follow – as regards transport, insurance and payment – should always accord with its provisions. The surest way to put the transaction on solid footing is to negotiate a precise contract of sale which deals unambiguously with all these key elements. Thus, the export contract should stipulate the delivery point and include a trade term under *Incoterms 2000*, such as FOB or FCA *Incoterms 2000*. Moreover, if payment is to be by letter of credit, it is helpful if the documentary requirements under the credit are already spelled out. If traders have any doubt about the completeness of their contracts, they are well–advised to compare their contracts with one of the standard form contracts, such as the *ICC Model International Sale Contract* (see infra Chapter 4).

b. CONTRACT OF CARRIAGE

Another basic contract is the contract of carriage, which is formed between the shipper (seller or buyer) and the carrier (transport company). The carrier may act through an agent or broker (e.g., freight forwarder). Legal recourse for damage to the goods during transport may be significantly affected by whether a freight forwarder was contracting as an agent or as a principal. The contractual terms and conditions of transport contracts are generally found in a transport document known as a bill of lading (or a similar but non–negotiable transport document, such as a sea waybill, air waybill, data freight receipt, cargo quay receipt, etc.). The bill of lading plays a triple role in the international sales transaction, acting as 1) transport contract, 2) evidence of receipt of goods, and 3) document conferring the right to control delivery of the goods. It is discussed in detail in Chapters 6 and 9.

c. PAYMENT–RELATED CONTRACTS

International payment mechanisms generate another series of contractual agreements. A letter of credit, for example, is based on an underlying contract of sale, which requires that the buyer then form a contractual agreement with its bank (credit application and issuance), and in the case of a confirmed credit, requires that the confirming bank irrevocably undertake to pay the beneficiary under the credit and that a further contract be formed between the issuing bank and confirming bank.

d. INSURANCE CONTRACTS

International shipments of goods are usually insured throughan insurance contract (e.g., a policy) between the insurer and the seller or buyer. When the seller is obliged under the sales contract to procure insurance, it is important that the conditions and insured amount under the policy be in accord with the conditions of the contract of sale. In particular, sellers under CIF or CIP

Incoterms 2000 need to be aware of requirements imposed by *Incoterms 2000* as regards the minimum insurance coverage which they must procure for the buyer.

2.1.5 Avoiding conflicts between contracts

Problems in international transactions will arise if one of the parties procures a letter of credit, bill of lading, or insurance policy that conflicts with the requirements of the contract of sale. Therefore, traders should strive to make sure that such subsidiary contracts are in harmony with the contract of sale.

a. AVOIDING CONFLICTS BETWEEN THE CONTRACT OF CARRIAGE AND THE CONTRACT OF SALE

Depending upon the Incoterm chosen in the contract of sale, one of the two parties (either seller or buyer) will incur transport obligations. For example, the CIF Incoterm requires the export seller to arrange and pay for international transport and also to provide the buyer with a negotiable bill of lading (as contract of carriage) conforming to "usual terms".

The party responsible for shipment must understand and be aware of the full extent of transport and documentary obligations required under the given Incoterm. For example, an FOB Incoterms seller should know that the goods must be safely loaded on board a vessel in the port of shipment. For further detail on this issue, see infra Chapter 4.4.

b. AVOIDING CONFLICTS BETWEEN THE PAYMENT MECHANISM AND THE CONTRACT OF SALE

If payment is by documentary credit, the importer may breach the contract if she fails to timely open the credit or if the credit that she opens does not precisely reflect the terms of the contract of sale. Thus, if the contract of sale specifies delivery on a lorry or railway wagon, the credit application must not require the exporter to provide a marine on board bill of lading. If the contract specifies that the letter of credit must be confirmed, then provision by the importer of any other kind of credit will constitute a breach of the contract. The safest practice is to prepare a contract of sale that adequately spells out the characteristics of the letter of credit to be required (e.g., is it to be confirmed, payable at sight, transferable, require an inspection certificate, etc.). Probably the surest way of eliminating a conflict between the contract of sale and the letter of credit is for the exporter to provide the importer with a sample filled–in application for a letter of credit, indicating exactly how the importer must apply for the credit.

c. AVOIDING CONFLICTS BETWEEN THE INSURANCE CONTRACT AND THE CONTRACT OF SALE

Two of the Incoterms – CIF and CIP – require the seller to procure an insurance contract. For example, an exporter under CIF Incoterms is required under the sales contract to conclude both transport and insurance contracts. As for the insurance contract, CIF Incoterms requires a minimum level of insurance (specifically: 110% of the contract value under the A, B, or C clauses of the London Institute of Underwriters – see Chapter 9 on Transport).

2.1.6 Jurisdiction and choice of law

In international contracts one has a choice (and therefore, potential uncertainty) as to the applicable national law and forum. Because of the great distances which may be involved in international transactions, this can be an important choice. An American company based in Cleveland will prefer not to have to send several key executives to testify in Ulan Bator in the event of a dispute with its Mongolian counterparty. Consequently, a well–drafted international contract of sale will contain clear answers to the following crucial questions:

a. WHAT LAW GOVERNS THIS CONTRACT OF SALE?

The parties are free in principle to choose an applicable law. If the parties make no election, a court or arbitral tribunal called upon to settle a dispute arising under the contract will first examine all elements related to the contract which may help in ascertaining the intention of the parties. The court will then apply the principles of that body of the law known as conflict of laws.[3] The arbitrators have a greater flexibility since they can apply the rules of law (including rules of conflict of laws) which they determine to be appropriate (see, for example, Article 17 of the *ICC Rules of Arbitration*).

Note that in the case of arbitration this question can be broken down further into two sub–parts: 1) procedural law, and 2) substantive law. It is possible to agree on the application of one national law to the substance of the contract and a different national law as to the procedure (usually the law of the place of arbitration).[4]

b. IN WHICH COURT OR ARBITRAL FORUM SHOULD A CASE BE BROUGHT IN THE EVENT OF A DISPUTE?

The parties have some freedom to choose the court or arbitral forum. However, certain types of cases, such as labour disputes, must be settled under national law or before specialized courts. If the parties choose arbitration, they should include in their contract an effective arbitration clause, such as the standard clause provided by ICC (see infra Chapter 3). Parties choosing arbitration are well advised to further specify the applicable law, the seat of arbitration, the language of arbitration and the number of arbitrators (1 or 3 generally).

Thus, a properly drafted contract between a French seller and a New York buyer will contain a clause making the transaction subject either to French law or to New York law, or even to the law of a third country. A further clause will very likely specify either the French or New York courts as the appropriate dispute–resolution forum, or may instead choose a type of commercial arbitration, such as ICC Arbitration. These contractual provisions are known as the "choice of law", "choice of forum", and "dispute resolution" or "arbitration" clauses.

2.1.7 Performance and remedies for breach of contract

Whether or not a particular act or omission is deemed a breach may depend on which national law applies to the contract. Moreover, in practical terms, whether or not there is anything that an aggrieved party can do about a breach will also depend on the stipulated forum and dispute–resolution method. In some cases, the expense and inconvenience of having to sue in a foreign court will rule out the possibility of fully enforcing a particular contract.

a. FACTORS AFFECTING THE RANGE OF REMEDIES AVAILABLE

The remedies for a breach of contract will vary according to the:

1) *Terms of the contract* – The contract may itself specify particular remedies, as for example, liquidated damages in the event of a particular default or breach.
2) *Applicable law* – National legal systems have different approaches to particular remedies. Common law courts, for example, have been less receptive to the application of the specific performance remedy (in essence, forcing a party to go through with their contract) than civil law courts.
3) *The nature and gravity of the breach* – In addition to the above factors, the remedies available to an aggrieved party will depend on the characteristics of the breach. In general, most legal systems seek to avoid creating harsh remedies for minor breaches. However, some breaches are so serious or flagrant that the aggrieved party should have access to the full range of possible remedies, such as those of consequential damages.

Two of the concepts that may be applied in this regard are:

- *Substantial performance* – if a party (the exporter, for example) has performed the bulk of his obligations, but has failed to perform only to a small degree or in unimportant matters (e.g., short–delivery by a commercially insignificant amount), the aggrieved party may only be allowed the remedy of a price reduction.
- *Fundamental breach* – if a breach is so serious that it deprives the aggrieved party of the intended benefits of the contract, the aggrieved party may be allowed to terminate the contract.

b. TYPES OF REMEDY AVAILABLE

Most legal systems make all of the following remedies available to some extent, depending on the circumstances of a particular case:

1) *Money damages* – An aggrieved party may be entitled to receive money in compensation for the contractual breach. The money may be calculated, inter alia, as a reduction in the price or as a lump–sum damages payment. If the breach was foreseeably likely to cause further or related damages (such as the lost sales occasioned by the shutting down of the aggrieved party's manufacturing operation), the aggrieved party may be able to obtain consequential damages as compensation for the results of the breach. The aggrieved party may have to mitigate damages, e.g., make reasonable efforts to reduce the extent of damages (thus, a buyer receiving a shipment of tomatoes of non–contract quality, but which are nonetheless merchantable, must make some efforts to sell the tomatoes rather than let them rot).

2) *Termination* – If the breach is a particularly serious one, it may entitle the other party to terminate the contract, and with it any remaining obligations she may have under it.

3) *Specific performance* – A party that has not performed according to her contractual obligations can be required to do so. A court may issue an order requiring that party to pay the contract price, deliver the contract goods or substitute goods, or otherwise fulfil that party's contractual obligations. Under common law legal systems, however, specific performance may be only available when damages are not an adequate remedy. Thus, a buyer who has not received the contract goods is expected to first terminate the contract and seek to buy the goods elsewhere. Specific performance is not often requested in practice.

2.1.8 Practical aspects of performance and breach

Most international agreements and contracts are successfully performed to the satisfaction of both sides. Professional business persons only invest in transactions they expect will prove profitable and practicable, and they are usually right. Unfortunately, this leads many traders to believe that many or all of the legal considerations spelled out in this text are mere technicalities that can be safely ignored. It is certainly worth the effort to convince such traders that a meticulous approach to contract drafting is the most prudent way of minimizing the risks from those unusual cases where a counterparty substantially breaches the contract.

Many minor contractual breaches are curable – the problem can be fixed or set right. Thus, if the seller delivers non–conforming goods before the delivery deadlines, and the non–conformity is pointed out, he may still make a second delivery of conforming goods. On other occasions, the aggrieved party will simply forgive a particular breach. Thus, if goods arrive a day or two late, and the time of delivery is not crucial, the buyer may simply overlook the breach. However, parties should be aware that by repeatedly forgiving a particular breach they may be taking the risk of establishing a waiver of their rights. One solution is to insert a clause in the contract to the effect that all modifications of the parties' rights under the contracts must be in writing signed by both parties (however, such provisions may not be enforceable in all cases or in all jursidictions, so they should be checked by experienced legal counsel). Another solution is for the aggrieved party to object in writing to the small breaches, thereby establishing a paper record that that party had no intention of waiving its right to insist on performance.

a. LAWYER'S FEES, COURT AND ARBITRATION COSTS
Usually, a party will only consult lawyers as regards legal remedies when all other means of obtaining satisfaction have been exhausted (i.e., repeated requests for performance or re–negotiation). At this point the party will be confronted with the practical reality of the cost of enforcing the contract. Legal fees and court or arbitration expenses come into the picture. The choice of law, forum and arbitration clauses becomes crucial.

Let us say, for example, that the cost to a Bolivian buyer of a particular breach by an American seller is USD10,000. Should the buyer sue for damages? If the lawsuit will cost the buyer more than USD10,000, it may make no sense to undertake it. While in many countries the winning party can oblige the losing party to pay attorneys' fees and court costs, there is always the possibility of losing in a foreign court – and being forced oneself to pay the other side's attorneys' fees! It may end up costing more to pursue a claim than to walk away from the contract. The aggrieved party must ask, how much would it cost to win this case – and how much to lose it? What are the chances of winning? The costs in lawyer's fees, court and arbitral costs, and lost executive time spent testifying, must be weighed against the potential money award. Depending on the circumstances of each transaction, there will be a threshold of money damages beneath which it will be impractical or dangerous to sue, and this calculation will depend on the convenience and cost of the appropriate forum. Hence, the practical importance of the choice of law and choice of forum clauses in the sales contract.

In order to have some security against small disputes (i.e., those involving damages beneath the threshold for which it becomes practical to sue), traders can only rely on other, extra–legal safeguards, such as: export credit insurance, advance deposits, bank guarantees or performance bonds by the counterparty, and good foreign credit information.

An additional practical observation is that it costs money to defend oneself against a lawsuit, regardless of whether or not one is in the wrong. In an international context, the inconvenience of defending a lawsuit can be magnified when the defence must take place in an expensive city across the globe. If a defendant chooses not to appear because of this expense, she runs the risk that a default judgement may be obtained against her, which might eventually result in a money judgement being enforced. Parties are thus justifiably wary of agreeing to a choice of forum clause specifying that claims must be brought in the counterparty's domestic courts, especially if the two countries are quite distant.

b. ADAPTATION AND FORCE MAJEURE CLAUSES

A common cause for failure to perform in international business transactions is that of sharp market swings during or before the time for performance. Long–term contracts, such as those for agency and distributorship, are especially exposed to these time–based contingencies. Prudent traders are therefore advised to build adaptation clauses into contracts likely to be affected by changing economic or commercial circumstances. Adaptation provisions allow for flexibility in prices and supply terms, enabling parties to avoid a total breakdown in their relationship.

It is also generally advisable to include a force majeure clause, which excuses non–performance in the event of unforeseeable events, such as earthquakes, wars or "acts of God".

2.2 Contract formation and pre–contractual liability

2.2.1 Pre–contractual actions

Under most legal systems, a contract is formed between exporter and importer when one party has made a sufficiently precise offer and the other has responded with an unconditional acceptance. However, the first contacts between the exporter and importer may arise far earlier, as for example when the importer views a catalogue or advertisement prepared by the exporter, and in response addresses a purchaser's inquiry to the exporter, requesting detailed product specifications or prices. Another possibility is that the importer will issue an invitation to submit tenders (offers) for a specific project. There are many possible variations, ranging from informal telephone contacts to highly detailed and binding offers. Initial contacts may lead to prolonged negotiations over prices or specifications, or may lead immediately to contract. Statements made during the course of these initial contacts (pre–contractual statements) may or may not have a legally binding nature.

In most cases, statements made during negotiation will not be contractually binding (unless they are later incorporated into the contract). Courts have generally allowed parties some freedom to negotiate without the fear of incurring pre–contractual liability.

However, there are several exceptions to this rule. If a contract results from the negotiations, and the pre–contractual statements made by one party turn out to have been misleading, the offending party may be held liable for the consequences of its misleading statements. While it is not possible to state a single, common legal principle that will apply in all jurisdictions, traders should apply commonsense notions of good faith to their pre–contractual negotiations and should take care not to make statements upon which the other party is likely to rely to its detriment.

2.2.2 Offers/tenders

In the parlance of the export trade, offers (or tenders) are those sufficiently precise communications – generally including product, price, payment and delivery elements – that an export seller specifically addresses to a particular buyer with the intention that a binding contract will be formed if the buyer accepts. The question may arise whether a price quotation made by an exporter amounts to a legally binding offer. Generally, the decisive criterion is whether or not the exporter intended to be bound by the offer.

Can an exporter change his mind and revoke the offer prior to acceptance? The answer varies widely according to the applicable law. Under certain legal systems the determining factor is whether the offer can be characterized as a firm offer. Under these systems, if the exporter specifically states that the offer will remain open for a given period of time, the exporter will be bound by any acceptance made within that time period, regardless of the exporter's attempts to revoke the offer. Different systems of law have different criteria for what constitutes a firm offer so that it is not possible to state a single, universal rule. In some jurisdictions an exporter may be able to preserve the right to revoke by stating in the offer that it will not become binding until a written acknowledgement of order has been sent.

Exporters and importers should also keep in mind that offers, tenders and other commercial proposals have a dual nature: they are not only legal instruments, they are also important sales and informational communications. The ideal tender will be professional–looking, detailed and complete. It will include such important sales information as key selling points, technical specifications, price, service conditions, as well as such legally significant items as general sales conditions, delivery time, and payment terms.

2.2.3 Acceptance

Generally, a buyer's acceptance must be unconditional in order to conclude a binding contract. A conditional acceptance may constitute a rejection and counteroffer, leaving it up to the exporter whether or not to accept the new condition. However, under some important systems of law (i.e., the Vienna Convention on the International Sale of Goods, or the US Uniform Commercial Code – the UCC), if the new condition concerns a minor or trivial matter, then the conditional acceptance will be valid and conclude a binding contract unless promptly objected to by the exporter.

Many tricky questions of law arise under different legal systems as to when and how an acceptance actually creates a contract, but it is not possible here to go into these in detail. In general, exporters and importers should make sure that both have expressly agreed to the same set of terms and conditions.

Unfortunately, in the rapid back–and–forth flow of international commerce, many traders do not take the time to be so rigorous.

The role of the exporter's general conditions of sale (and the buyer's general conditions of purchase) in the formation of contract will be considered below.

2.2.4 Letters of intent and other preliminary agreements

In certain complex transactions, the parties may wish to come to a preliminary agreement, sometimes called an "agreement to agree", which may or may not be enforceable, depending on circumstances and applicable law. Such an agreement may take the form of a "letter of intent," "memorandum of under–standing," "heads of agreement," "agreement with open terms," "commitment letter" or "binder". These preliminary agreements may be necessary when a certain major issue (such as obtaining bank approval for a loan, or obtaining a government authorization) is not yet known or definite. The preliminary agreement itself may be useful in getting a bank officer or government official to grant an approval or authorization. Another possibility is that the parties will use the preliminary agreement to resolve certain basic issues, while continuing to negotiate on more complicated matters.

One danger of preliminary agreements is that the courts of some countries will interpret them as being legally binding, even though one of the parties had no intention of being bound. One way of avoiding this problem is to include express language in the agreement to the effect that "this document is not intended to constitute a binding contract," or "this document is only intended to indicate the parties' willingness to negotiate and nothing more".[5] However, not all courts will consider such language to be decisive.

In some cases, both parties intend to conclude a contract, but will intentionally leave a term or terms to be agreed upon in further negotiations. Here, the critical issue for courts will be whether, in the event that the further negotiations fail, there is a suitably definite mechanism or "fall–back" standard enabling the court to supply the missing term(s).

It should be clear from the above that an instrument such as the letter of intent should be used with some discretion. If the document is too vague or contains too many disclaimers, banks or government officials may not wish to rely on it. However, if it is highly detailed and contains no disclaimers, it may be held to bind the parties as a valid contract. Ultimately, parties should generally refrain from signing even a preliminary document unless they are truly ready to conclude a binding agreement on terms that they are reasonably likely to obtain from the other party.

2.3 Model or standard contracts in international trade

2.3.1 Model or standard form contracts

The use of standard form contracts is quite common in international trade. For example, various commodity and raw materials markets use highly specific form contracts, which are virtually obligatory for market participants.

a. FIDIC AND ORGALIME CONTRACTS

A typical contractual standard is found in the FIDIC (Fédération Internationale des Ingénieurs–Conseils) form contracts. These are intended to serve as models for international engineering projects, primarily those based on competitive bidding in developing countries. Perhaps the best known of the FIDIC Contracts is generally known as the Red Book (official name: "Conditions of Contract for Works of Civil Engineering Construction"). The Red Book includes a standard form of tender, a form of agreement, general conditions, and conditions of particular application. It is available in a variety of languages. Orgalime (Liaison group of the European mechanical, electrical, electronic and metalworking industries) also produces a series of model general conditions for the supply of mechanical and electronic products.

Similarly, the United Nations Economic Commission for Europe (UNECE) has developed a series of standard terms and conditions for contracts for the construction of plant and machinery (mixed transactions involving supply of goods and services).

Yet another type of model is to be found in the professional form books published by legal publishers, such as Matthew Bender and Kluwer. These references are primarily intended as drafting guides for international trade lawyers, but they may prove useful in a trader's export library. Most law firms and company legal departments also find ways to stockpile and classify their contracts and forms over the years, so that lawyers working on repetitive transactions or parts of transactions can make use of detailed contracts that have been previously drafted and tested in actual transactions.

Great care should be used by beginning lawyers and non–specialists in the use of forms. The worst way to use a form is simply to sign it without reading it (although in some markets or sectors this may be common). The better approach is to prepare for negotiations by going through each clause of the various models that are available, seeking to determine whether the clause is favourable or not, and developing negotiating strategies as a function of one's conclusions.

b. THE ICC MODEL CONTRACTS (currently available for Sale, Agency, Distributorship, Franchising, Occasional Intermediary Contracts, with model clauses for Selective Distribution in progress)

These ICC Model Contracts respond to the need of international traders for a neutral, uniform framework for their contractual dealings.

Generally, international traders mustbase their contracts on the national law of one or the other parties, or must otherwise apply an international treaty or convention. The latter course may well be impossible, because in areas such as agency or distributorship there is no worldwide convention or treaty currently available that could provide a comprehensive international frame-work. In such casesthe only solution is to subject the contract to the national law of one of the contracting parties. Generally, this is satisfactory for the stronger party in the negotiations and less desirable for the other party. The weaker party is forced to adhere to a contract despite its relative ignorance of the substantive and procedural intricacies of the other country's law – a significant practical disadvantage should a dispute arise. The ICC Model Contracts provide a reliable alternative for parties faced with this problem. These ICC Contracts are developed on neutral premises, independent of any specific national legislation. Instead, they are based insofar as possible on prevailing standards of international trade practice.

1) *Balanced contracts* – An essential aspect of the ICC Model Contracts is that they seek to provide balanced instruments which do not give undue advantage to either side. This means that they may not be ideal for parties in extremely strong negotiating positions who are able to impose virtually any conditions. There are many other model contracts available on the marketplace, some of which may provide better protection for one or the other parties under particular circumstances. For example, a national commercial agents' association may publish a model agency contract which gives stronger protection to the agent than the ICC contract, while a manufacturers' association may publish a contract giving stronger protection to the principal. Seeking the middle way, the ICC contracts attempt to provide a neutral, fair and equitable document. Both sides can sign an ICC contract with a certain peace of mind, knowing that it was specifically designed to provide reasonable protection for both sides without either taking undue advantage.

2) *Application of the Lex Mercatoria in ICC Model Contracts* – The ICC Model
Contracts rely to some extent on Lex mercatoria or internationally accepted
general trade practices as the groundwork for interpretation of the contract,
unless the parties have otherwise agreed. In the event of a dispute arising
under an ICC Model Contract, the respective rights and obligations of the
parties will be determined by reference firstly to the contract itself, and
secondly to the lex mercatoria. This solution implies that in some cases an
arbitrator trying a case based on the ICC Model Contract will have a certain
degree of freedom to decide the case on those commonly accepted legal
principles which constitute the lex mercatoria, rather than upon specific,
national statutes.

The ICC Model Contracts are sufficiently detailed that the greater part
of possible disputes are covered by their provisions. National statutes
and jurisprudence are generally more detailed and precise than the
combination of ICC contract and lex mercatoria, but this advantage in
precision is outweighed by the potential conflicts and misunderstandings
that may arise when parties from different countries try to negotiate and
perform an international contract. Nonetheless, ICC Model Contracts do
provide for the possibility of expressly submitting the contract to a specific
national law. In any event, the mandatory laws of particular countries may
apply in certain situations regardless of contract provisions.

While it is possible that some provisions of an ICC Model Contract may
conflict with mandatory principles of the national law of one or the other
parties (in which case the national law might override the Model Contract,
depending upon whether the national provision is a matter of strong public
policy or "ordre public"), this is rather unlikely, given the Contracts' reliance
on widely accepted principles. Such a case appears to be an exception
since whenever there is a doubt, recommendations are made to users to
check that the clauses of the model contract conform to the mandatory
rules of the law.

3) *The central role of international arbitration* – Like many standard
international contracts, ICC Model Contracts prescribe international
commercial arbitration as the preferred mode of dispute resolution.
Arbitration is especially suitable for truly international projects. Moreover,
arbitrators, who come from a neutral background, are more likely to be
comfortable with the ICC Model Contracts' reference to lex mercatoria,
and feel unhindered by the lack of application of a specific national

legislation. It remains to be seen whether an arbitrator would consider reliance on an ICC Model Agency Contract as evidence that the parties were willing to have the dispute resolved with reference to lex mercatoria independently or reference to an applicable national law. National courts might have difficulty in applying the lex mercatoria to a dispute. Certain kinds of disputes, nonetheless, are considered "non–arbitrable" under the New York Convention of 1958.

NOTES

(1) See Richard Schaffer et al., International Business Law and Its Environment (5th Ed.), West Legal Studies in Business (2002), p.59–61.

(2) MCC Marble Ceramic v. Ceramica, 144 F.2d 1384 (1998).

(3) As to contractual obligations, please refer to the Rome Convention on the Law Applicable to Contractual Obligations (1980).

(4) Note however, that courts will always apply their own procedural law.

(5) See Fox, *International Commercial Agreements*, p. 128.

CHAPTER THREE

Resolving International Disputes

The basics: International traders should prepare their dispute resolution strategy while negotiating or concluding a contract. After a dispute has arisen, some methods of dispute–resolution may become unavailable.

DISCUSS DISPUTE–RESOLUTION DURING CONTRACT NEGOTIATION AND DRAFTING

Ideally, parties should ensure that their contract partners are trustworthy and reliable, thereby avoiding many disputes. The ideal contract will be sufficiently precise so that surprises are unlikely, and sufficiently flexible so that foreseeable contingencies can be handled by adaptation clauses. If the parties desire a long–term commercial relationship, they may wish to specify in their contract that disagreements be initially addressed by renegotiation, mediation or conciliation (sometimes called "alternative dispute resolution» or "ADR"). A well–drafted contract will also contain a clear and precise clause specifying the conditions of binding dispute–resolution. For major international transactions, commercial arbitration will generally be preferred to litigation because arbitration is considered to be more neutral, faster, cheaper, less adversarial and more confidential than litigation.

AFTER A DISPUTE ARISES

Even if the parties have failed to stipulate contractually a form of dispute–resolution, they may still come to an agreement after a dispute has arisen. This, however, becomes more difficult when the parties have adopted hostile, defensive postures. It often happens that a party conscious of his own responsibility or liability will seek to delay justice. In such cases the absence of prior agreement on issues such as applicable law and appropriate forum will multiply the opportunities for dilatory tactics.

3.1 Working it out – contractual foresight and adaptation clauses

Adaptation clauses are useful in contracts expected to last for a period of years or which are expected to begin a continuing commercial partnership. These have already been discussed above as regards the contract of sale. *Force majeure* and *excusable delay* clauses are what might be termed automatic adaptation clauses, in that certain future events automatically trigger a suspension of contract responsibilities. Under typical *force majeure* clauses, wars, strikes and natural catastrophes will excuse non–performance by one or both parties.

Price provisions are often linked to an *escalation clause* in the case of long–term contracts. A given price may remain in effect, for example, for six months, and thereafter be pegged to a publicly available inflation index. Thus, a buyer may be given a "best price" or "most favoured" clause, according to which the buyer is assured that it will never pay a higher price than any other customer. Product specifications may be subject to updating of catalogues or verifiable changes in market conditions. *Variation* and *substitution* clauses may allow a party to deliver goods which are functionally as good as the contract goods, but which may differ slightly in composition. Delivery provisions may be made flexible by allowing for excusable delays or time extensions, particularly in the event of unexpected occurrences. Specific clauses are often drafted to excuse non–performance as a result of significant changes in government policy, legislation or tax rules.

3.2 Talking it over – waiver, renegotiation, assistance of an expert and ADR

3.2.1 Waiver

A possible response to a minor contractual breach is for the other party to excuse the breach. It is quite common for minor breaches to be forgiven, as for example with respect to lateness in delivery, or with failure to reach minimum sales targets in agency and distributorship contracts. Such forgiveness may amount, from a legal point of view, to a "waiver" or abandonment of the aggrieved party's right to object.

One way of preserving one's rights and avoiding an unwitting waiver is to insert a clause in the contract specifying that all contractual modifications must be in writing. Another option, in the event that a party may wish to tolerate a particular breach on a single occasion, but not as a general rule, is to object in writing in response to each event of breach.

3.2.2 Renegotiation

The parties can always *mutually* agree to modify an existing contract. In some cases, the parties may wish to expressly include a clause that requires executives of the two parties to meet for formal renegotiation in the event of a disagreement. Under such a clause, the parties commit themselves to a concerted effort to avoid more acrimonious forms of dispute resolution, such as litigation.

3.2.3 Seeking the assistance of an expert

An independent expert in the relevant field can often assist parties in resolving their controversies. An expert could be requested to give an opinion on, for example, questions of a financial or technical nature. The typical fields of activity in which experts are well known include:

- technical assessment of machinery or processes;
- testing the quality of a product or construction artifact;
- investigating the performance or conformity of industrial plants;
- investigating the causes of failures; and
- investigating the causes and consequences of delays.

The role of an expert in advising on such matters could include:

- during the construction of a plant, advice on the conformity of materials or services with contractual specifications which may later be used as a "record of the factual situation" or could later form the basis of recommendations; and
- assisting lawyers in the preparation of a legal submission.

The purpose of the expert's findings, decisions or recommendations varies according to the parties requesting them. Alone, they will usually not form the basis of a binding, enforceable decision. However, such findings, decisions or recommendations, whether embodied in a report or not, made close to the time of the disputed events, can be highly persuasive for judges or arbitral tribunals.

The selection of competent experts, especially in an international context, is a delicate task and is vital to the success of the expertise.

Parties who require the services of an expert may request the ICC International Centre for Expertise (the "Centre") to furnish the name of such an expert in the particular field required. The Centre, established in 1976, operates under the *ICC Rules for Expertise* (available at www.iccexpertise.org). The Centre deals with technical, financial, legal, or other questions calling for specialized knowledge. Parties may agree to apply to the Centre for the appointment of an expert to provide a report on such a question. The expert's intervention can help the parties to resolve questions amicably or simply to establish certain facts.

The parties may refer to the Centre's Rules for Expertise in their contracts or at a later date. The Rules include the basic procedures applicable from the Request to appoint an expert up to the notification of a complete expert's report. Examples of the Centre's cases include: assessing the operational capacity of a product unit, assessing corrosion of materials, the financial audit of a company during a takeover, revaluation of a contract price, and assistance relating to dispute adjudication boards in international construction projects.

As an alternative to seeking the appointment of an expert, any party (or Arbitral Tribunal) may independently request the Centre to propose the name of an expert. A party could require an expert's opinion in various situations either inside or outside a dispute. For example, outside a dispute, a party may seek advice on technical matters before entering into a contract. An Arbitral Tribunal, in resolving a dispute, may seek an expert opinion on a technical matter or a specific point of law.

3.2.4 DOCDEX

The International Centre for Expertise also administers the *ICC Rules for Documentary Credit Instruments Resolution Expertise* (DOCDEX). DOCDEX was established by the ICC Commission on Banking Technique and Practice to facilitate the rapid settlement of disputes arising under the *Uniform Customs and Practice for Documentary Credits (UCP)* and the *Uniform Rules for Bank–to–Bank Reimbursement under Documentary Credits (URR)*. The revised version of the DOCDEX Rules, that entered into force in 2002, also provides for the settlement of disputes relating to the *Uniform Rules for Collections (URC)* and the *Uniform Rules for Demand Guarantees (URDG)*.

DOCDEX is a speedy and reliable dispute settlement mechanism providing for a document–based expert decision made by three experts, scrutinized by the technical adviser of the ICC Banking Commission and issued by the Centre for Expertise. The DOCDEX decision is not binding unless the parties have agreed otherwise. In most instances, the parties can expect the final opinion six to twelve weeks after the ICC has received the request, but exceptionally complex cases could take longer.

3.2.5 ADR

Mediation and conciliation are sometimes distinguished as being different legal concepts. However, they are usually considered to be synonymous terms. They refer to an amicable method of resolving disputes with the assistance of a neutral third party. Mediation/conciliation is theoretically a cheap and fast form of dispute resolution. Whether it succeeds or not will depend on such variable factors as the commitment of the two sides to a friendly resolution and the personal skills and dedication of the mediator/conciliator. The weakness of mediation/conciliation is the absence of enforcement powers. The procedure is usually not binding so the parties can simply walk away from the mediation/conciliation if they are unhappy with the result.

3.3 The ICC ADR Rules

3.3.1 General

The 1988 *ICC Rules of Conciliation* were replaced in July 2001 by the *ICC ADR Rules*. The *ICC ADR Rules* provide a flexible framework for amicable resolution of business disputes and differences with the help of a third party, known as a Neutral. The ICC ADR Secretariat supervises proceedings under the *ICC ADR Rules*. The *ICC ADR Rules* and the ADR Secretariat build on the experience gained by ICC in administering the *ICC Rules of Conciliation*.

3.3.2 Commencing ICC ADR proceedings

The *ICC ADR Rules* provide for two alternative methods for commencing ADR proceedings. The first is mutual request, whereby the parties may insert an ICC ADR clause into their contract or agree to ICC ADR at some time after the dispute has arisen.

The second occurs when there is no previous agreement for ICC ADR and the party wishing to commence ICC ADR proceedings files a unilateral Request with the ICC ADR Secretariat. In this scenario the ICC ADR Secretariat then notifies the Request to the other party (or parties). If the other party accepts to engage in ICC ADR proceedings, the proceedings commence. If there is no agreement, the proceedings cannot commence. Four alternative ICC ADR clauses have been proposed by ICC for the parties to insert into their contracts. They are not model clauses but rather suggestions that may be adapted to the parties' needs. They are presented in order of increasing obligations upon the parties, from purely optional to binding, and according to whether or not the ADR proceedings are combined with ICC arbitration proceedings.

3.3.3 The procedure in ICC ADR proceedings

The *ICC ADR Rules* allow the parties to choose whatever settlement technique they consider best suited to resolving their dispute. Possibilities include mediation, whereby the Neutral acts as facilitator to help the parties see eye–to–eye; referral to the Neutral for an opinion on one or more matters; a mini–trial, whereby a panel comprising the Neutral and an executive of each party gives an opinion or seeks a solution acceptable to all concerned; or a combination of various techniques. Under the Rules, mediation will be the fallback technique if the parties do not express a preference for a particular method.

Whatever technique is adopted, the success of the procedure will depend largely on the Neutral's personality, professional skills and human qualities. The parties may jointly designate the Neutral or agree upon the qualifications or attributes required of the Neutral to be appointed by ICC. In appointing the Neutral, ICC will appoint a person who is independent of the parties. A party who is dissatisfied with the appointment of the Neutral can submit a reasoned objection to the appointment of the Neutral within 15 days of her/his appointment and ICC will appoint another Neutral.

Once the proceedings have begun, an initial discussion takes place between the parties and the Neutral in order to define the procedure to be followed.

3.3.4 Result of ICC ADR proceedings

ICC ADR proceedings aim for a settlement or compromise agreement that finally settles all or some of the disputes between the parties. If the parties do not reach a settlement agreement, ADR proceedings do not result in any binding outcome. This is in contrast to arbitration, which results in a final award that is enforceable against the opposing party. ADR may, however, complement binding procedures such as arbitration. For instance, parties may turn to ADR in the course of arbitration proceedings if it seems likely that their dispute could be settled amicably. Alternatively, parties may choose a dispute resolution method which provides first for ADR and, in the event of failure to reach an amicable settlement, finally for arbitration.

Confidentiality is a key characteristic of ICC ADR, as it is of ICC Arbitration.

3.3.5 Further information on ICC ADR

Further information on the ICC ADR system can be obtained from the ADR website www.iccadr.org or by sending an e–mail to adr@iccwbo.org.

3.4 The final recourse: international litigation

3.4.1 Litigation

Dispute resolution via recourse to public courts or tribunals is generally the most costly and confrontational of the various dispute resolution options. Experienced traders and their counsel often try to avoid the possibility of court actions by negotiating for the inclusion of ADR or arbitration clauses in their contracts.

Considering the limitations of litigation, it may seem surprising that there are still traders and lawyers who appear to work from the assumption that litigation is the principal means of resolving commercial disputes, even minor ones. Some companies, and some countries, appear to be more litigious than others. This may be partially due to training, or lack of it (i.e., an ignorance of procedures like international commercial arbitration, ADR and the benefits of adaptation and re–negotiation clauses).

In some cases, practical or economic considerations may play a role in dictating the choice of litigation: the more powerful party can use the threat of costly court procedures to intimidate the weaker party.

International litigation can be slow, complicated, unfriendly, and expensive. It is technically difficult and requires professional counsel. Litigation is final after appeals are exhausted and enforceable in the country in which it takes place. However, in an international context, arbitration is often more effective than litigation in terms of enforcement, because arbitral awards are supported by the widely ratified 1958 New York Convention on the Recognition and Enforcement of Foreign Arbitral Awards.

In particular cases, the reputed drawbacks of litigation can be beneficial to one of the parties. A party which is in the wrong and expects to ultimately lose a case may prefer to stall the case in a national court system and delay judgement as long as possible.

3.4.2 Where to bring suit: jurisdiction and choice of forum

a. INTRODUCTORY

Lawsuits must be brought in the proper courts of the proper country. This is referred to as jurisdiction, the power or competence of a particular court to hear a case. The first thing an aggrieved party must do in an international dispute is choose a court or tribunal (a "forum") which has jurisdiction over the case.

Under the Roman law principle, *actor forum rei sequitur*[1], the plaintiff was required to bring suit in the defendant's local courts. As modern international trade developed, companies and their assets spread across the globe, fundamentally altering the underlying economic context. It became a matter of practical interest for an aggrieved trader to assert jurisdiction over a foreign defendant in any jurisdiction where that defendant had assets. While under the Roman jurisdictional rule the plaintiff followed the physical defendant, modern plaintiffs sought the freedom to follow the defendant's money or tangible assets. As international centres of commerce, particularly London and New York, grew in the 19th and early 20th centuries, their courts developed legal theories for sustaining this exercise of jurisdiction over foreign defendants.

Today, most courts asked to hear a case arising out of an export–import dispute will look first to the contract to see if it contains a choice of forum clause (see below), and will then determine in light of the circumstances and national law whether to assert jurisdiction.

b. CHOICE OF FORUM AND FORUM–SHOPPING

If a contract is silent on the country of the proper court, the parties involved in a dispute may to invoke the jurisdiction of the national courts in which they think they have the highest likelihood of success, or the courts which are most convenient for them. This practice, known as "forum–shopping", can create problems. A party might try to bring suit in a country only tangentially related to the contract, or, after a lawsuit has commenced in one country, bring a counter–suit in yet another country.

In order to avoid these uncertainties, parties to an international contract will frequently include a *forum selection* or *choice of forum* clause. Commonly, the party with the stronger negotiating position will propose a choice of forum clause stipulating that lawsuits must be brought in the stronger party's domestic courts.

Choice of forum clauses are usually subject to a test of *reasonableness*: the chosen forum must bear some logical relation to the subject of the contract. Thus, in a lawsuit arising under a distribution contract between a large German manufacturer and a small Puerto Rican distributor, it was held that a choice of forum clause specifying Mexico as the appropriate forum was unreasonable. The tacit effect of such a provision was, the court held, to render it difficult for the Puerto Rican distributor to undertake any legal action. However, even where the choice is reasonable, choice of forum clauses may not be respected in all countries or in all situations.

c. TYPES OF JURISDICTION – THE COMPETENCE OF A FORUM TO RECEIVE A CASE

1) *Subject matter jurisdiction* – this term refers to the power of a particular court to hear a particular *type* of case. In some countries, for example, only special commercial courts are empowered to decide commercial cases. This scope for receiving cases is sometimes also referred to as the *competence* of the particular court.

2) *Personal jurisdiction* – Crucial in international cases is the issue of *personal jurisdiction* over foreign parties – whether a court has judicial power over a person or company domiciled in another country. A court's personal jurisdiction is generally said to extend to all physical persons present, residing or domiciled in the forum state, as well as to any individuals who have *consented* to such jurisdiction. A foreign party manifests *express* consent to jurisdiction by signing an appropriate forum selection clause. In the absence of a forum selection or choice of law clause, some courts resort to a theory of *implied consent* to assert personal jurisdiction over foreign parties. For example, US courts will consider whether the foreign party has sufficient "minimum contacts" with the US, such as a branch office or regular commercial dealings in the US.

Ultimately, one option, which is almost always available, is simply to bring the lawsuit in the jurisdiction where the defendant is legally domiciled (a return to the Roman law principle). Unfortunately, this can involve great expense and inconvenience for the plaintiff.

3.4.3 Choice of law and applicable law

The parties may choose the law which they wish to govern their contract so long as it is not contrary to the public policy of the place where suit is brought.

If the contract does not specify the applicable law, or if the choice of law is unreasonable or contrary to public policy, then the court that hears the case will have to choose the applicable law. In doing so, courts refer to a body of legal theory known as "conflict of laws," which can involve complex analysis, beyond the scope of this book. However, the basic elements of conflict of laws analysis are grounded in common sense – the court will primarily look to the place where the contract was negotiated and/or signed, the place where it is to be performed, and the domiciles of the parties involved. Some countries leave great latitude to the courts to decide the most appropriate law (commonly, the law which bears "the most significant relationship" to the contract). Various international treaties provide a certain measure of harmonization of conflict of laws principles. Amongst the most important is the EC Convention on the Law Applicable to Contractual Obligations (Rome 1980), which applies in most European Union courts.

3.4.4 Enforcement of judgements

Winning a lawsuit is not enough. The legal judgement must then be *enforced*. If the complaining party obtains a judgement directing the other party to pay money damages, the prevailing party must also apply for a court order compelling the loser to pay over the funds. The likelihood of ultimately being able to enforce a judgement is something that must be thoroughly considered before the lawsuit begins. It may be useless to receive a money judgement against a party who is likely to declare bankruptcy or disappear. Thus, a party wishing to begin a lawsuit should assure himself that the other party has sufficient assets to satisfy a money judgement. It may be necessary to apply for an *injunction* – a court order – freezing those assets until the case is decided.

Difficulties often arise when a judgement is obtained over a foreign party who has no assets in the jurisdiction where the judgement is rendered. In this case, the successful party will look for countries in which the loser has assets to satisfy the judgement. Such assets can often be found in the jurisdiction where the losing party is domiciled. A court procedure commonly known as an *exequatur* or "execution of judgement" must then be held in that country. An exequatur involves a hearing by a court that is being asked to recognize a foreign court's judgement. Will the exequatur result in enforcement of the foreign judgement? The situation varies widely from country to country. In Europe, the Brussels and Lugano Conventions have made enforcement of foreign judgements from other signatory countries a fairly routine matter. In other countries, the courts will often ask whether there is a relationship of *reciprocity* between the courts of the two countries. In essence, this means, "we will enforce your judgements if we find you have enforced ours".

3.5 International commercial arbitration

3.5.1 Benefits of international commercial arbitration

International commercial arbitration is often the most appropriate dispute resolution mechanism for major international transactions where a binding decision is required. The advantages of arbitration are numerous:

a. NEUTRALITY

The choice of arbitration allows the parties to deal with the otherwise troublesome negotiating point of deciding where a lawsuit should be brought in the event of a dispute. Many traders may hesitate to take the risk that they would have to sue in a foreign court, where they may not only be unfamiliar with language, procedure, law, and customs, but where they may even have doubts about the neutrality of the judges or judicial system. With arbitration, the parties may agree that the case will be heard in a neutral country (although arbitration can take place anywhere, including the country of one of the contract parties).

b. CONFIDENTIALITY

Arbitration is private, confidential, and does not generate publicly available records of decisions. Companies may not wish to take the risk that unfounded charges against them gain publicity by being debated in open court.

c. EXPENSE, TIMING AND FINALITY

Arbitration is generally faster and cheaper than litigation. Experienced lawyers can sometimes take advantage of complicated court procedures to stall and delay the resolution of a case, while arbitral procedures are less amenable to dilatory tactics. In many countries the courts are so backlogged that even getting to the initial phases of hearing a case can take years. Moreover, arbitral awards are normally final, whereas court judgements can usually be appealed to higher courts. Finality in arbitration means that the dispute resolution process is less disruptive to business because the dispute will usually be resolved after only one set of proceedings.

d. LANGUAGE

Arbitration proceedings can be held in any language. As well as providing added convenience, this may reduce costs related to translations.

e. ARBITRATOR'S EXPERTISE

The parties in a dispute may be able to designate an arbitrator who is an expert in the relevant technical field, or who at least has experience in the relevant business sector. Experienced trial attorneys often complain that judges, on the other hand, do not really understand the technical issues upon which they are called to rule. The expertise of the arbitrator may also contribute to obtaining a more rapid final decision, because the arbitrator will not have to receive as much "education" as a judge.

f. ENFORCEMENT

Enforcing international arbitral awards may be simpler than enforcing judgements from foreign courts due to the existence of international conventions, in particular the UN convention on the recognition and enforcement of foreign arbitral awards known as the 1958 New York Convention"[2].

3.5.2 Potential disadvantages

Despite the foregoing, certain reservations are also sometimes voiced about arbitration.

a. COST AND DELAY

Although it is said that arbitration is relatively cheaper and faster than litigation, there are many examples of arbitral proceedings that were very expensive or dragged on for many years (which is not to say that those cases, had they been litigated, would not have been even more expensive and time–consuming). With litigation, by comparison, there is no need to pay the judges' salaries nor the rental of the courtroom. Nonetheless, arbitration is widely believed to be less expensive than litigation overall because the procedure is swifter and not open to appeal. Moreover, arbitration permits greater flexibility and party control over the procedures. In a sense, with arbitration you get what you pay for. However, parties are well–advised to understand that the assertion that arbitration is cheaper and faster does not necessarily mean that it is always cheap or fast.

b. PROCEDURAL SAFEGUARDS

The many procedural devices allowed in litigation, while often having the effect of slowing the progress of a case, are not without potential benefits for both sides. Some lawyers experienced in civil litigation have found themselves frustrated by what they perceived as the relative informality of arbitration, which in their eyes constituted a lack of "rigor" or "order". However, the inherent flexibility of arbitration means that whenever the parties agree that it is in their interests, proceedings can be pre–structured so as to have effective procedural safeguards. For example, complex arbitration proceedings can be conducted with transcripts or written records.

c. FINALITY

In litigation, losing parties may appeal to a higher court to have the matter reconsidered. However, in arbitration, the enforcement of an arbitral award may be challenged only to a limited extent in the appropriate court. In general, recourse against an arbitral award is much more limited than against an initial court judgement.

3.6 ICC Arbitration

3.6.1 Introduction

Arbitration under the auspices of the ICC International Court of Arbitration ("ICC Arbitration") is the most widely used form of institutional international arbitration. More than 12,000 cases have been submitted for ICC Arbitration since it was first made available in 1923. Over the past three years, more than 500 new Requests for Arbitration per year have been received by ICC. More than 1000 cases are currently pending, with a total amount–in–dispute value of approximately USD 30 billion. This caseload is growing at a steady annual rate.

ICC arbitration is distinguished by certain key features:

a. UNIVERSALITY

Unlike certain other forms of institutional arbitration, ICC is not limited in terms of technical or geographical scope. ICC arbitral proceedings have covered the full range of business sectors, involving parties from all corners of the globe, including both private and government entities. Although the International Court of Arbitration (the "Court") is based in Paris, and has meeting rooms and other infrastructure support there, the proceedings may take place anywhere in the world. In fact, the majority of proceedings take place outside of Paris. Arbitrators and counsel may come from almost anywhere; more than 60 nationalities were represented among ICC arbitrators in the year 2001. In 2001, the seat of the arbitration was fixed, either by the Court or the parties, in more than 40 different countries.

b. SUPERVISION

Especially as compared with ad hoc arbitration, ICC Arbitration distinguishes itself by virtue of its support from a professional staff. ICC Arbitration is the most highly supervised form of institutional arbitration. The Court employs more than 50 staff members. ICC staff relieves the arbitrators of the need to oversee such case management issues as supervising payment of fees and expenses. The Secretariat also handles much of the work involved in distributing necessary documentation. The Court scrutinizes the arbitral awards prior to their approval – a unique and important feature of ICC

Arbitration. Moreover, it is the Court, rather than the arbitrators, that notifies the parties of the ultimate award. The Court relies on a state–of–the–art computer system to file and track all arbitration documents.

c. STATURE

After seven decades as the world's pre–eminent arbitral institution, ICC has acquired a reputation for neutrality and integrity. This reputation may be of practical relevance in certain cases. For example, during negotiations parties are relieved of convincing their opponents of the neutrality of ICC Arbitration.

3.6.2 ICC arbitration clause

Although it is possible for parties to mutually decide on submitting a case for ICC Arbitration after the dispute has arisen, it is more common for the choice of ICC Arbitration to be made earlier, by including the appropriate arbitration clause in the contract. ICC recommends the use of the following standard clause:

> "All disputes arising out of or in connection with the present contract shall be finally settled under the *Rules of Arbitration* of the International Chamber of Commerce by one or more arbitrators appointed in accordance with the said Rules."

This clause can be complemented by the addition of stipulations as to the place of arbitration, the number of arbitrators (one or three), the applicable law, and the language to be used. In particular, parties who wish to make sure that the process is as fast and cheap as possible should seek to incorporate these precise stipulations in the contract. Thus, if parties can agree on an applicable law, it will save time wrangling about applicable law in the event of a dispute. One common solution is to stipulate the applicable law of a neutral country. The stipulation of a sole arbitrator is one way to make sure that the cost of arbitration is kept to a minimum.

If the contract involves multiple (i.e., more than two) parties, special provisions should be considered.

Parties should take care that any additions to the basic standard clause do not create ambiguity. For example, parties have been known to add the words "in Paris" after "International Chamber of Commerce". This may cause confusion as to whether they mean that the place of arbitration should be Paris.

3.6.3 ICC Court and Secretariat

The Court consists of a Chairman, several Vice–Chairmen, and more than 115 members from 77 different countries. The Secretariat is composed of a Secretary General, Deputy Secretary General, General Counsel, and seven teams each headed by a Counsel. There are also special Counsel and support staff.

The Court does not itself decide disputes; rather it oversees the conduct of proceedings and ensures that they conform to the ICC Rules. The Court's main tasks are:

1) In certain circumstances, to examine whether there is a prima facie agreement to arbitrate under the ICC Rules.
2) To appoint the arbitrators when the parties have not done so. For sole arbitrators and chairmen, the Court first determines that a particular nationality is desirable (that is, an appropriate nationality which is different from those of the parties), then requests the relevant ICC national committee to recommend an arbitrator. The recommendations are usually, although not obligatorily, followed. The Court also reviews and decides on parties' challenges to arbitrators on grounds of an alleged lack of independence or otherwise.
3) To fix the place of arbitration, unless agreed upon by the parties.
4) To examine and in some circumstances approve the arbitrators' Terms of Reference (see further on).
5) To determine the costs of the arbitration, including the arbitrators' fees, and establish appropriate deposits.
6) To decide on any necessary extensions of time limits.
7) To scrutinize and approve the draft arbitral Awards.

3.6.4 The Arbitrator(s)

In ICC Arbitration the parties are free to nominate the arbitrators for confirmation by the Court. If the parties do not choose the arbitrators, the Court will appoint a neutral arbitrator from a neutral country. The Court requires all arbitrators to be completely independent from both parties and the arbitrators must make an initial statement to this effect.

The dispute is decided generally by one or three arbitrators. If the parties do not specify the number of arbitrators, the Court will appoint a sole arbitrator save where it appears to the Court that the dispute is such as to warrant the appointment of three arbitrators. In deciding the number of arbitrators, the

Court takes into account factors like the complexity of the case and the amount of money in dispute. The contractual choice of three arbitrators is very common, perhaps because it allows each party to nominate one arbitrator. When drafting an arbitration clause specifying the number of arbitrators, the parties should also keep in mind that stipulating three arbitrators will clearly increase the overall cost of resolving the dispute, and may cause delay. Parties who believe that an arbitrator may not be completely independent may challenge the arbitrator by submitting the matter to the Court. If the Court finds that the arbitrator may not be independent, or is not otherwise properly fulfilling his or her duties, the arbitrator will be replaced.

3.6.5 ICC arbitration procedure

There is a large degree of flexibility, according to the will of the parties, with respect to the procedure in ICC Arbitration. Pursuant to the *ICC Rules of Arbitration* (the "Rules"), the procedure is generally as follows:

a. REQUEST FOR ARBITRATION

At least one party ("Claimant") must send a written Request for Arbitration (the "Request") to the Secretariat of the Court accompanied by a non-refundable advance of USD 2500 on administrative expenses. The Rules require that the Request identify all the relevant parties and describe the case. The Secretariat will then notify the other party or parties "respondent(s)" of the Request, forwarding all relevant documents. The respondent(s) must submit an "Answer" to the Request within 30 days, setting forth its defence, any counterclaims, and any comments on the constitution of the arbitral tribunal. The claimant is allowed 30 days to reply to any counterclaim. After receipt of the respondent's Answer, the Secretariat submits the case to the Court. The Court reviews the relevant documents and, unless the parties have made specific provisions, fixes the place of arbitration and chooses the arbitrator(s). In cases where the respondent(s) do(es) not answer or raises jurisdictional objections, the Court may decide that the arbitration will proceed if the Court is prima facie satisfied that an agreement to arbitrate under the ICC Rules may exist.

b. TERMS OF REFERENCE

A key feature of ICC Arbitration is the Terms of Reference, drafted by the Arbitral Tribunal in consultation with the parties, which describe the case, define the issues and indicate the place and applicable rules for the arbitration. The Terms of Reference are submitted to the parties for comment (the Arbitral

Tribunal may or may not amend the document according to the parties' input), then submitted to the parties for signature and ultimately to the Court. If any of the parties refuses to sign the Terms of Reference, the Court will decide whether or not to approve them. If all parties sign, the Court will only take note of the Terms of Reference. The arbitration can go forward regardless of the refusal by a party to sign the Terms of Reference.

Whether or not the Terms of Reference are a necessary part of arbitral proceedings has been a long–standing debate within the international arbitration community. It has been claimed that the usefulness of Terms of Reference is not sufficient to justify the time spent on their preparation. In recent years, however, there has developed an emerging international consensus that some form of preliminary procedure – such as that of the ICC Terms of Reference – is useful. ICC considers that Terms of Reference are an essential part of the ICC procedure and that they contribute significantly to refining the issues in dispute, thereby increasing the effectiveness of later hearings. Moreover, Terms of Reference can be prepared very quickly indeed if it is the desire of the parties to do so.

c. TIME LIMITS

The Terms of Reference must be submitted to the Court within two months after the Arbitral Tribunal receives the case file, and the Arbitral Tribunal must make its award within six months after the signature of the Terms of Reference. However, the Court may authorize extensions of the time limits following a reasoned request or on its own initiative. Such extensions are granted whenever necessary.

d. PROCEEDINGS

The ICC Rules are designed to be very flexible with respect to the proceedings. The parties are free to agree on the rules of procedure. If they fail to agree, however, the procedure will be decided by the Arbitral Tribunal, which will further decide on the need for hearings (although the parties have a right to be heard if they so request), examination of witnesses, or the appointment of experts. Once the Secretariat has transmitted the file to the Arbitral Tribunal, the Arbitral Tribunal may, at the request of a party, grant interim or conservatory measures (for example a party may seek an injunction to freeze assets or force the other party to refrain from certain actions). Before the file is transmitted to the Arbitral Tribunal, and in appropriate circumstances even after the file is transmitted, the parties may seek such measures from any competent judicial authority without affecting their right to arbitrate their dispute.

e. APPLICABLE LAW

If the parties do not agree upon the applicable law, for example in the contract, it will be decided by the Arbitral Tribunal.

f. AWARD

Final or interim decisions by the Arbitral Tribunal are called awards. Awards must be in writing and are rendered either by unanimous decision, by majority, or failing these, by the Chairman. In some cases with three arbitrators, dissenting opinions may also be rendered. If the parties are able to work out a settlement between themselves, they may wish to have such a settlement formalized as an award, thereby facilitating enforcement; such awards are called "awards by consent". The award also decides the apportionment of costs of the arbitration, including legal costs.

The award is first submitted in draft form to the Court, which may modify the form of the award and, without affecting the Arbitral Tribunal's liberty of decision, make suggestions as to the substance of the award. The parties are then notified of the award, but only after they have fully paid the costs of the arbitration.

If one of the parties refuses to comply with the award, the other party may seek enforcement in a competent court. Such recourse is simplified by the existence of the 1958 New York Convention on the Recognition and Enforcement of Foreign Arbitral Awards, which has been signed by more than 125 countries.

g. COSTS

Costs include the arbitrators' fees and expenses, the ICC's administrative expenses, the fees of any experts, and lawyers' fees and expenses.

Upon receipt of the Request for Arbitration, the Secretary General fixes a provisional advance which is designed to cover the Arbitral Tribunal's fees and expenses and the ICC's administrative expenses until the Terms of Reference have been drawn up. The file will not be transmitted to the parties until this provisional advance is paid. When the case is first submitted to the Court, the Court fixes the amount for the required advance on costs. Ultimately each side (i.e., claimant(s) and respondent(s)) is required to pay 50% of the advance on costs. ICC's administrative expenses and the range of possible fees for the arbitrators are calculated depending on the amount in dispute and according to a fixed Schedule of Costs and Fees contained in the ICC

Rules. An arbitration cost calculator, for estimating the costs of a future arbitration proceeding, can be found on the International Court of Arbitration's website (www.iccarbitration.org). If one party fails to pay its share of the advance on costs the other party is given the opportunity to pay it, or to supply a bank guarantee, so that the arbitration can proceed.

h. ICC "FAST–TRACK" ARBITRATION

A fast–track arbitration is one where both parties have agreed to a specific form of expedited arbitral proceeding. What distinguishes a fast–track arbitration is that within the framework of the *ICC Rules of Arbitration* the parties agree to a faster arbitration proceeding with respect to all or certain of their disputes. Care should be taken in drafting a fast track arbitration clause and it is recommended that parties engage experienced counsel for this purpose.

3.7   Other arbitration institutions and rules

Other well–known arbitration institutions include the London Court of International Arbitration (LCIA), the American Arbitration Association (AAA), the Stockholm Court of Arbitration, and the China International Economic and Trade Arbitration Commission (CIETAC).

The United Nations Commission on International Trade Law (UNCITRAL) has promulgated a very important set of rules for international commercial arbitration which allow arbitration proceedings conducted independently of an arbitration institution ("ad hoc" arbitration). Since the UNCITRAL rules were developed without reference to a specific arbitration institution, they are somewhat general as regards costs and fees, merely establishing a standard of "reasonableness". A notable success of the UNCITRAL rules involved their use as the basis of proceedings at the US–Iranian Claims Tribunal at The Hague.

"Ad hoc" arbitration refers to an arbitration that is structured by the parties themselves. The parties may base themselves in part on rules and procedures such as those of UNCITRAL, or they may create their own procedure. Ad hoc arbitration proceedings can be useful, particularly where the parties are cooperative, but parties should be aware that ad hoc proceedings require expertise on behalf of the legal counsel who negotiates the arbitration structure and can require recourse to national courts where one party refuses to take part in the proceedings.

Notes

(1) "the plaintiff follows the forum of the defendant."

(2) The New York Convention on the Recognition and Enforcement of Foreign Arbitral Awards – more than 125 countries are parties; the full list of signatory countries can be found on the UNCITRAL website (www.uncitral.org).

CHAPTER FOUR

International Contracts of Sale and General Conditions

The basics: The international sale contract is the central contract in export transactions. In law, a contract is created by the conjunction of offer and acceptance. In international trade, this offer and acceptance may be manifested in a variety of fashions, such as by the exchange of exporter's pro forma invoice (offer) and importer's purchase order (acceptance). A good sale contract or set of general conditions of sale will cover all the principal elements of the transaction, so that surprises and uncertainties are avoided. The parties' respective duties as concern the payment mechanism, transport contract and insurance responsibilities, inter alia, will all be clearly detailed in the contract.

4.1 The law governing the contract of sale

The rights of buyers and sellers in international merchandise transactions are governed either by national law (usually, the law of either the seller or the buyer's domicile) or by an international treaty, the Vienna Convention on the International Sale of Goods (described further on). Since the Vienna Convention and most national sales laws are based on the distilled experience of centuries of commerce, it is not surprising that they exhibit a great degree of similarity. This substantial international uniformity in commercial practice is at the heart of the concept of lex mercatoria, the international law of merchants. The lex mercatoria covers not only transnational rules but also international trade usages which can assist traders, arbitrators and judicial bodies in resolving commercial disputes.

Despite the emergence of a certain level of international uniformity as regards national commercial laws, there remain important differences. Such differences can be determinative of the outcome in a particular case, so that redress for a particular party may depend on which national law applies. For this reason, it is quite common for the party in the stronger negotiating position to seek to impose a choice of law clause stipulating that its national law governs the contract.

4.1.1 The Vienna Convention on Contracts for the International Sale of Goods (CISG)

Commonly referred to as "the Vienna Convention", or by its initials (CISG), this Convention provides a unified set of rules on the formation and execution of contracts for the international sale of goods. As of 2001, 60 countries had ratified CISG, including most of the major trading nations. The pace of ratification has been such that all international trade professionals should acquire a basic familiarity with the provisions of this key document.

a. SCOPE

CISG applies to international commercial transactions. Four important constraints limit its application:

1) It only applies to international sales – CISG applies if both parties to the contract are in different Contracting States (countries which have ratified CISG); or if only one of the parties is in a Contracting State but conflict of laws rules point to the application of the law of a contracting state; or if both parties expressly agree to submit their contract to the application of CISG (conceivably, even if neither is in a Contracting State).

2) CISG expressly excludes coverage of: consumer sales; sales of ships, aircraft and electricity; securities transactions; sales where services play a preponderant role (although in this latter case the two parties may specifically state that they wish to override the exclusion and subject their contract to CISG).

3) CISG does not cover certain important aspects of international sales, most notably:
   - trade terms (terms for the delivery of the goods and the fixing of the price, such as FOB and CIF, where CISG defers, inter alia, to Incoterms – see further on); and
   - the passing of property in the goods (the point at which the title to the goods is transferred from the exporter to the buyer – see further on).

4) CISG provides that parties may "contract out" of CISG or any of its provisions; this is in recognition of the principle of freedom of contract or the autonomy of the parties. Parties may also use CISG as a primary law governing the contract, but agree to resort to a specific national law as a "gap–filling" device.

b. KEY PROVISIONS

CISG is composed of 101 articles which take up approximately 20 printed pages. Exporters and importers should especially be aware of the following points (keeping in mind that it is possible to expressly vary or exclude CISG provisions if both parties agree):

1) *Oral contracts* – These are permitted and enforceable under CISG; signed writings are not required.

2) *Prior course of dealings and trade usages* – CISG provides that the "parties are bound by any usage to which they have agreed and by any practices they have established between themselves".

3) *Contract formation* – An offer is any proposal that is "sufficiently definite", meaning that it at least "indicates the goods and expressly or implicitly fixes or makes provision for determining the quantity and the price". Acceptance of an offer is effective when it reaches the offeror; however, the offeror may not revoke an offer once the offeree has dispatched his acceptance.

4) *The "Battle of the Forms"* – When the parties exchange printed forms that differ on certain terms, the question arises of which form prevails, the seller's or the buyer's? The CISG rule is that a buyer's acceptance that differs materially (e.g., on a key point such as price, quantity, quality or delivery date) from the seller's offer amounts to a rejection and counter–offer, which the seller must expressly accept. If the buyer's acceptance only differs on points that are not material, then the acceptance is deemed to form a valid contract unless the seller objects. Ultimately, the easiest option is to try to always be the one who "fires the last shot". Thus, exporters may wish to provide a printed acknowledgement form – including the general conditions of sale – in response to buyers' purchase orders. Obviously, if either party believes that a provision contained in the other's general conditions is material and unacceptable, they should openly negotiate for a modification of that provision (see discussion on general conditions of sale further on).

5) *Delivery and risk of loss/Incoterms 2000/UCP 500* – Delivery and risk of loss are covered much less fully than by *Incoterms 2000*; traders, therefore, should explicitly incorporate Incoterms into the sale contract (see further on). Moreover, in contracts involving letters of credit, banks will generally follow rules in the International Chamber of Commerce's *UCP 500*, which require that "all parties deal in documents, not goods". To avoid discrepancy between CISG and the UCP 500, a prudent approach would be to specifically refer to UCP 500 in that part of the sale contract setting out the seller's documentary duties.

6) *Passage of property/title* – Not covered by CISG (nor Incoterms), therefore a matter of applicable domestic law; traders should specify the point at which they wish title to pass, after having checked the compliance of said provision with domestic law.

7) *Warranties* – CISG provides that the seller must deliver goods that are "of the quantity, quality and description required by the contract ... The goods do not conform with the contract unless they ... are fit for the purposes for which goods of the same description would ordinarily be used [or] are fit for any particular purpose expressly or impliedly made known to the seller at the time ... of the contract".

8) *Inspection of the goods* – The buyer must inspect the goods and "loses the right to rely on a lack of conformity of the goods if he does not give notice... within a reasonable time after he has discovered [the non–conformity] or ought to have discovered it". The exporter may wish to expressly specify a limited period for notification of defects. Moreover, the exporter may wish to expressly override the CISG article 27, under which the exporter bears the risk of delay or non–receipt of notices from the buyer.

9) *Remedies* – CISG allows for the full scope of remedies, including specific performance, delivery of substitute goods, price reduction, and compensatory damages. Exporters may wish to expressly limit recourse to these remedies, as, for example, by limiting liability and by excluding consequential damages, price reduction or specific performance options.

As is inevitably the case with attempts at international harmonization, CISG may not be to the benefit of all traders in all sales transactions. CISG is sometimes said to be more favourable to buyers and to parties in developing countries than to sellers or parties in industrialized countries.

Nonetheless, CISG is undeniably a landmark document which plays a central role in international commerce. It is sufficiently comprehensive and balanced that more and more parties are likely to turn to it as an alternative to protracted negotiating contests in which each side seeks to impose its own domestic law.

4.2 The contract of sale

4.2.1 Basic elements

Under most legal systems, an international contract of sale comes into existence when a sufficiently precise offer by one party is accepted unconditionally by the other party. A sufficiently precise offer generally includes:

- a clear description of the goods
- price and payment terms
- delivery terms, including packing, invoicing, transportation and insurance instructions.

Whether or not an offer in a particular case is adequately precise will depend on the applicable law and circumstances of the case. Even if one or more of the above "essential" terms is absent from an agreement, a court may nonetheless find a binding contract. A variety of devices can be used to "fill in the gaps".

Either the exporter or importer can be the one who makes the first legally binding offer. To take one example: an exporter replies to an inquiry from a prospective importer with a quotation that is clearly only intended to be an invitation to contract (and therefore not a binding offer). In such a case, the importer's purchase order is considered the offer. If the exporter wishes to conclude a contract, he will accept the offer, which is usually done via a confirmation.

However, to take a slightly different example, suppose that the exporter's sales proposal is extremely concrete, contains all the above essential elements, is addressed to a specific importer and the exporter clearly intends to be bound thereby. Here, the exporter's proposal amounts to a legally binding offer and the importer's purchase order constitutes an acceptance, concluding a binding contract.

4.2.2 Checklist – Key clauses in international sales contracts

The following clauses are often included in international contracts of sale and general conditions of sale:
- preamble
- identification of parties
- description of goods
- price and payment conditions
- delivery periods and conditions
- inspection of the goods – obligations and limitations
- quantity or quality variations in the products delivered
- reservation of title and passing of property rights
- transfer of risk – how accomplished
- seller's warranties and buyer's complaints
- assignment of rights
- force majeure clause
- requirement that amendments or modifications be in writing
- choice of controlling language of the contract
- choice of law
- choice of dispute resolution mechanism

4.2.3 Elements of a sale contract; the ICC Model Contract

The discussion of sale contract clauses will frequently refer to the *ICC Model International Contract of Sale* (hereafter, the "ICC Model"). Note, however, that the ICC Model contract is two–part in nature. The first part, the Special Conditions, contains the basic information commonly found in export quotes or pro forma invoices. The Special Conditions set out terms which are specific to a particular contract. The second part, the General Conditions, sets out standard terms. Many international contracts, however, do not follow this two–part structure. Therefore, the discussion below assumes a contract based on a single set of clauses. We will examine the specific ICC provisions in greater detail in section 4.3.3 on general conditions of sale or purchase.

a. PARTIES TO THE CONTRACT; PREAMBLE

These introductory types of clauses generally identify the parties and the effective date of the contract. It is important that the parties, and their correct legal denomination, be carefully and exactly specified. In some countries corporations, especially family–owned ones, can be knit into a network of cross–owned companies. Some of these companies may be mere "shells" without assets, which means that a lawsuit against them could prove fruitless.

Therefore, the party identified in the contract should be exactly the same company for which credit and bank references have been fully checked, and not one of its sister companies with a similar name. Likewise, an individual signing a contract on behalf of a company should do so in such a fashion that it is clear which party is to be bound by the contract – the company or its representative.

b. SUBJECT MATTER; PRODUCT DESCRIPTION AND/OR "SCOPE OF WORK"
In a sale contract, the minimum "scope of work" is the seller's supply of the specified products. Where the contract calls for a preponderant part of the seller's obligations to involve services or labour, CISG (the Vienna Convention) is no longer applicable, unless the parties expressly decide to incorporate CISG notwithstanding the non–merchandise characteristics of the contract. As in the ICC model contract, introductory clauses may set forth basic definitions and/or explanations of the structure of the contract.

c. DESCRIPTION
The question of preciseness of description of the contract goods is worthy of attention. Generally, exporters should be cautious and brief in describing products. In some legal systems, if the goods delivered vary from the description given in the contract it may be possible for an importer faced by a falling market to terminate the contract, claiming that the seller has not fulfilled the contractual duty to deliver goods of the contract description. A buyer acting in bad faith might seek to seize upon irrelevant details which the seller has unwisely and unnecessarily placed in the contract. Thus, it can be dangerous to deliver goods which are "too good" – that is, goods of a superior but slightly different nature to that specified in the contract. Example: a buyer contracts to buy a shipment of used personal computers containing Intel "Pentium II" chips. The seller ultimately delivers – for the same price – computers containing "Pentium III" chips (which are technically superior). The buyer, for commercial reasons, is no longer able to pay for the shipment. Some systems of law would allow the buyer to terminate such a contract, on the grounds that the seller has delivered goods which are different to those required by the contract.

Risks resulting from excessively detailed product description can also arise in connection with a letter of credit. If a contract of sale is based on a pro forma invoice which contains an excessively detailed description of the products, the chances are increased that some aspect of that description will conflict with other documents required under the credit, thereby leading to a discrepancy and rejection by the bank of the documents. Certainly, if the seller delivers merchandise which is "too good", as in the previous paragraph, and the commercial invoice then differs from the product description in the letter of credit, the bank will initially reject the documents and it will be up to the importer to decide whether or not to waive the discrepancy.

The importer, on the other hand, is faced with contrary imperatives. She will want to negotiate a description which identifies the goods with sufficient precision such that the exporter cannot deliver goods which are "almost" good enough. Vague and general locutions are not helpful in the event of a later dispute and should be replaced by objective or documentary criteria (e.g., "top quality fish meal" will not be as useful in a court dispute under a documentary credit as "inspection certificate issued by XX company to indicate fish meal with a minimum 70.75% protein content"). Some contracts include a separate Definitions section, for technical terms or terms with legal connotations, such as "delivery", "shipment", "acceptance", or "confirmation".

Exporters may wish to stipulate in their sale contracts or general conditions of sale that variations in quality or quantity that are of minimal importance should not be grounds for termination of the contract. For minor defects in the products, which do not prevent the buyer from using them more or less as intended, the buyer and seller may agree that it is fair that the buyer pay a reduced price or get a refund, because the goods delivered were of lesser quality than those specified in the contract at the contract price.

For defects which make it impossible for the buyer to use the goods at all, the buyer will commonly wish to negotiate for a right to a full refund, although she may find herself obliged to accept a corresponding duty to take care that any goods under her control are not improperly stored or disposed of, assuming that they have any residual value. The question of whether or not the buyer should also be entitled to consequential damages (damages which result from the contract breach, such as lost profits or production) is one that will vary according to the commercial context and legal system.

Case Example

How old is this chicken? A fowl misunderstanding.

Frigaliment Importing Co., Ltd v. B.N.S. International Sales Corp.

An American exporter of chickens entered into a contract with a Swiss importer for the sale of some 125,000 lbs. of chickens varying in weight from 1° to 3 lbs. When the initial shipment arrived, the importer discovered to its dismay that the birds were not young chickens suitable for broiling or frying, but were older "fowl" suitable only for stewing. The importer brought suit in US Federal Court. The bemused judge noted, "The issue is, what is chicken?" The contract did not resolve the issue, referring generally only to "chicken". The judge heard contradictory testimony from various chicken experts (that is, humans in the poultry trade). The exporter's witness testified, somewhat unhelpfully, "Chicken is everything except a goose, a duck, and a turkey." In the end, the judge held that the burden of persuasion was on the plaintiff – the importer. If the importer wanted young chickens, he should have so specified in the contract.[1]

Comment: This case demonstrates the importance of a properly drafted description of the goods in the contract of sale.

---

d. PRICING

Whenever the contract is one for long duration, or when inflation or currency fluctuations otherwise make it sensible, exporters should consider including price escalation or adaptation clauses. One possibility is to make the price firm for a given period of time, and beyond that time to peg the price to publicly available labour and/or commodities indexes. There are thus situations in which it is acceptable to the parties to leave some uncertainty in the price – as of the date of conclusion of the contract; but the mechanism for fixing the price later should be clear.

For examples of price escalation clauses and formulae there are numerous industry and trade–association instruments. Thus, the Federation of British Electrotechnical and Allied Manufacturer's Associations (BEAMA) has issued a series of Contract Price Adjustment (CPA) clauses, which set precise arithmetical formulae for calculating price variations resulting from fluctuations in the cost of materials and labour. The United Nations Economic Commission for Europe has issued a series of general conditions of sale for the erection of plants and machinery abroad (sometimes called "turnkey" contracts), which contain a straightforward price revision formula that allows the parties to negotiate the degree of price adjustment and to agree on the public indexes or other sources of economic statistics upon which the revisions will be based.[2]

e. DELIVERY, TRANSPORT, INSURANCE

In international contracts, these items are best covered by reference to Incoterms 2000, trade terms defined by ICC (see section on *Incoterms 2000* further on), such as FCA (Free Carrier), FOB (Free on Board) or CIF (Cost, Insurance and Freight). Incoterms 2000 principally cover allocation of international transport costs, transfer of risk, responsibility for customs clearance and duties, and responsibility for obtaining insurance coverage. Incoterms 2000 are nonetheless fairly general terms, and parties may be well advised, particularly when dealing with new counterparties, to make additional specifications with respect to the exact manner of delivery, the amount and duration of insurance, and necessary limitations on suitable transport. The ICC model stipulates the Ex Works (EXW) term as a fallback provision when the parties have not otherwise chosen a specific trade term.

The importer will be wise to describe precisely the point of delivery. A failure to do so will allow the exporter to exploit general terms – thus, "FOB Spain" will ultimately allow the exporter to deliver at any Spanish port.

The question of timeliness of delivery is often dealt with by specific provisions in the contract of sale. With some products, late delivery is not a cause of concern, and the payment of a small percentage penalty by the exporter in such cases seems reasonable. However, with other products, late delivery is a serious breach, depriving the importer of the entire value of the product. In such cases, the importer will want to insist in the contract that time of delivery is "of the essence". The importer may further wish to make the exporter liable for consequential damages flowing from late delivery. Such provisions will be strongly resisted by exporters, but in certain jurisdictions some liability for consequential damages may be inescapable regardless of contractual provisions.

f. RETENTION OF TITLE AND TRANSFER OF PROPERTY

The transfer of legal title to goods in international transactions is covered neither by Incoterms nor the Vienna Convention, but by national law. Consequently, the parties are free to specify how title passes, but they should be careful to verify that the method they have chosen is permitted by the applicable national law.[3]

The retention of title (ROT) clause is a common one in international trade. It provides that the seller retains legal ownership of the goods until the full purchase price is paid. In a sales transaction without a retention of title clause, title passes from the seller to the buyer independently of the payment of the purchase price. In some countries, title will pass at the moment of physical delivery of the goods, while in others title passes according to the agreement reached between seller and buyer. If a buyer who has received goods is unwilling or unable to pay the price, the seller may find himself barred from claiming title to the goods. These considerations become crucial when buyers become insolvent and other creditors are competing for the buyer's remaining assets. With a valid ROT clause, the seller can reclaim the goods even if the buyer is bankrupt.

There are several variations of the ROT clause, but two major types can be distinguished:

1) The simple ROT clause, under which the seller retains title until the price is paid, and
2) The extended clause, under which the seller seeks to extend its title to include:
    i. the proceeds from any sale of the goods
    ii. any goods commingled with, or manufactured from, the contract goods
    iii. any other indebtedness owed to the seller by the buyer
    iv. any combination of the foregoing

The availability of recourse to extended–type clauses will depend on the applicable national law. Contract drafters therefore should prepare the ROT clause in light of the national law as regards the transfer of title, as previously indicated.

g. PENALTY AND LIQUIDATED DAMAGES CLAUSES

The contract may provide that a party which fails to comply with obligations, or is late in doing so, will pay a fixed sum. The purpose may be to compensate the damaged party (liquidated damages) or to stimulate compliance via the threat of punishment (penalties). In some jurisdictions, penalties are not allowed and consequently liquidated damages that are held to be punitively harsh will be invalid. It is therefore prudent to provide a pre–estimate of likely damages, even if these are difficult to calculate, so that courts will be more likely to respect the fixed sum as a form of liquidated damages.

h. FORCE MAJEURE AND HARDSHIP/EXCUSABLE DELAYS

Under most systems of law, a party can be excused from a failure to perform a contract obligation that is caused by the intervention of a totally unforeseeable event, such as the outbreak of war, or an "act of God" such as an earthquake or hurricane. Under the American Uniform Commercial Code

(UCC) the standard for this relief is one of "commercial impracticability". In contrast, many civil law jurisdictions apply the term force majeure to this problem. Under CISG, the standard is based on the concept of "impediments" to performance. Because of the differences between these standards, parties might be well advised to draft an appropriate clause in the contract to minimize the damages, should disruption later occur. ICC *Force Majeure Clause 2003 and ICC Hardship Clause 2203*[4] (ICC Publication 650), provides a model force majeure clause that could be incorporated by reference in the contract. When the seller wishes to devise his own excusable delays clause, he will seek to anticipate in its provision such potential difficulties as those related to obtaining government authorizations, changes in customs duties or regulations, drastic fluctuations in labour, materials, energy, or transportation prices, etc.

4.3 General conditions of sale (or purchase)

4.3.1 The purpose of general conditions of sale (or purchase)

Many international contracts are made up of two parts: 1) a precise commercial offer in the form of a pro forma invoice or memorandum, which is subject to 2) certain standard legal terms known as "general conditions", "general conditions of sale/purchase", or "general terms and conditions". The general conditions often appear as a pre–printed set of clauses on the back of, or attached to, specific tenders, proposals, price lists, catalogues, acceptances, confirmations or purchase orders.

The purpose of general conditions is to complement business forms or correspondence which do not cover all important legal aspects of the transaction. General conditions are not used whenever a unique, detailed contract is to be specifically drafted. General conditions save time by establishing a standard legal framework which will then apply to a multitude of repeated, individual transactions. This enables exporters to carry on and conclude negotiations on the key practical issues of price, delivery terms and quality, leaving the legal "fine points" to be covered by the general conditions. Those contractual provisions which are not appropriate for inclusion in general conditions are those that will vary from contract to contract, such as price, product specification and delivery details. These contractual provisions should be incorporated in the special conditions of the sale contract.

4.3.2 The "battle of the forms": obtaining agreement to general conditions

With general conditions, as with other provisions of the contract of sale, one must obtain the agreement of one's counterparty. Thus, if a seller were to send the general conditions along with the commercial invoice <u>after</u> the goods had been dispatched, the conditions would have no legal effect. However, if one party transmits general conditions along with the offer or acceptance, the silence or performance of the contract by the other party may be construed as acceptance of the general conditions. It is nonetheless preferable that the counterparty agree to the general conditions in writing. One way to obtain written agreement is to include a confirmation slip along with the order or acceptance form (to which the general conditions are attached). The counterparty is requested to return the confirmation slip, duly signed. As a result, some exporters have a rule that sales personnel are not authorized to sign customer purchase orders without management review (because to do so could indicate assent to the buyer's general conditions of purchase).

Many international traders do not systematically address the battle of forms issue. Instead, a series of printed forms are exchanged between seller and buyer (proposal, purchase order, acknowledgement, confirmation, etc.), and performance follows without further reflection. Only when a dispute arises and the lawyers are called in do parties begin to consider the significance of discrepancies between their general conditions.

Example

An exporter's general conditions (printed on the back of the sales offer) contain a broad clause admitting various possible excuses for minor delays, whereas the importer's general conditions (printed on the back of the purchase order) contain a much more restrictive force majeure clause under which most foreseeable delays are inexcusable. The exporter's shipment arrives late, for reasons excused by the exporter's clause – but not the importer's. In such a case, the exporter who has not bothered to demand written confirmation of acceptance of his general conditions could find himself faced with a suit for damages.

The only absolutely "safe" procedure is to refuse to conclude the contract until the other side signs your general conditions. However, since this may be viewed as impractical or unwieldy, some traders resort to the "last shot" theory. Under this approach, whichever party transmits the last printed form ("fires the last shot") has a better chance of imposing its general conditions.

This is by no means as legally secure as a negotiated, signed agreement, since the availability of the last shot theory will depend on applicable law.

4.3.3 ICC Model General Conditions of Sale, a balanced set of clauses

As described in the preceding sections, ICC has developed a set of Model General Conditions of Sale in conjunction with the *ICC Model International Sale Contract* (the "ICC Model"). The ICC Model consists of two parts:

- *Special Conditions* – This part corresponds to the role of a form sale contract or pro forma invoice; and
- *General Conditions* – This part provides a detailed legal background to complement the basic provisions on price, product description, payment and delivery terms contained in the Special Conditions.

As previously mentioned (see supra section 4.2.3), the Special Conditions set out terms which are specific to a particular contract. The General Conditions set out standard terms, namely defaulting clauses that are applicable in absence of any choice by the parties.

It is intended that parties be free to use the ICC General Conditions independently, even if they do not use the Special Conditions.

The ICC Model as a whole is intended to dovetail with the provisions of the Vienna Convention, thereby creating a "CISG–compatible" instrument. Although the ICC Model differs substantially from other, more specifically targeted general conditions, it can serve as a useful example of one way of dealing with the issues usually covered by general sales conditions.

a. SCOPE

Because general conditions will vary according to the nature of the products, ICC decided to focus on a single key sector of international trade: mass–produced manufactured goods intended for ultimate re–sale to consumers. This would cover everything from toasters to toothbrushes, but would not apply to goods for industrial use such as large machine tools, nor to custom–made goods, raw materials or commodities.

b. INCORPORATION BY REFERENCE

It is intended that parties be able to incorporate the ICC Model by a simple reference, such as: "This contract is subject to the general conditions of the ICC Model International Contract of Sale". Theoretically, an exporter could make a sales offer, "100USD/container blue widgets FOB New York Incoterms 2000 under the general conditions of the ICC Model International

Contract of Sale", and expect thereby to conclude, with buyer's acceptance, a detailed and complete international contract of sale. However, whether or not courts would enforce the reference to the ICC General Conditions could depend on whether it could be established that the buyer was familiar with those terms. So it is probably better to include the full text of the general conditions, at least in early communications to the counterparty. Moreover, in light of the discussion above on the battle of forms, it is preferable to obtain the counterparty's signed agreement to the General Conditions.

c. PRODUCT CHARACTERISTICS

How strictly will the exporter be bound to deliver the exact qualities and specifications he mentions in his sales literature and in his catalogues? The ICC Model provides that product characteristics (e.g., dimensions, capacities, prices, colours, etc.) contained in catalogues and brochures, or evidenced in samples, will only be binding upon the seller if they are expressly referred to in the sales contract.

d. PRE–SHIPMENT INSPECTION (PSI) AND EXAMINATION OF THE GOODS

The ICC Model provides the following rule: if the parties have agreed to PSI, the seller must notify the buyer within a reasonable time before shipment that the goods are ready for inspection.

e. PRICE AND PAYMENT CONDITIONS

Under the ICC Model, the current list price of the seller applies unless otherwise agreed. The price is net of VAT (value–added tax) and is not subject to price adjustment.

The ICC Model permits use of all payment modes, including open account, documentary collection, documentary credit, and payment in advance. If the parties fail to specify any form of payment, a default provision is based on an open account payment by electronic funds transfer.

f. RETENTION OF TITLE

If the parties have agreed on retention of title, the goods shall remain the property of the seller until the complete payment of the price or as otherwise agreed (see supra, discussion of retention of title in section 4.2.3 f.).

g. DELIVERY

Unless otherwise agreed, delivery is at seller's place of business (EXW Incoterms 2000). The ICC Model also makes highly specific provisions with respect to calculation of liquidated damages in the event of the buyer's claim for lateness or non–delivery, the idea being to limit the amount of damages available to the buyer in the event of a delayed shipment. In essence, the seller must pay liquidated damages of 0.5% of the price per week of lateness up to a maximum of 5% of the price.

h. TRANSFER OF RISK

According to the rules of Incoterms.

i. NON–CONFORMITY OF THE GOODS

Products with tolerances which are reasonable or within the range of usages or common practices shall not be deemed non–conforming. The buyer must notify the seller in writing of any non–conformity within a specified period of time.

i. FORCE MAJEURE

Failure of performance by either party is excused in the event of "force majeure", which in essence amounts to reasonably unforeseeable and unavoidable circumstances, beyond its control, which make it substantially impossible for a party to fulfil its obligations.

k. APPLICABLE LAW AND ARBITRATION

Any questions not covered by the ICC Model are to be resolved by reference to CISG, and if these are not covered by CISG, to general principles of international trade or lex mercatoria (see section 4.1). Dispute resolution is by arbitration under the *ICC Rules of Arbitration.*

4.3.4 Industry–specific general conditions – UN ECE and others

Many trade associations and international organizations have developed general conditions which are specifically suited for a particular industrial sector. The United Nations Economic Commission for Europe (UN ECE), in particular, has developed a series of these instruments. A typical example is UN ECE 188, entitled "General Conditions for the Supply of Plant and Machinery for Export". UN ECE 188 resembles the ICC Model in many key respects, but is understandably much more detailed when it comes to such items as delivery (which can be particularly complicated when the product is an entire manufacturing plant), technical drawings, and guarantees. Traders should check with their relevant industry association for the existence of specifically adapted general conditions.

4.3.5 Sales contracts online: the way of the future

A web–based application launched by ICC in 2002 is an innovative new step in negotiating a sales contract. The application is marketed under the brand name Paction, and it combines the benefits of a neutral model contract with the advantages of the global market opened up through the Internet.

The online dealing enables both buyer and seller to prepare, negotiate and complete contracts for the international sale and purchase of goods, keeping track of every stage of the negotiation via the Internet and – once both parties are satisfied – sealing the deal by digital signature.

The Internet version brings a number of advantages:
Based on the clauses of the *ICC Model International Sale Contract*, Paction provides the same level of flexibility and authority as the paper version, combined with the speed and convenience of dealing over the web, rather than transmitting printed documents. Every phase of the negotiation can be monitored, with revisions preserved under time and date stamps. Both buyer and seller can sign online, using digital ID. The contracts can be securely stored. The application can be found at *www.modelcontracts.com*. Other ICC contracts are expected to join the program.

4.4   Trade terms for international contracts – *Incoterms 2000**

The basics: Incoterms 2000 are internationally standardized "trade terms" (such as FCA, FOB, and CIF), which enable exporters to quote prices that clearly allocate the costs and risks of international transport between seller and buyer. Insurance responsibilities (under CIF and CIP) and customs formalities are also covered by Incoterms.

Incoterms should be explicitly incorporated into contracts of sale by reference, e.g., "FOB Rotterdam Incoterms 2000". Incoterms govern certain responsibilities between seller and buyer under the contract of sale; they should not be confused with the allocation of responsibilities between shipper, carrier and consignee under the contract of carriage.

When goods are containerized, when transport is multi-modal, or when delivery is to an inland terminal, traders should not use the traditional set of maritime terms, FOB – CFR – CIF, but should instead use the more appropriate terms, FCA – CPT – CIP.

---

* Incoterms™ 2000 (ICC Publication 560) is an ICC registered trademark.
  For more information, please visit www.iccwbo.org/index_incoterms.asp

Reflecting the general trend in international trade and transport to "house–to–house" service, the "delivered" or "D"–terms" Incoterms (especially DDU and DDP) are becoming more prevalent.

4.4.1 Introductory

a. HOW WERE INCOTERMS DEVELOPED? HOW ARE THEY USED?

ICC derived Incoterms (International Commercial Terms) from studies of prevailing international trade practices, publishing the first version of Incoterms in 1936. Subsequent revisions were published in 1953, 1967, 1976, 1980 and 1990. The current valid version is *Incoterms 2000*. Incoterms can be incorporated into contracts by simple reference, e.g., "FOB Liverpool Incoterms 2000".

The most recent version of Incoterms, *Incoterms 2000*, takes into account the latest changes in contemporary commercial practice. *Incoterms 2000* also seeks to update and clarify any provision of *Incoterms 1990* that had given to misunderstandings or disputes (e.g., the loading obligation under EXW, the application of FOB for containers, the terminal handling charges under FCA, etc.).

The introduction of *Incoterms 2000* as well as the preambles to the terms were redrafted to be more precise. A new section on terminology was added to define the most important concepts used in the new version. The parties' obligations, such as loading and unloading, were more precisely detailed.

Substantive changes were also made in two areas: the customs clearance and payment of duty obligations under FAS and DEQ, and the loading and unloading obligations under FCA (see infra 4.4.3).

The Incoterms tell the buyer what is "included" in the sales price, by allocating transport costs and risks, as well as the responsibility for insurance and customs formalities, between the seller and buyer.

There are 13 Incoterms. They can be thought of as representing a stepladder of increasing responsibility from seller's premises to buyer's premises. Thus, the Incoterm which represents the minimum responsibility for the seller is EXW (Ex Works), which is generally used in cases involving delivery at the seller's factory or warehouse. At the other extreme, the Incoterm DDP (Delivered Duty Paid) represents maximum responsibility on the part of the seller, with delivery generally at the buyer's premises.

A buyer on EXW terms knows that nothing "extra" (in terms of transport, customs clearance or insurance) is included in the sales price – the buyer must handle the entire transport operation themselves. A buyer on DDP terms ("Delivered Duty Paid"), knows the quoted price includes all transport costs, risks and formalities up to the final destination. In between these two extremes, there are 11 other Incoterms, representing a range of options for the division of costs/risks between the parties.

b. HOW DOES ONE INCORPORATE INCOTERMS INTO A CONTRACT?

Key reminder: traders should explicity refer to "INCOTERMS 2000".

Traders should link their contracts to Incoterms by explicitly referring to Incoterms. The common practice of quoting a price as follows, "$100/ton FOB New York" (without an explicit reference to "*Incoterms 2000*") can be DANGEROUS. In the absence of a specific reference to Incoterms the trader may lose the right to apply Incoterms to the contract. The contract may consequently be subjected to a national legal definition, with surprising results (e.g., the American definition of FOB can be quite different from the "Incoterms" definition). The correct formulation of the above contract would be "$100/ton FOB New York Incoterms 2000".

c. ARE INCOTERMS THE LAW?

The legal nature of Incoterms is frequently misunderstood. Incoterms are creatures of contract, not legislation. Incoterms apply to a contract whenever the parties can demonstrate that they both intended Incoterms to apply. If the parties fail to incorporate Incoterms into the sales contract, they may not be able to invoke Incoterms once a dispute has arisen; instead, national legal interpretations may apply.

There are, however, exceptions. If trade customs, general sales conditions, commercial usages or previous contractual dealings indicate that the parties intended to use Incoterms, then Incoterms may apply even in the absence of a specific mention in the sale contract. Under some legal systems great weight is given to customs of trade and there may be a presumption that Incoterms constitute a custom of trade. In such countries, courts or arbitrators might take judicial notice of an Incoterms rule to resolve a case although Incoterms had not been incorporated into the contract.

d. WHY SHOULD IMPORTERS AND EXPORTERS UNDERSTAND THE INCOTERMS IN DETAIL?

Many international traders, unfortunately, have only a general idea of the differences between Incoterms such as EXW, FOB, CIF or DDP. As a result, they are unprepared for certain common contingencies with respect to transfer of risk, loading/unloading, customs clearance and insurance. For example, one of the more common uncertainties arising in international sales is, who is responsible for loading (or unloading) the goods? An understanding of Incoterms will generally allow the matter to be solved.

e. WHAT IMPORTANT MATTERS ARE NOT COVERED BY INCOTERMS?

The Incoterms do not cover all possible legal or transport issues arising out of an international sale. Incoterms are a sort of contractual shorthand that allows the parties to easily specify their understanding as to: 1) the transport costs that the seller will cover; 2) the point at which risk of loss will be transferred from seller to buyer; 3) who must handle customs formalities and pay duties; and, 4) in the case of CIF and CIP, the seller's responsibility to provide insurance cover.

Other details must be dealt with specifically in the contract. Thus, there is nothing in the Incoterms on how the seller should transport the goods to the agreed delivery point. If the sale is "FOB Buenos Aires *Incoterms 2000*" the buyer has no control – under Incoterms – over how the seller gets the goods to Buenos Aires. But it may be very important to the buyer that the goods be transported in a certain way, for example, in refrigerated containers. If this is the case, the buyer should specify in the contract how the goods must be transported to the delivery point.

Key reminder: Incoterms cannot be expected to make up for a contract which is not sufficiently precise. In many cases it is advisable to include in the sale contract precise details on exact place and method of delivery, loading and unloading charges, extent of insurance, and mode of transport.

Moreover, Incoterms only cover those cases where one party has an obligation to the other party to do something. Incoterms do not indicate when a trader should do something because it is prudent or advisable. Thus, a buyer of merchandise in an FOB contract has no obligation to take out insurance, and Incoterms are silent on this matter. But since the risk of loss is on the buyer once the goods have been loaded, she would be very foolish not to take out insurance.

f. TRANSFER OF PROPERTY OR TITLE

One of the key areas not governed by Incoterms is that of the transfer of property or title to goods. In fact, there is no international legal harmonization as regards the transfer or title or property in international transactions. Thus, the matter is not resolved by the Vienna Convention on the International Sale of Goods.

Since the law on transfer of property rights differs from country to country, the parties to a contract of sale may wish to specifically provide for this matter in the contract, but only after determining what is permissible under the applicable law. Under many jurisdictions it is possible for the seller to retain title and ownership of the property until the purchase price is paid in full, even if this takes years. This "retention of title" by the seller is usually set out in a clause in the contract of sale (see supra, discussion in section 4.2.3.f).

4.4.2 The contract of sale and the contract of carriage: Incoterms, liner terms and charter party terms

Perhaps the most common misunderstanding related to Incoterms involves confusion of the contract of sale with the contract of carriage. Note the distinction:

- *Contract of sale* – Incoterms are embedded in this contract, an agreement between the seller and the buyer.
- *Contract of carriage* – This contract is between the shipper and the carrier (or his agent). Depending on the contract of sale and the chosen Incoterm, the shipper may be either the seller or the buyer.

Incoterms are not part of the contract of carriage. However, the choice of Incoterm may oblige the shipper to obtain a contract of carriage with particular conditions. One cause of confusion in this area is that terms in the contract of carriage resemble Incoterms (for example, in their usage of the word "free" as in "free in and out"), but traders should remember that these are separate contracts with separate sets of responsibilities.

Many traders appear to expect that the transport contract will automatically accord with the Incoterm in the sales contract. Although it is indeed important that the transport responsibilities required by the Incoterm in the contract of sale accord with the terms of the contract of carriage, there is nothing automatic about it. It is up to the shipper to give precise instructions to the carrier or freight forwarder so that the proper transport arrangements are made and so that the invoices are prepared accordingly. In some cases, inexperienced traders do not even inform the carrier as to the Incoterm in the contract of sale, then profess surprise later when the billing for transport services does not accord with the Incoterm.

a. LINER TERMS

With "liner" transport the shipper entrusts his goods to a "shipping line" which often is a member of one of the large "conferences" (groups of shipping companies that have associated to assure levels of service at specified price ranges on particular ocean routes). Not all shipping companies belong to the conferences – those that do not are called "outsiders" or "tramps". Certain costs may be included in the freight (such as loading or unloading charges) levied by regular shipping lines – hence, "liner terms". With liner terms, for example, discharging expenses are frequently included in the freight. Shippers should take care to ensure that the charges included in the liner terms accord with the shipper's transport responsibilities under the given Incoterm (see also Chapter 9 on sea freight).

b. CHARTER PARTIES

Another basic form of maritime transport is via charter party, under which the shipper hires a ship or part of a ship. In this context, "free in" and "free out" mean that the loading or unloading obligations are not included in the charter party hire.

Thus, when a seller under CIF has chartered the vessel on "free out terms", he will have assumed the costs of loading and discharge vis–a–vis the shipowner. It will be in the seller's interest to require the buyer to discharge the goods within a certain number of days (referred to as the "laytime"). Conversely, a shipowner may provide for a bonus (known as "dispatch money") to the seller (when the seller is the charterer) for timely discharging, which the seller may pass on as an incentive to the buyer. The relationship of these charter party arrangements to the agreement between seller and buyer should be clarified in the contract of sale.

Finally, under CFR and CIF Incoterms, where a bill of lading "contains a reference to a charter party", the charter party must also be tendered by seller to buyer. In this requirement Incoterms departs from the rule under certain national legal systems, such as that of the United Kingdom.

4.4.3 Summary of *Incoterms 2000*

The Four Basic Incoterms Groups: "E"–, "F"–, "C"– and "D"–Terms

"E"–terms:
The goods are placed at the disposal of the buyer at the seller's premises/factory.
"F"–terms:
The buyer is responsible for the cost and risk of the main international carriage.
"C"–terms:
The seller pays for the main international carriage, but does not bear the risks during that carriage.

▓ "D"–terms:

The seller bears all transport–related costs and risks up to the delivery point at the agreed destination, which may be in the buyer's country or even at the buyer's premises.

Incoterms definitions – the preambles to the 13 current Incoterms

> **Please note:** The preambles to *ICC Incoterms 2000* provide an excellent introduction and overview of each Incoterm, but they do not constitute the full, definitive text of *Incoterms 2000*, which is somewhat more detailed (available from www.iccbooksusa.com or from your local ICC national committee or chamber of commerce). Please also note that a few of the Incoterms preambles contain footnotes which refer to particular sections of the Introduction to Incoterms. These sections from the Introduction are reprinted at the end of this chapter.

▓ "E"–Terms

EXW

EX WORKS (... named place)

"Ex works" means that the seller delivers when he places the goods at the disposal of the buyer at the seller's premises or another named place (i.e., works, factory, warehouse, etc.) not cleared for export and not loaded on any collecting vehicle.

This term thus represents the minimum obligation for the seller, and the buyer has to bear all costs and risks involved in taking the goods from the seller's premises.

However, if the parties wish the seller to be responsible for the loading of the goods on departure and to bear the risks and all the costs of such loading, this should be made clear by adding explicit wording to this effect in the contract of sale*. This term should not be used when the buyer cannot carry out the export formalities directly or indirectly. In such circumstances, the FCA term should be used, provided the seller agrees that he will load at his cost and risk.

▓ "F"–Terms

FCA

FREE CARRIER (... named place)

"Free Carrier" means that the seller delivers the goods, cleared for export, to the carrier nominated by the buyer at the named place. It should be noted

---

* Note: refer to *Incoterms 2000* Introduction, paragraph 11 found at the end of this chapter.

that the chosen place of delivery has an impact on the obligations of loading and unloading the goods at that place. If delivery occurs at the seller's premises, the seller is responsible for loading. If delivery occurs at any other place, the seller is not responsible for unloading.

This term may be used irrespective of the mode of transport, including multimodal transport.

"Carrier" means any person who, in a contract of carriage, undertakes to perform or to procure the performance of transport by rail, road, air, sea, inland waterway or by a combination of such modes.

If the buyer nominates a person other than a carrier to receive the goods, the seller is deemed to have fulfilled his obligation to deliver the goods when they are delivered to that person.

FAS
FREE ALONGSIDE SHIP (... named port of shipment)
"Free Alongside Ship" means that the seller delivers when the goods are placed alongside the vessel at the named port of shipment. This means that the buyer has to bear all costs and risks of loss of or damage to the goods from that moment.
The FAS term requires the seller to clear the goods for export.
This is a reversal from previous Incoterms versions which required the buyer to arrange for export clearance.
However, if the parties wish the buyer to clear the goods for export, this should be made clear by adding explicit wording to this effect in the contract of sale*.
This term can be used only for sea or inland waterway transport.

FOB
FREE ON BOARD (... named port of shipment)
"Free on Board" means that the seller delivers when the goods pass the ship's rail at the named port of shipment. This means that the buyer has to bear all costs and risks of loss of or damage to the goods from that point. The FOB term requires the seller to clear the goods for export. This term can be used only for sea or inland waterway transport. If the parties do not intend to deliver the goods across the ship's rail, the FCA term should be used.

---

* Note: refer to *Incoterms 2000* Introduction, paragraph 11 found at the end of this chapter.

The distinction between two key groups of Incoterms

FCA · CPT · CIP

(general, multimodal /containerized transport)

FOB · CFR · CIF

(maritime transport only)

The key difference is in the point of **TRANSFER OF RISK** :

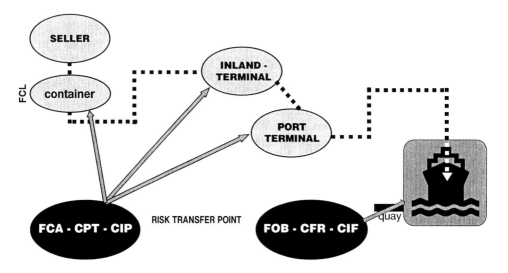

Since containerized and multimodal shipments are often delivered to the carrier far <u>inland</u> from the ship's rail, it makes sense to move the point of risk transfer accordingly. Pursuant to the sale contract, delivery may take place at any one of a number of stipulated points.

Risks are transferred at ship's rail

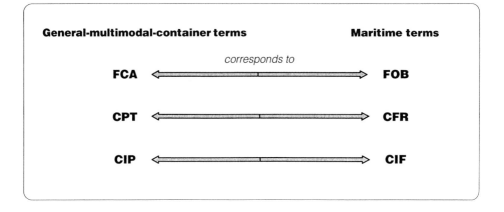

▬ "C"–Terms

CFR
COST AND FREIGHT (... named port of destination)

"Cost and Freight" means that the seller delivers when the goods pass the ship's rail in the port of shipment.

The seller must pay the costs and freight necessary to bring the goods to the named port of destination BUT the risk of loss of or damage to the goods, as well as any additional costs due to events occurring after the time of delivery, are transferred from the seller to the buyer.

The CFR term requires the seller to clear the goods for export.

This term can be used only for sea and inland waterway transport. If the parties do not intend to deliver the goods across the ship's rail, the CPT term should be used.

CIF
COST, INSURANCE AND FREIGHT (... named port of destination)

"Cost, Insurance and Freight" means that the seller delivers when the goods pass the ship's rail in the port of shipment.

The seller must pay the costs and freight necessary to bring the goods to the named port of destination BUT the risk of loss of or damage to the goods, as well as any additional costs due to events occurring after the time of delivery, are transferred from the seller to the buyer. However, in CIF the seller also has to procure marine insurance against the buyer's risk of loss of or damage to the goods during the carriage.

Consequently, the seller contracts for insurance and pays the insurance premium. The buyer should note that under the CIF term the seller is required to obtain insurance only on minimum cover*. Should the buyer wish to have the protection of greater cover, he would either need to agree as much expressly with the seller or to make his own extra insurance arrangements.

The CIF term requires the seller to clear the goods for export.

This term can be used only for sea and inland waterway transport. If the parties do not intend to deliver the goods across the ship's rail, the CIP term should be used.

---

* Note: refer to *Incoterms 2000* Introduction, paragraph 9.3 found at the end of this chapter.

CPT
CARRIAGE PAID TO (... named place of destination)

"Carriage paid to..." means that the seller delivers the goods to the carrier nominated by him but the seller must in addition pay the cost of carriage necessary to bring the goods to the named destination. This means that the buyer bears all risks and any other costs occurring after the goods have been so delivered.

"Carrier" means any person who, in a contract of carriage, undertakes to perform or to procure the performance of transport, by rail, road, air, sea, inland waterway or by a combination of such modes.

If subsequent carriers are used for the carriage to the agreed destination, the risk passes when the goods have been delivered to the first carrier.

The CPT term requires the seller to clear the goods for export.

This term may be used irrespective of the mode of transport including multimodal transport.

CIP
CARRIAGE AND INSURANCE PAID TO (... named place of destination)

"Carriage and Insurance paid to..." means that the seller delivers the goods to the carrier nominated by him but the seller must in addition pay the cost of carriage necessary to bring the goods to the named destination. This means that the buyer bears all risks and any additional costs occurring after the goods have been so delivered. However, in CIP the seller also has to procure insurance against the buyer's risk of loss of or damage to the goods during the carriage.

Consequently, the seller contracts for insurance and pays the insurance premium.

The buyer should note that under the CIP term the seller is required to obtain insurance only on minimum cover*. Should the buyer wish to have the protection of greater cover, he would either need to agree as much expressly with the seller or to make his own extra insurance arrangements.

"Carrier" means any person who, in a contract of carriage, undertakes to perform or to procure the performance of transport, by rail, road, air, sea, inland waterway or by a combination of such modes.

---

* Note: refer to *Incoterms 2000* Introduction, paragraph 9.3, following Preambles

If subsequent carriers are used for the carriage to the agreed destination, the risk passes when the goods have been delivered to the first carrier.

The CIP term requires the seller to clear the goods for export.

This term may be used irrespective of the mode of transport including multimodal transport.

▦ "D"–Terms

DAF
DELIVERED AT FRONTIER (... named place)
"Delivered at Frontier" means that the seller delivers when the goods are placed at the disposal of the buyer on the arriving means of transport not unloaded, cleared for export, but not cleared for import at the named point and place at the frontier, but before the customs border of the adjoining country. The term "frontier" may be used for any frontier including that of the country of export. Therefore, it is of vital importance that the frontier in question be defined precisely by always naming the point and place in the term.

However, if the parties wish the seller to be responsible for the unloading of the goods from the arriving means of transport and to bear the risks and costs of unloading, this should be made clear by adding explicit wording to this effect in the contract of sale*.

This term may be used irrespective of the mode of transport when goods are to be delivered at a land frontier. When delivery is to take place in the port of destination, on board a vessel or on the quay (wharf), the DES or DEQ terms should be used.

DES
DELIVERED EX SHIP (... named port of destination)
"Delivered Ex Ship" means that the seller delivers when the goods are placed at the disposal of the buyer on board the ship not cleared for import at the named port of destination. The seller has to bear all the costs and risks involved in bringing the goods to the named port of destination before discharging. If the parties wish the seller to bear the costs and risks of discharging the goods, then the DEQ term should be used.

This term can be used only when the goods are to be delivered by sea or inland waterway or multimodal transport on a vessel in the port of destination.

---

* Note: refer to *Incoterms 2000* Introduction, paragraph 11, found at the end of this chapter.

DEQ
DELIVERED EX QUAY (... named port of destination)

"Delivered Ex Quay" means that the seller delivers when the goods are placed at the disposal of the buyer not cleared for import on the quay (wharf) at the named port of destination. The seller has to bear costs and risks involved in bringing the goods to the named port of destination and discharging the goods on the quay (wharf).The DEQ term requires the buyer to clear the goods for import and to pay for all formalities, duties, taxes and other charges upon import.

This is a reversal from previous Incoterms version which required the seller to arrange for import clearance.

If the parties wish to include in the seller's obligations all or part of the costs payable upon import of the goods, this should be made clear by adding explicit wording to this effect in the contract of sale[*].

This term can be used only when the goods are to be delivered by sea or inland waterway or multimodal transport on discharging from a vessel onto the quay (wharf) in the port of destination. However if the parties wish to include in the seller's obligations the risks and costs of the handling of the goods from the quay to another place (warehouse, terminal, transport station, etc.) in or outside the port, the DDU or DDP terms should be used.

DDU
DELIVERED DUTY UNPAID (... named place of destination)

"Delivered duty unpaid" means that the seller delivers the goods to the buyer, not cleared for import, and not unloaded from any arriving means of transport at the named place of destination. The seller has to bear the costs and risks involved in bringing the goods thereto, other than, where applicable[**], any "duty" (which term includes the responsibility for and the risks of the carrying out of customs formalities, and the payment of formalities, customs duties, taxes and other charges) for import in the country of destination. Such "duty" has to be borne by the buyer as well as any costs and risks caused by his failure to clear the goods for import in time.

However, if the parties wish the seller to carry out customs formalities and bear the costs and risks resulting therefrom as well as some of the costs payable upon import of the goods, this should be made clear by adding explicit wording to this effect in the contract of sale[***].

---

[*] Note: refer to *Incoterms 2000* Introduction, paragraph 11, found at the end of this chapter
[**] Note: refer to *Incoterms 2000* Introduction, paragraph 14, found at the end of this chapter
[***] Note: refer to *Incoterms 2000* Introduction, paragraph 11, found at the end of this chapter

This term may be used irrespective of the mode of transport but when delivery is to take place in the port of destination on board the vessel or on the quay (wharf), the DES or DEQ terms should be used.

DDP
DELIVERED DUTY PAID (... named place of destination)
"Delivered duty paid" means that the seller delivers the goods to the buyer, cleared for import, and not unloaded from any arriving means of transport at the named place of destination. The seller has to bear all the costs and risks involved in bringing the goods thereto including, where applicable, any "duty" (which term includes the responsibility for and the risks of the carrying out of customs formalities and the payment of formalities, customs duties, taxes and other charges) for import in the country of destination.

Whilst the EXW term represents the minimum obligation for the seller, DDP represents the maximum obligation.

This term should not be used if the seller is unable directly or indirectly to obtain the import licence.

However, if the parties wish to exclude from the seller's obligations some of the costs payable upon import of the goods (such as value–added tax: VAT), this should be made clear by adding explicit wording to this effect in the contract of sale[**].

If the parties wish the buyer to bear all risks and costs of the import, the DDU term should be used.

This term may be used irrespective of the mode of transport but when delivery is to take place in the port of destination on board the vessel or on the quay (wharf), the DES or DEQ terms should be used.

4.4.4 Incoterms categories

In order to understand how to properly use them, it is helpful to be familiar with certain fundamental distinctions in Incoterms.

a. MARITIME TERMS VS. GENERAL/MULTIMODAL TERMS

■ *"General/container/multimodal" Incoterms: FCA – CPT – CIP*
These Incoterms are the modern counterparts of older, maritime terms (FOB – CFR – CIF) and were specifically developed for containerized and multimodal

---

[*] Note: refer to *Incoterms 2000* Introduction, paragraph 14, found at the end of this chapter
[**] Note: refer to *Incoterms 2000* Introduction, paragraph 11, found at the end of this chapter.

Note the Difference between C- and D- terms !

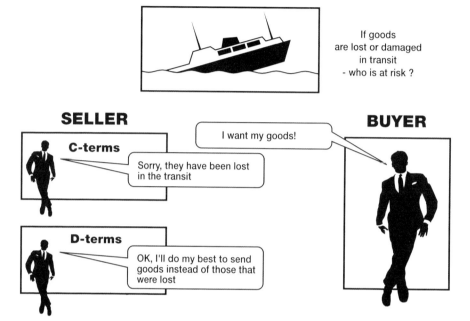

The basic distinction between C- and D- terms becomes crucial when goods are lost or damaged in transit. With C-terms, the seller has already fulfilled his delivery obligations, while with D-terms the seller may be liable for breach of contract.

transport – but they are suitable for all modes of transport. Only FCA, CPT or CIP should be used when transport is containerized or multimodal. Multimodal transport refers to that which involves a sequence of different modes of transport – e.g., goods are first hauled by road carrier, then shipped on a container vessel, then transferred to rail transport. However, it should be noted that these modern terms were designed for a maximum of flexibility, so that they can be used for virtually all modes of transport, including traditional bulk maritime transport.

The terms DDU and DDP are suitable for all forms of transport, but their use often implies multimodal transport.

The DAF term is a unique case, used primarily for road/rail transport.

- *"Maritime only" Incoterms: FAS – FOB – CFR – CIF – DES – DEQ*

These six Incoterms have derived from long–standing tradition in sea transport. Today, they should be used only for sales in which the principal international transport will be by seagoing vessel. Nonetheless, the three most common terms, FOB, CFR and CIF, are widely over–used and mis–used by exporters, who quote them even in regard to transactions in which the goods are containerized or will be delivered at an inland point rather than on board a vessel.

The key distinction between the maritime terms and the multimodal terms is the different point of transfer of risk and division of cost. With the traditional maritime terms, FOB, CFR and CIF, the division of risks and costs between seller and buyer is at the ship's rail. If a crate, being hoisted over the ship's rail by means of a crane, were to slip and fall onto the wharf, destroying the merchandise, the loss would be the seller's, and the seller would not have fulfilled the sales contract.

In modern transport practice, non–bulk goods are frequently shipped in containers that are mechanically stacked in immense container yards. Furthermore, "roll–on roll–off" (RO–RO ships) allow lorries to drive container loads directly onto the ship. With the increasing prevalence of these practices, it was no longer appropriate to divide responsibilities at the ship's rail, for reasons linked to both risk and cost.

With containerized transport, the seller commonly delivers the full container (FCL) or the goods to be grouped into a container (LCL) at a point inland from the ship's rail. Often the goods are delivered to a container terminal, which may be located at the port or even far inland. Since goods are leaving the seller's control earlier, it no longer makes sense to divide risk at the ship's rail. Goods may be lost or damaged in between the time they are delivered to the container terminal and the time they are loaded on board (it does happen that port terminals suffer from fire damage). In such a case, the unwary seller who has not required a sufficiently inclusive insurance policy may find that he is not insured for the loss of the goods.

However, even if the goods have been fully insured under an "open" cover or "floating" policy, the seller who is unable to load goods in good condition on board commits a breach of the sale contract. Under FOB, CFR, or CIF, the seller is required to deliver the goods on board.

Moreover, the seller of a containerized shipment under FOB or CIF may not be able to comply with the requirement to furnish the "usual" transport contract required under clause A3 of Incoterms, because the buyer will not receive complete legal rights against the carrier. That is, there may be a gap in the coverage provided by the bill of lading, between the delivery to the inland container terminal (which may be operated by someone other than the carrier) and the loading on board the vessel provided by the carrier.

In response to the difficulties of adapting traditional Incoterms to modern transport practices, ICC developed the "modern" trade terms appropriate for containers, RO–RO ships, and multi-modal transport. Under these terms, delivery is considered to occur when the goods are received into the transportation system. Thus, the FCA, CPT, and CIP terms move the crucial transfer point inland, to the point where the seller hands the goods over to the carrier, as at a container or port terminal.

The ship's rail had proven troublesome, not only with respect to the transfer of risks, but also to the division of costs. Technically, costs under FOB, CFR and CIF are to be divided precisely at the ship's rail. But it is virtually never the case that port authorities or stevedores divide the charges for loading operations at the ship's rail. Thus, either the seller or buyer will pay entirely for these operations, although technically they are not required to. The only alternative is a cumbersome division between the parties. In contrast, FCA, CPT and CIP shift the transfer point inland, allowing for a simpler allocation of costs.

Problems with division of terminal handling charges (THC)
While it is true that the transport handling charges are split between the seller and the buyer, there is no authoritative definition of this term. It is recommended, therefore, that the parties clarify in the contract of sale how such costs should be distributed between themselves.

b. SHIPMENT VS. ARRIVAL CONTRACTS
Incoterms can be divided into those that dictate shipment or arrival contracts.

1) *Shipment Contracts – "E"–, "F"–, and "C"–terms* – The seller fulfils his delivery obligation at the point of shipment, hence, "shipment contracts". Shipment contracts were the norm of international trade in previous centuries, when the risks of ocean travel were much higher. Sellers did not wish to gamble that the goods would reach the overseas destination or that foreign buyers would pay after receipt. Instead, sellers preferred to be paid (and to transfer all risks) once they had delivered the goods on board a ship at the port of loading.

   The letter of credit system developed in tandem with the practice of shipment contracts, allowing the seller to receive prompt payment against documents proving that the goods had indeed been shipped. However, it is a very common misconception amongst traders that there is a difference between "F"–terms and "C"–terms contracts with respect to transfer of risk. Both FOB and CIF terms dictate shipment contracts.

2) *Arrival contracts – Only the "D"–terms make for arrival contracts.* Under "D"–terms, the seller is responsible for the goods until they arrive in the country of destination (hence "arrival contracts"). The seller not only pays the cost of transport to the ultimate destination, he is also at risk for any damage that may occur to the goods up to that point.

   Compare CIF (a shipment contract) and DDU (an arrival contract) in the case of a maritime shipment to a foreign port. Under CIF, there are two critical points: i) the point of division of risks (at the ship's rail in the port of loading) and ii) the point to which freight is paid, the destination port. With DDU, on the other hand, the seller bears all risk until the goods arrive at destination, and he also pays for the carriage all the way to the destination. This distinction becomes crucial if the goods are lost or damaged in transit. Under CIF, the seller is safe, because he fulfilled his delivery obligation when the goods were loaded on board the ship.

The buyer must pay the contract price even if the goods arrive damaged or are lost. The buyer can rely only on the insurance to recompense herself (and bear any losses not covered by insurance, should the insurance prove insufficient). Under DDU, on the other hand, if the goods are damaged in transit, the seller has not fulfilled his delivery obligation under the contract. He may, therefore, be liable for breach of contract, meaning he would be required to pay damages, provide substitute goods, or make some other kind of restitution.

Since "D"–terms thus involve greater risk for the seller than "C"–terms,this will generally be reflected in higher prices.

Case Examples: Incoterms in Practice

Case 1 – Phillips Puerto Rico Core, Inc. v. Tradax Petroleum, Ltd
Phillips, an importer with offices in Puerto Rico, agreed to buy approximately 25,000 tons of naphtha from Tradax, a corporation doing business in Switzerland. The contract was done under so–called "C&F" terms and also incorporated Incoterms ("C&F" corresponds to CFR Incoterms). The naphtha was loaded on a vessel called the Oxy Trader in the port of Skikda, Algeria, and the vessel departed bound for the destination port in Puerto Rico. A few days after embarkation the boat was detained by the Coast Guard at Gibraltar. The authorities discovered a latent defect in the Oxy Trader and refused to allow the vessel to proceed. Phillips informed Tradax that the goods would have to be transshipped (transferred to another vessel). Phillips refused to pay under the contract and announced to Tradax that it was "terminating" the contract. Tradax sued in US Federal Court. The judge observed that under the rule of Incoterms a C&F (that is, CFR) seller has two obligations: to deliver the goods to an appropriate carrier with which it has contracted for shipment and to tender proper documents to the buyer. In this case the seller had fulfilled these two obligations. Hence, the judge found in favor of Tradax and ordered Phillips to pay the damages that Tradax had suffered, which amounted to over USD 1 million.[5]

Comment: With "C"–terms (CFR, CIF, CPT, CIP) the seller is obliged to properly deliver the goods to the carrier in the country of destination, but does not bear the risk for any damages incurred during transit. Buyers wishing to place all risks for transport–related damage on the seller should choose one of the "D"–terms (DAF, DES, DEQ, DDU, DDP).

Case 2 – <u>Kumar Corp. v. Nopal Lines, Ltd</u>

Kumar, a television exporter, contracted under CIF terms to sell 700 TV sets to a customer in Venezuela. The contract stated the buyer would not pay Kumar until the buyer actually sold the goods. After Kumar delivered the goods to his freight forwarder in Florida, the goods were stolen. Despite the CIF term, Kumar had neglected to obtain marine insurance for the goods. Consequently, Kumar sued his freight forwarder and the carrier. At trial, the judge ruled that once Kumar had turned the goods over to the carrier, the risk of loss had passed to the buyer and Kumar had no standing to sue. On appeal, however, the appellate court held that when a CIF seller fails to procure insurance, the risk of loss remains with the seller. Therefore, Kumar did have standing to sue the carrier.

Comment: This case shows how thoroughly some traders fail to understand or heed the choice of Incoterm. By failing to obtain insurance, Kumar breached his contract to the buyer and could have been liable to a suit for damages from the buyer. Kumar is reduced to seeking compensation from the freight forwarder, a lawsuit which is unlikely to make him whole (due to statutory limitations on carrier's liability).

4.4.5 Division of costs, risks and responsibilities

Incoterms allocate costs, risks and responsibilities between seller and buyer according to the provisions of 10 numbered articles, divided into two parallel series – "A" for seller's responsibilities, and "B" for buyer's responsibilities:

A – Seller's responsibilities	B – Buyer's responsibilities
A1 Provision of goods in conformity with the contract	**B1** Payment of price
A2 Licences, authorizations and formalities	**B2** Licences, authorizations and formalities
A3 Contract of carriage and insurance	**B3** Contract of carriage and insurance
A4 Delivery	**B4** Taking delivery
A5 Transfer of risks	**B5** Transfer of risks
A6 Division of costs	**B6** Division of costs
A7 Notice to the buyer	**B7** Notice to the seller
A8 Proof of delivery, transport document or equivalent electronic message	**B8** Proof of delivery, transport document or equivalent electronic message
A9 Checking – packaging – marking	**B9** Inspection of goods
A10 Other obligations	**B10** Other obligations

A1/B1 Delivery of goods and payment of price

The seller must deliver the goods specified in the contract, along with a commercial invoice. The buyer must pay the purchase price.

A2/B2 Customs clearance and formalities

Incoterms allocate the responsibilities for export and import customs clearance and formalities between seller and buyer. Traders should take particular care whenever the chosen Incoterm makes them responsible for customs formalities in the other party's country.

A3/B3 Contracts of carriage and insurance

- *Contract of carriage*

Incoterms allocate between seller and buyer the responsibility for procuring a contract of carriage for the main international transport of the goods (with the exception of EXW; of course, the EXW buyer will normally procure the contract of carriage). The following are the range of options under Incoterms:

EXW – neither party is under an obligation.

FCA, FAS and **FOB** – the buyer is under an obligation to "contract at his own expense for the carriage of the goods". However, it is fairly common for the seller, at buyer's request, to contract for carriage at the buyer's risk and expense – although the seller is under no obligation to do so.

CFR, CIF, CPT, CIP – the seller is under an obligation to "contract on usual terms at his own expense for the carriage of the goods". The carriage must be for transport by a "usual route" and in a "customary manner" (or in the specific case of sea transport under CFR or CIF, "in a vessel ... of the type normally used for the transport of goods of the contract description").

DAF, DES, DEQ, DDU, DDP – the seller is under an obligation to "contract at his own expense for the carriage of the goods by a usual route and in a customary manner" to the named place, port or quay at destination.

- *Contract of insurance*

Only under CIF and CIP is insurance required: the seller must obtain at his own expense cargo insurance entitling the buyer to claim directly from the insurer. The minimum insurance coverage required under CIF and CIP is 110% of the value of the goods (the extra 10% is meant to account for the potential profit to the buyer from the transaction). The Incoterms insurance requirements are based on the Institute Cargo Clauses drafted by the Institute of London Underwriters. There are three alternatives: clauses, A, B, or C, with clause A representing the so–called "all–risk" insurance (traders should not be deceived by this term into thinking that "all" risks are covered – they are not; see further on).

The Incoterms principle of minimum coverage is a potential trap for the inexperienced trader, because minimum coverage is only appropriate when the risk of loss is solely from such casualties as collision or fire; such coverage does not include damage resulting from theft, pilferage or improper handling of the goods. Consequently, minimum cover is not suitable for manufactured goods, especially if they are of high value. The buyer may want to go even further than clause A, by requiring insurance against war, riots, and strikes (as in so–called "SRCC" clauses – coverage for "strikes, riots and civil commotions"), but these and similar items must be included specifically, and cannot be added simply by using a formula such as "maximum insurance". If the buyer agrees to a CIF or CIP term with "maximum insurance", he will in effect be leaving it to the seller to determine which of the possible and available covers this could be, with a resultant level of uncertainty.

Model Insurance Clause

In light of the foregoing, ICC recommends that partners specifically agree in their contracts as to the precise extent of coverage, as in the following example clause:

Insurance cover on the basis of ....*(clearly identified)* conditions

from....................*(place of commencement of insurance)*

to...................... *(place of termination of insurance)*

Extensions:

plus .... days of storage at buyer's option

plus .... War, SRCC, etc.

plus % .... profit anticipated

plus .... *(named currency – if not currency of contract)*

plus .... *(other particularities)*

A4/B4 Delivery and taking of delivery

Who is responsible for loading/unloading operations? One of the practical issues influenced by the different delivery provisions is that of determining who is responsible for loading and unloading/discharging operations. The loading/unloading obligation is also covered by clause A6/B6, which deals with the division of costs, because the party with a responsibility for loading or unloading will generally have to pay the costs as well. For reasons of unity of presentation, we will consider both aspects together.

Traders should understand that with certain Incoterms the loading or un–loading obligations are generally clear, while with other Incoterms additional contractual provisions may be advisable.

■ *Loading*

DELIVERY AT SELLER'S PREMISES – Under EXW, the seller is not required to load the goods upon vehicles provided by the buyer; the buyer wishing to have the loading operations included in the seller's obligations should add a contractual stipulation to that effect (note that it is also possible to deliver at seller's premises with FCA, which is discussed below).

DELIVERY ON BOARD VESSEL – Under FOB, CFR, and CIF, the seller must load goods on board the named vessel. Technically, under Incoterms the cost of transport operations is divided at the ship's rail. However, in practice the attribution of the cost of loading and related operations (such as stowage and trimming) may vary according to local custom of port. Buyers who are unfamiliar with the custom of the port of loading should consider adding contractual stipulations as to the distribution of loading costs.

DELIVERY ALONGSIDE SHIP – Under FAS, the seller is not required to load the goods on board the vessel (although he must do any unloading of the goods necessary to place them alongside the named vessel in the port of shipment).

DELIVERY INTO CUSTODY OF THE CARRIER – Under FCA, CPT, and CIP, the delivery is accomplished when the goods are placed "in the custody" of the carrier.

In *Incoterms 1990*, the delivery provisions under FCA A4 formed the longest article in all of the Incoterms, specifying delivery under seven transport modalities (rail, road, air, sea, inland waterway, multimodal, unnamed). *Incoterms 2000* clarifies the seller's obligation to load the goods on to the buyer's collecting vehicle. When the seller has to deliver to a place – to a terminal or some similar spot – he now has to arrive with the goods on his vehicle not unloaded.

- *Unloading/discharging*

DELIVERY AT BUYER'S PREMISES – Under DDU and DDP Incoterms 2000, the allocation of these costs is very precise: the seller must place the goods at the disposal of the buyer … on any arriving means of transport not unloaded at the named place of destination.

UNLOADING/DISCHARGING UNDER "C"–TERMS – Under CFR, CIF, CPT and CIP the allocation of the costs for unloading at the point of destination can be complicated and even troublesome (note that, technically, this issue is not one of delivery under A4/B4 – delivery being accomplished when the goods are loaded on board or delivered to the carrier for shipment; rather this is a question of the division of costs under A6/B6).

In *Incoterms 2000*, CFR and CIF terms provide that the seller must pay, at the agreed port of discharge, those costs that are for his account under the contract of carriage – including the costs of loading the goods on board and any charges for unloading. The principle is the same for CPT and CIP, for which *Incoterms 2000* has new wording, indicating that the seller must pay the costs of loading and unloading at the place of destination only when such costs are for the seller's account under the contract of carriage.

A5/B5 Transfer of risks

The rule for the transfer of risks from seller to buyer directly follows upon the applicable rule under A4/B4 as to delivery. In general, the seller is liable for the risks of loss up to the delivery point, the buyer is responsible thereafter. The most significant consequence of the transfer point is that if goods fail to reach the point of transfer of risk, the seller has not fulfilled his delivery obligation, and may, in some legal systems, be liable for breach of contract unless substitute goods can be procured within the contractual time for delivery.

- *Premature transfer of risk*

Under several of the Incoterms, the buyer has a duty to take certain actions which will enable the seller to accomplish delivery. The buyer's failure to perform any of the duties necessary for the seller to accomplish delivery can result in a premature transfer of risk, provided that the contract goods have been "clearly set aside or otherwise identified as the contract goods".

A6/B6 Division of costs

Generally, seller pays costs up to the point of delivery, and buyer pays costs after that point. If a party is under a duty to perform a function, that party must normally pay the costs of accomplishing that function. However, in practice there are exceptions to the basic rule and particular commercial practices or trading customs may require a different principle. Thus, traders may wish to clarify the distribution of costs in the contract of sale.

▪ *Services and assistance*

Often one party will be required to assist the other in performing a certain task, and may be entitled to reimbursement. Examples: 1) seller's assistance for the buyer's export clearance under EXW; 2) buyer's assistance for the seller's clearing of goods under DDP.

A7/B7 Notice provisions

▪ *Buyer must give notice*

Unless there is a specified time or place in the contract, the buyer must give the seller sufficient notice of the following:

- the time and place to take delivery under EXW or "D"–terms;
- the nomination of the carrier and delivery time under "F"–terms;
- the time for shipping the goods and/or the destination under "C"–terms.

▪ *Seller must give notice*

The seller must give the buyer notice of:

- when and where the goods will be placed at the buyer's disposal under EXW;
- when and where the goods have been delivered to the carrier under "F"– and "C"–terms;
- when and where the goods are expected to arrive under "D"–terms so that the buyer can take appropriate measures in time to receive them.

A8/B8 Proof of delivery and transport document

Under all Incoterms except EXW, the seller must submit proof of having fulfilled the delivery obligation. This proof is usually found in some sort of transport document, such as a bill of lading or waybill. Under CFR and "CIF, as with FOB, the seller is under an obligation to deliver the goods on board the named vessel. Since the transport document should prove that delivery on board has been accomplished, the only acceptable transport document is an "on board" bill of lading.

However, with containerized or multimodal shipments, obtaining the on board bill of lading can be cumbersome. First, the container line will issue a "received for shipment" bill of lading; then, the seller will have to request that the "received for shipment" bill be converted to an "on board" bill by virtue of an "on board" notation once the goods have actually been loaded. The time which elapses while the seller waits for the onboard notation can be quite costly for the seller, because the seller may only have a very limited time to present the shipping documents in order to receive payment under a documentary credit.

There is only an absolute need for an onboard bill of lading – which may be a negotiable document – in those cases where the buyer intends to resell the goods afloat, by endorsing the bill of lading. If there is no such need, the seller would be well advised to consider use of CPT or CIP instead of CFR or CIF, so that only a "received for shipment" bill of lading or waybill would be required under Incoterms. Alternatively, it is possible to use CFR or CIF, but with a specific stipulation to the effect that the particular transport documents envisaged will be acceptable.

A9/B9 Checking–packaging–marking/inspection of goods

Checking – the seller must "pay the costs of those checking operations (such as checking quality, measuring, weighing, counting) ... necessary for ... delivering the goods".

Packaging – the seller must provide any packaging which is appropriate for the type of goods and the type of transport intended. Under EXW or "F"–terms, where the seller may not know what the type or conditions of international transport will be, the seller will only be required to provide appropriate packaging to the extent that the buyer has informed the seller of specific circumstances related to the transport.

Pre–shipment inspection (PSI) – If the inspection is required by the authorities of the buyer's countries, then the buyer will normally bear the cost, unless otherwise specified in the contract.

On the other hand, in cases where the inspection is performed to make sure that the goods are conforming or to make sure that there has been no maritime fraud, either the seller or buyer may pay, depending on trade customs or contractual stipulations. In any event, Incoterms section B9 specifies that the buyer will pay unless otherwise agreed.

A/B10 Other obligations

Both parties must render their counterparty – at the counterparty's cost – any assistance necessary for obtaining necessary documents or for performing their contractual obligations.

Examples:

- seller's assistance for the buyer's export clearance under EXW and FAS;
- buyer's assistance for the seller's clearing of goods under DEQ and DDP. Moreover, parties must provide all information necessary for their counterparty to obtain insurance for the shipment.

4.4.6 Miscellaneous points

a. OPTIMAL TRANSPORT ECONOMY AND THE TREND TOWARD D–TERMS

An essential principle of transport cost is that prices decline according to the amount or volume of transport services purchased. Thus, the total cost of transport between seller and buyer will in general be cheaper if it is arranged entirely either by seller or buyer. This would seem to militate in favour of either EXW or the "D"–terms.

In fact, delivered terms have become more popular in international trade over the past decades. In addition to the advantage of optimizing transport economy, "D"–terms allow for greater control by the seller of the quality of transport. In the case of high–value manufactured goods, it may be very important for the seller to be in a position to assure that the goods arrive in time and in good condition. Control of the entire transport chain is facilitated for seller under "D"–terms. Moreover, in highly competitive markets, buyers may insist on being quoted "D"–terms, which facilitates the comparison of offers from different countries.

b. SHIP ARRIVES BEFORE BILL OF LADING

In cases involving documentary credit payments, the ship often arrives in the port of discharge before the buyer has received the bill of lading entitling her to take possession of the goods. Frequently, the ship's master accepts to hand over the goods to the buyer (despite the absence of a bill of lading) against the security provided by a bank guarantee, standby credit (sometimes called a "steamer" guarantee), or letter of indemnity ("LOI"). ICC recommends avoiding this practice, as it reduces the security of the documentary credit transaction, which is based on the firm principle that under no circumstances should the goods be delivered except in return for an original bill of lading.

c. INCOTERMS VARIANTS AND ADDITIONS: "STOWED", "TRIMMED", "UNCLEARED", "LOADED", "LANDED", ...

Traders should note that *Incoterms 2000* do not contain standard definitions of those additional terms which are sometimes appended to trade terms, as for example, "stowed" or "trimmed" in the common variation, "FOB stowed and trimmed".

WARNING

Traders should be aware that the use of Incoterms variants can be dangerous, because the careless use of a variant can result in an ambiguous or even self–contradictory term. In particular, traders should be aware that by altering the cost element of a particular Incoterm, they may also be altering the transfer of risk. It is strongly recommended, therefore, that they clarify the meaning of the variations.

To illustrate the difficulties which may arise from the use of an Incoterms variant, consider "FOB stowed". Incoterms do not define exactly what is meant by the word "stowed". Although it may seem clear that "FOB stowed" requires the seller to stow the goods aboard the ship and to pay all of the loading costs, it is unclear whether the seller also intended to bear the risks of loss and damages to the goods in the process of stowage. In other words, if the goods are damaged during the stowage, traders will not be able to rely on Incoterms to determine whether the seller or buyer is responsible.

The only solution for the trader wishing to modify or vary the basic distribution of responsibilities or risks under Incoterms is to think carefully through the potential consequences, and in particular:

- are both cost and risk intended to be shifted?
- if the variant affects customs clearance or duties, is it intended to shift responsibility for a) customs duties, b) administrative clearance, c) risk of non–clearance or d) all of the preceding?

CHECKLIST

1) Explicitly incorporate Incoterms into your sales contracts, as by the specific mention "FCA ...*Incoterms 2000*". Always include the words "*Incoterms 2000*" in your contracts.

2) Have access to a copy of the full set of definitions of Incoterms, contained in the ICC Publication 560 *Incoterms 2000*. These can be obtained directly from www.iccbooksusa.com, from a local ICC national committee, or from an international business book store or local chamber of commerce.

3) Recognize the 13 valid Incoterms, and refer to them by their three–letter abbreviations:

EXW – Ex Works

FCA – Free Carrier

FAS – Free Alongside Ship

FOB – Free On Board

CFR – Cost and Freight

CIF – Cost, Insurance and Freight

CPT – Carriage Paid To *(named place)*

CIP – Carriage and Insurance Paid To *(named place)*

DAF – Delivered At Frontier

DES – Delivered Ex Ship

DEQ – Delivered Ex Quay

DDU – Delivered Duty Unpaid

DDP – Delivered Duty Paid

Note that the terms "FOB Airport" and "FOR/FOT" (free on rail/free on truck) have been replaced by the more general term, FCA. Avoid other, non–standard variations, such as "franco [named place]", "free [named place]", or C&F.

4) Distinguish between those Incoterms which should be used exclusively for traditional maritime transport (for example, bulk goods and commodities loaded over the ship's side), and the more general Incoterms that are appropriate for all modes of transport, particularly containerized and multimodal transport:

- *Maritime* – Use FAS, FOB, CFR, CIF, DES, and DEQ only for traditional maritime transport (goods lifted over ship's side).
- *Containerized/multimodal/general* – Use EXW, FCA, CIP, CPT, DAF, DDU and DDP for all modes of transport.

5) Understand that Incoterms are meant for use in the contract of sale between buyer and seller, which should not be confused with the related contract of carriage between the shipper and carrier/transporter. Traders should give precise directions to their transporters as to the Incoterm they have chosen in a particular contract of sale; this will ensure that the contract of carriage is in conformity with the contract of sale.

6) Understand that Incoterms cover the allocation between seller and buyer of risks and costs, as well as certain customs and insurance responsibilities. However, several other important conditions of a sales contract may need to be specified in addition to Incoterms. You may be well advised to:

- Specify how delivery will take place, and specifically who must load and who must discharge.

- Specify how much insurance coverage you want, and the geographical and time extent of the insurance coverage (where and when coverage begins and ends).
- Specify any necessary limitations on what kind of transport is appropriate (i.e., refrigerated containers, not carried on deck, etc.).
- Make sure that your contract contains force majeure, exoneration, or time–extension clauses if you are responsible for customs clearance or foreign delivery at an inland point.

7) Understand that CIF, CFR, CIP and CPT are NOT "arrival contracts"; they are "shipment contracts". This means that the point of transfer of risk with these "C"–terms is the same as with "F"–terms: in the country of departure.

4.4.7 Extracts from the Introduction to *Incoterms 2000*

To be read in conjunction with the Preambles to *Incoterms 2000* (see 4.4.3. Summary of *Incoterms 2000*).

Extracts
---

9. The terms

9.3 The "C"–terms require the seller to contract for carriage on usual terms at his own expense. Therefore, a point up to which he would have to pay transport costs must necessarily be indicated after the respective "C"–term. Under the CIF and CIP terms the seller also has to take out insurance and bear the insurance cost. Since the point for the division of costs is fixed at a point in the country of destination, the "C"–terms are frequently mistakenly believed to be arrival contracts, in which the seller would bear all risks and costs until the goods have actually arrived at the agreed point. However, it must be stressed that the "C"–terms are of the same nature as the "F"–terms in that the seller fulfils the contract in the country of shipment or dispatch. Thus, the contracts of sale under the "C"–terms, like the contracts under the "F"–terms, fall within the category of shipment contracts.

It is in the nature of shipment contracts that, while the seller is bound to pay the normal transport cost for the carriage of the goods by a usual route and in a customary manner to the agreed place, the risk of loss of or damage to the goods, as well as additional costs resulting from events occurring after the goods having been appropriately delivered for carriage, fall upon the buyer. Hence, the "C"–terms are distinguishable from all other terms in that they contain two "critical" points, one indicating the point to which the seller is bound to arrange and bear the costs of a contract of carriage and another one for the allocation of risk. For this reason, the greatest caution must be observed when adding obligations of the seller to the "C"–terms which seek to extend the seller's responsibility beyond the aforementioned "critical" point for the allocation of risk. It is of the very essence of the "C"–terms that the seller is relieved of any further risk and cost after he has duly fulfilled his contract by contracting for carriage and handing over the goods to the carrier and by providing for insurance under the CIF and CIP terms.

The essential nature of the "C"–terms as shipment contracts is also illustrated by the common use of documentary credits as the preferred mode of payment used in such terms. Where it is agreed by the parties to the sale contract that the seller will be paid by presenting the agreed shipping documents to a bank under a documentary credit, it would be quite contrary to the central purpose of the documentary credit for the seller to bear further risks and costs after the moment when payment had been made under documentary credits or otherwise upon shipment and dispatch of the goods. Of course, the seller would have to bear the cost of the contract of carriage irrespective of whether freight is pre–paid upon shipment or is payable at destination (freight collect); however, additional costs which may result from events occurring subsequent to shipment and dispatch are necessarily for the account of the buyer.

If the seller has to provide a contract of carriage which involves payment of duties, taxes and other charges, such costs will, of course, fall upon the seller to the extent that they are for his account under that contract. This is now explicitly set forth in the A6 clause of all "C"–terms.

If it is customary to procure several contracts of carriage involving tran-shipment of the goods at intermediate places in order to reach the agreed destination, the seller would have to pay all these costs, including any costs incurred when the goods are transhipped from one means of conveyance to the other. If, however, the carrier exercised his rights under a transhipment – or similar clause – in order to avoid unexpected hindrances (such as ice, congestion, labour disturbances, government orders, war or warlike operations) then any additional cost resulting therefrom would be for the account of the buyer, since the seller's obligation is limited to procuring the usual contract of carriage.

It happens quite often that the parties to the contract of sale wish to clarify the extent to which the seller should procure a contract of carriage including the costs of discharge. Since such costs are normally covered by the freight when the goods are carried by regular shipping lines, the contract of sale will frequently stipulate that the goods are to be so carried or at least that they are to be carried under "liner terms". In other cases, the word "landed" is added after CFR or CIF. However, it is advisable not to use abbreviations added to the "C"–terms unless, in the relevant trade, the meaning of the abbreviations is clearly understood and accepted by the contracting parties or under any applicable law or custom of the trade.

In particular, the seller should not – and indeed could not, without changing the very nature of the "C"–terms – undertake any obligation with respect to the arrival of the goods at destination, since the risk of any delay during the carriage is borne by the buyer. Thus, any obligation with respect to time must necessarily refer to the place of shipment or dispatch, for example, "shipment (dispatch) not later than...". An agreement for example, "CFR Hamburg not later than..." is really a misnomer and thus open to different possible interpretations. The parties could be taken to have meant either that the goods must actually arrive at Hamburg at the specified date, in which case the contract is not a shipment contract but an arrival contract or, alternatively, that the seller must ship the goods at such a time that they would normally arrive at Hamburg before the specified date unless the carriage would have been delayed because of unforeseen events.

It happens in commodity trades that goods are bought while they are at sea and that, in such cases, the word "afloat" is added after the trade term. Since the risk of loss of or damage to the goods would then, under the CFR and CIF terms, have passed from the seller to the buyer, difficulties of inter-pretation might arise. One possibility would be to maintain the ordinary meaning of the CFR and CIF terms with respect to the allocation of risk between seller and buyer, namely that risk passes on shipment: this would mean that the buyer might have to assume the consequences of events having already occurred at the time when the contract of sale enters into force. The other possibility would be to let the passing of the risk coincide with the time when the contract of sale is concluded. The former possibility might well be practical, since it is usually impossible to ascertain the condition of the goods while they are being carried. For this reason the 1980 United Nations Convention on Contracts for the International Sale of Goods article 68 stipulates that "if the circumstances so indicate, the risk is assumed by the buyer from the time the goods were handed over to the carrier who issued the documents embodying the contract of carriage". There is, however, an exception to this rule when "the seller knew or ought to have known that the goods had been lost or damaged and did not disclose this to the buyer". Thus, the interpretation of a CFR or CIF term with the addition of the word "afloat" will depend upon the law applicable to the contract of sale. The parties are advised to ascertain the applicable law and any solution which might follow therefrom. In case of doubt, the parties are advised to clarify the matter in their contract.

In practice, the parties frequently continue to use the traditional expression "C&F" (or C and F, C+F). Nevertheless, in most cases it would appear that they regard these expressions as equivalent to CFR. In order to avoid difficulties of interpreting their contract the parties should use the correct Incoterm which is CFR, the only world–wide–accepted standard abbreviation for the term "Cost and Freight (... named port of destination)".

CFR and CIF in A8 of Incoterms 1990 obliged the seller to provide a copy of the charterparty whenever his transport document (usually the bill of lading) contained a reference to the charterparty, for example, by the frequent notation "all other terms and conditions as per charterparty". Although, of course, a contracting party should always be able to ascertain all terms of his contract – preferably at the time of the conclusion of the contract – it appears that the practice to provide the charterparty as aforesaid has created problems particularly in connection with documentary credit transactions. The obli-gation of the seller under CFR and CIF to provide a copy of the charter–party together with other transport documents has been deleted in Incoterms 2000.

Although the A8 clauses of Incoterms seek to ensure that the seller provides the buyer with "proof of delivery", it should be stressed that the seller fulfils that requirement when he provides the "usual" proof. Under CPT and CIP it would be the "usual transport document" and under CFR and CIF a bill of lading or a sea waybill. The transport documents must be "clean", meaning that they must not contain clauses or notations expressly declaring a defective condition of the goods and/or the packaging. If such clauses or notations appear in the document, it is regarded as "unclean" and would then not be accepted by banks in documentary credit transactions. However, it should be noted that a transport document even without such clauses or notations would usually not provide the buyer with incontrovertible proof as against the carrier that the goods were shipped in conformity with the stipulations of the contract of sale. Usually, the carrier would, in standardized text on the front page of the transport document, refuse to accept responsibility for information with respect to the goods by indicating that the particulars inserted in the transport document constitute the shipper's declarations and therefore that the information is only "said to be" as inserted in the document. Under most applicable laws and principles, the carrier must at least use reasonable means of checking the correctness of the information and his failure to do so may make him liable to the consignee. However, in container trade, the carrier's means of checking the contents in the container would not exist unless he himself was responsible for stowing the container.

There are only two terms which deal with insurance, namely CIF and CIP. Under these terms the seller is obliged to procure insurance for the benefit of the buyer. In other cases it is for the parties themselves to decide whether and to what extent they want to cover themselves by insurance. Since the seller takes out insurance for the benefit of the buyer, he would not know the buyer's precise requirements. Under the Institute Cargo Clauses drafted by the Institute of London Underwriters, insurance is available in "minimum cover" under Clause C, "medium cover" under Clause B and "most extended cover" under Clause A. Since in the sale of commodities under the CIF term the buyer may wish to sell the goods in transit to a subsequent buyer who in turn may wish to resell the goods again, it is impossible to know the insurance cover suitable to such subsequent buyers and, therefore, the minimum cover under CIF has traditionally been chosen with the possibility for the buyer to require the seller to take out additional insurance. Minimum cover is however unsuitable for sale of manufactured goods where the risk of theft, pilferage or improper handling or custody of the goods would require more than the cover available under Clause C. Since CIP, as distinguished from CIF, would normally not be used for the sale of commodities, it would have been feasible to adopt the most extended cover under CIP rather than the minimum cover under CIF. But to vary the seller's insurance obligation under CIF and CIP would lead to confusion and both terms therefore limit the seller's insurance obligation to the minimum cover. It is particularly important for the CIP – buyer to observe this: should additional cover be required, he should agree with the seller that the latter could take out additional insurance or, alter-natively, arrange for extended insurance cover himself. There are also particular instances where the buyer may wish to obtain even more protection than is available under Institute Clause A, for example insurance against war, riots, civil commotion, strikes or other labour disturbances. If he wishes the seller to arrange such insurance he must instruct him accordingly in which case the seller would have to provide such insurance if procurable.

10. The expression "no obligation"

As appears from the expressions "the seller must" and "the buyer must" Incoterms are only concerned with the obligations which the parties owe to each other. The words "no obligation" have therefore been inserted whenever one party does not owe an obligation to the other party. Thus, if for instance according to A3 of the respective term the seller has to arrange and pay for the contract of carriage we find the words "no obligation" under the heading "contract of carriage" in B3 a) setting forth the buyer's position. Again, where neither party owes the other an obligation, the words "no obligation" will appear with respect to both parties, for example, with respect to insurance.

In either case, it is important to point out that even though one party may be under "no obligation" towards the other to perform a certain task, this does not mean that it is not in his interest to perform that task. Thus, for example, just because a CFR buyer owes his seller no duty to make a contract of insurance under B4, it is clearly in his interest to make such a contract, the seller being under no such obligation to procure insurance cover under A4.

11. Variants of Incoterms

In practice, it frequently happens that the parties themselves by adding words to an Incoterm seek further precision than the term could offer. It should be underlined that Incoterms give no guidance whatsoever for such additions. Thus, if the parties cannot rely on a well–established custom of the trade for the interpretation of such additions they may encounter serious problems when no consistent understanding of the additions could be proven.

If for instance the common expressions "FOB stowed" or "EXW loaded" are used, it is impossible to establish a world–wide understanding to the effect that the seller's obligations are extended not only with respect to the cost of actually loading the goods in the ship or on the vehicle respectively but also include the risk of fortuitous loss of or damage to the goods in the process of stowage and loading. For these reasons, the parties are strongly advised to clarify whether they only mean that the function or the cost of the stowage and loading operations should fall upon the seller or whether he should also bear the risk until the stowage and loading has actually been completed. These are questions to which Incoterms do not provide an answer: consequently, if the contract too fails expressly to describe the parties' intentions, the parties may be put to much unnecessary trouble and cost.

Although *Incoterms 2000* do not provide for many of these commonly used variants, the preambles to certain trade terms do alert the parties to the need for special contractual terms if the parties wish to go beyond the stipulations of Incoterms.

EXW	the added obligation for the seller to load the goods on the buyer's collecting vehicle;
CIF/CIP	the buyer's need for additional insurance;
DEQ	the added obligation for the seller to pay for costs after discharge.

In some cases sellers and buyers refer to commercial practice in liner and charter party trade. In these circumstances, it is necessary to clearly distinguish between the obligations of the parties under the contract of carriage and their obligations to each other under the contract of sale. Unfortunately, there are no authoritative definitions of expressions such as "liner terms" and "terminal handling charges" (THC). Distribution of costs under such terms may differ in different places and change from time to time. The parties are recommended to clarify in the contract of sale how such costs should be distributed between themselves.

Expressions frequently used in charterparties, such as "FOB stowed", "FOB stowed and trimmed", are sometimes used in contracts of sale in order to clarify to what extent the seller under FOB has to perform stowage and trimming of the goods onboard the ship. Where such words are added, it is necessary to clarify in the contract of sale whether the added obligations only relate to costs or to both costs and risks.

As has been said, every effort has been made to ensure that Incoterms reflect the most common commercial practice. However in some cases – particularly where Incoterms 2000 differ from Incoterms 1990 – the parties may wish the trade terms to operate differently. They are reminded of such options in the preamble of the terms signalled by the word "However".

14. Customs clearance

The term "customs clearance" has given rise to misunderstandings. Thus, whenever reference is made to an obligation of the seller or the buyer to undertake obligations in connection with passing the goods through customs of the country of export or import it is now made clear that this obligation does not only include the payment of duty and other charges but also the performance and payment of whatever administrative matters are connected with the passing of the goods through customs and the information to the authorities in this connection. Further, it has – although quite wrongfully – been considered in some quarters inappropriate to use terms dealing with the obligation to clear the goods through customs when, as in intra–European Union trade or other free trade areas, there is no longer any obligation to pay duty and no restrictions relating to import or export. In order to clarify the situation, the words "where applicable" have been added in the A2 and B2, A6 and B6 clauses of the relevant Incoterms in order for them to be used without any ambiguity where no customs procedures are required.

It is normally desirable that customs clearance is arranged by the party domiciled in the country where such clearance should take place or at least by somebody acting there on his behalf. Thus, the exporter should normally clear the goods for export, while the importer should clear the goods for import.

Incoterms 1990 departed from this under the trade terms EXW and FAS (export clearance duty on the buyer) and DEQ (import clearance duty on the seller) but in *Incoterms 2000,* FAS and DEQ place the duty of clearing the goods for export on the seller and to clear them for import on the buyer respectively, while EXW – representing the seller's minimum obligation – has been left unamended (export clearance duty on the buyer). Under DDP the seller specifically agrees to do what follows from the very name of the term – Delivered Duly Paid – namely to clear the goods for import and pay any duty as a consequence thereof.

Notes

(1) Frigaliment Importing Co., Ltd. v. B.N.S. International Sales Corp., 190 F.Supp. 116 (1960).
(2) See *International Contract Manual*, Kritzer ed., Kluwer, Farringdon Looseleaf.
(3) See *Transfer of Ownership in International Trade*, ICC Publication 546.
(4) *Force Majeure and Hardship*, 1985, ICC Publication 421 (revised in March 2003, ICC Publication 650).
(5) US Court of Appeals, Second Circuit. 782 F2 314 (1985).

CHAPTER FIVE

Agency, Distributorship, Franchising and Occasional Intermediary Contracts

The basics: Agency, distributorship, franchising and occasional inter-mediary are four important and distinct modes for export and the international expansion of firms. Traders should be familiar with the benefits and disad-vantages of each particular mode, and understand the differing legal frameworks underlying each of them. A foreign agent markets the exporter's products, leaving the contract of sale to be concluded directly between the exporter and the foreign customer. The agent's income is usually derived from a percentage commission on sales made in his territory. A distributor buys the exporter's products and then resells them in the distributorship territory. The distributor's earnings come from the difference between the purchase price from exporter and the re–sale price to the domestic customer. Exporters, agents and distributors may wish to refer to the Model Contracts developed by the International Chamber of Commerce (ICC).

5.1 Agency

5.1.1 Agency and distributorship in the range of possible distribution options

Agency and distributorship relationships represent a common phase in the internationalization of the export firm. They require relatively more investment than mere direct exporting, because the exporter must go to the expense of evaluating and contracting with the representative, and must further concede an important share of the profits to the representative. However, the agency/distributorship option is cheaper and less risky than establishing a joint venture or a branch.

The difference between agency and distributorship relationships

Agency

The agent proposes the principal's product to the customer, but the principal concludes the sale contract directly with the customer.

Distributorship

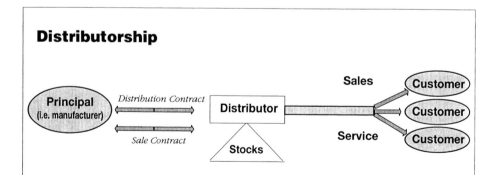

The distributor buys the principal's products, then resells them on his own account. The distribution agreement sets the framework for the sales between the principal and distributor. There is no direct sales contract between the principal and the customers, although the principal may be subject to warranties.

Agency and distributorship relations have traditionally been a good place for small importers to begin. By representing a high–quality foreign manufacturer, it may be possible to get a business off the ground with a small initial capital investment.

Let us consider the range of options for international distribution:

a. BRANCH OFFICE

An exporter could opt for a mode of commercial distribution with a high level of control, investment and risk, by opening a branch office. However, this might entail extensive formalities. The registration of the branch in some countries exposes the exporter's entire legal entity to taxation on worldwide profits (as in the unitary taxation systems of some US states).

b. SUBSIDIARY

A subsidiary is an independent company set up under the laws of the foreign country. Subsidiaries are also a high–investment, high–risk form of inter-nationalization. Subsidiaries have several potential disadvantages: they may generate unwieldy overhead structures caused by the degree of centralized control required from the home office; or the exporter may have difficulty supervising and motivating local employees, who may have a work ethic distinct from that of the exporter's home country. Moreover, the employees of the subsidiary are frequently protected by strict labour laws, so that laying off employees may be difficult.

c. JOINT VENTURE

Another option is that of the joint venture, where a foreign company joins forces with a local company. A joint venture is an attractive option when a local company offers assets such as manufacturing plants, corporate clients, or government contacts, which are difficult for a foreign company to easily develop. Despite the popularity of this structure, a high rate of failure is reported with international joint ventures. At the corporate level, it is frequently difficult for the distinct managerial cultures of the two companies to reach a compromise on business strategies and procedures. Moreover, the joint venture may be subject to national requirements of majority ownership by the local partner. Also, it may be difficult or expensive to withdraw from the venture. Because of the venture's limited legal liability, other parties may be unwilling to contract with it.

d. AGENT OR DISTRIBUTOR

Thus, one arrives at the option of the agent or distributor – independent contractors who do not bind the principal. No partnership or joint venture is created. The exporter avoids the risks of unwanted contractual obligations, the need to register a branch office, and the possibility of local taxation. The exporter often hopes to rely on the expertise of the local agent to introduce a product rapidly throughout a market, but does not want to go to the expense or risk of investing more heavily, as via a subsidiary.

5.1.2 Choosing between agency and distributorship

Many international business executives do not observe any significant distinction between the terms "agency" and "distributorship". The two terms are often used interchangeably, as if they were synonymous and equivalent to yet another general term, "foreign representative". There are, however, under most systems of law, some fundamental distinctions between agency and distributorship:

- In commercial agency relationships, the principal will ultimately contract directly with the customers. The agent only, as it were, "introduces" them, by conducting marketing and prospecting activities in the territory. He is an intermediary. Conversely, in distributorship relationships, the distributor stands between the principal and the ultimate customers – the distributor buys the goods and then resells them on its own account to the final purchaser. He is a buyer–reseller. The key difference is therefore that the agent does not buy the goods and take title to them in his own name.

- In actual practice, the two roles may both be played by the same firm: a firm may act as an agent and a distributor at the same time, but for different products. It is even possible to be both agent and distributor for the same principal, acting as an agent for certain products and as a distributor for others. In the event of a dispute, the legal consequences of a particular transaction may turn on whether the representative was acting as an agent or a distributor.

Although there are no general principles applicable to all jurisdictions, the reader may find some guidance in the following simple rule of thumb for determining whether an agency or distributorship structure is more suitable for a given project.

■ *Agency preferable*

If the final purchasers are likely to want to deal directly with the principal (for example, as with products that are unique or must be customized, or machinery which is complicated, expensive, or maintenance–intensive), then agency is more appropriate.

■ *Distributorship preferable*

If the distributor needs to keep a very large stock of goods on hand for resale to a large number of customers, the appropriate contract is likely to be one for distributorship.

The exporter's choice of distribution structure may change over time. Many exporters begin with direct export sales, then move to international sales via an agent, then later on to sales via a distributorship relationship, and then finally, if the market has become extremely well developed, to a branch or subsidiary.

5.1.3 Drafting agency and distributorship contracts

Agency and distributorship contracts require careful drafting because they will govern long–lasting relationships and significant mutual investments. Agency and distributorship contracts must allow for a wide range of contingencies and a variable range of products over a period of time. Not only products but also parties may change over time – prospering or declining, or being purchased by third parties. How does the contractual agreement respond to such changed situations? The contract must be precise enough to provide clear solutions for predictable price and product–line variations, but flexible enough to adapt to contingencies.

Agency and distributorship commercial relationships usually require work, patience, and investment of time and money by both parties. Consequently, an eventual separation can be quite painful. Under some systems of law, the exporter is required to pay the agent an indemnity, an equitable compensatory payment for the financial loss the agent is deemed to suffer as a result of the separation. If an exporter becomes unhappy with the agent and wishes to terminate the contract, he may be surprised to discover that an indemnity payment is necessary.

Agents or distributors should be selected with great care, after a thorough analysis of the foreign market and all potential representatives in that market. Agents and distributors are like ambassadors. If they give customers a bad impression of the exporter's products and services, the exporter's sales to that market may suffer for years. Moreover, an unsatisfied or dismissed agent may establish relations with a rival exporter.

Case Example

How to find a foreign representative

- George S. Parker, founder of the Parker Pen Co., took meticulous care in appointing foreign distributors. After appointing the first foreign distributor in 1902, Parker Pen grew steadily until it became one of the world's most recognizable brands. By the late 1980s, Parker Pen had appointed distri-butors in 153 countries and was doing over 80% of its business outside its home base of the United States.

- George Parker's procedure was as follows. He would first select his next target market, then do careful preparatory research. He would then visit the market, planning to spend up to three weeks there. He would visit a number of stores where pens were sold, carefully examining how they were presented and marketed. Then he would ask store owners which brands sold best, and why. Gradually, he would develop a firm under-standing of the pen market in that country. After establishing a list of the key pen wholesalers, he would then visit banks, as well as the American embassy, to check on the backgrounds of the prospective partners. Only after such exhaustive research would he prepare a short list of candidates. Then he would begin to personally call on each of the them. He would carefully interview each potential candidate, then return to the US for further research. He would contact other exporters who sold into the particular market, asking them to evaluate the various candidates. When asked why he performed such exhaustive research, he explained that appointing a distributor was like entering into a marriage – he wanted to be absolutely sure of long–term commitment. The success of Parker's system can be found in the remarkably durable nature of the relationships he established: the very first distributor he appointed in 1902 is still associated with Parker.[1]

5.1.4 Legal principles of agency contracts

Agency contracts impose substantial legal commitments on both sides. The exporter should realise that agents may – in some jurisdictions and under certain conditions – acquire the authority to contract in the exporter's name. The exporter should, therefore, take care that the agent is a well–established professional with a good reputation. The exporter or manufacturer (called the "principal" in the agency context), may wish to provide for further contractual precautions, such as by requiring a trial period in which to evaluate the agent's competence, or by holding the agent to a minimum sales figure.

On the other side, the agent will invest a great deal of time and energy in promoting the products of the principal, in creating a good reputation for them, and in advertising them throughout the national territory. If these efforts are properly executed, the principal's products will accumulate "goodwill" (a good professional reputation) worth a significant amount of money in future sales for the principal. Moreover, the principal may eventually acquire the names and addresses of the main customers the agent has prospected with his time and effort. At a later point in time, once the goods are well–established in the territory, the principal may seek to eliminate the agent and deal directly with the customers, saving himself the agent's commission fees.

From the foregoing, it may be seen that the termination provisions of the contract can provide certainty and protection for both sides. For the agent, a termination indemnity will ensure that if he is terminated he will at least receive a percentage of the financial value of the goodwill generated for the principal. Moreover, the contractual or legally required length of notice – which the principal must give before termination – may allow the agent sufficient time to find other principals for whom to work. Conversely, the principal will generally wish for his own protection to have a short minimum notice period for termination, and if possible, to avoid paying any termination indemnity whatsoever. However, even in many cases where the principal has in a particular jurisdiction both the legal right and the negotiating leverage to impose an earlier termination or lower indemnity, he may still wish to provide for a "fair" period of notice and indemnity.

a. TERMINOLOGY

The use of the word "agency" in international trade does not always accord with the strict legal meaning of the term; therefore, it is recommended that the parties clearly qualify their relationship in the contract. There are different categories of agents (e.g., "buying agent" or "service agent") and in some countries, special rules govern contracts with agents categorized as employees. In such cases, the rules applicable to employed agents will apply.

b. DISCLOSURE OF PRINCIPAL

An agent may or may not disclose the fact that he is acting on behalf of a foreign exporter, his principal. In many civil law countries, the principal may not be able to directly sue the customer if the agent has not disclosed the principal's existence to the customer – only the agent can sue the customer. If an exporter wishes to avoid this constraint, he should contractually require the agent to disclose during any sales or professional communications the fact that he is acting as an agent, or contractually require the agent to assign to the principal any relevant claims against customers.

c. ACTUAL AND APPARENT AUTHORITY

Actual authority refers to authority which the principal gives expressly to the agent; *apparent authority* (or *ostensible authority*) is the authority that an agent appears to have to others. Under certain circumstances, a third party may rely on an agent's apparent authority to bind the agent or principal to the contract. Thus, the principal should avoid giving the impression to third parties that the agent has full authority to bind the principal.

5.1.5 Basic duties of agent and principal

a. DUTIES OF THE AGENT

To use reasonable diligence – The agent must carry out his duties with customary and reasonable care, skill and diligence, and is responsible to the principal for any loss caused by a failure to observe such standards. For example, an agent cannot give a buyer any warranty unless the principal has given him the authority to do so.

To disclose all material facts – The agent must pass on all information likely to be of interest to the principal in deciding whether or not to accept the customer's order. Clearly, the agent may have a financial incentive to neglect this duty if he feels that certain information will result in the principal refusing to accept the order. However, such a violation of the duty to disclose makes the contract voidable at the principal's option. Thus, for example, the agent cannot act simultaneously as an agent for the buyer and seller, thereby receiving a double commission.

Not to make secret profits – The agent cannot accept a bribe or make other secret profits. The standards of honesty that an agent must respect are very high.

Not to divulge confidential information – The agent must not reveal privileged information about the principal and the principal's business operations.

To account to the principal – The agent must keep proper business records so that the principal can verify the terms and obligations of the agreement. The agent must pay over all moneys received on behalf of the principal.

b. DUTIES OF THE PRINCIPAL

To pay commission – The commission system is meant to provide an incentive for the agent to maximize sales. The principal may provide in the contract that the commission will only be paid when the purchase price is received in cash by the principal. Another alternative is to arrange a contract on *del credere* terms, which means that the agent undertakes to indemnify the principal for losses resulting from sales made to customers who turn out to be insolvent or fail to pay for whatever reason. Obviously, the calculation of the agent's commission is at the very heart of the contract. It is vital that the parties express themselves with absolute precision on this point.

Agent's expenses and indemnity – The self–employed sales agent normally cannot claim his expenses from the principal unless they have agreed to this effect in the agency contract.

Orders emanating from the agent's territory but not procured by him – The basic principle is that the agent is remunerated for orders placed that are derived from his efforts. However, if the order is placed directly with the principal by a customer within the agent's territory, the agent may or may not be entitled to commission, depending on the law governing the contract and the specific contractual provisions.

Commission on repeat orders – The contract should provide whether the agent is entitled to commission on repeat orders during the period of the agency agreement, as well as after the termination of the contract.

Principal's ability to accept or reject orders – If the agent has not been given the authority to do more than introduce customers, then the principal may either accept or reject the customer's order. Commission will only be paid if the principal accepts the order.

5.1.6 Agency and law/regulation: the case of the European Agency Directive 86/653 of 18 December 1986.

The European Commission Directive on Commercial Agents – Under the European Commission Directive on Commercial Agents (the "Directive"), which is a key example of a regulation which provides protection for agents, an agency contract cannot be valid unless evidenced in writing. The Directive also has some important items concerning the agent's commission; notably, it shall not be paid any later than the last day of the month following the quarter in which the commission became due; derogations are not permitted.

The Directive also sets forth notice requirements for termination. Under Article 17 of the Directive the agent is entitled to a certain indemnity after termination of the contract, provided that he requests it in writing within one year of the termination of the contract. The agent will be entitled to an indemnity which corresponds to the amount of business he brought the principal. The indemnity can be lost if the agent is guilty of culpable behaviour. Finally, the agent can seek damages if, for example, he has not been able to amortize the investments he has undertaken pursuant to the principal's advice.

5.1.7 Agency – antitrust rules of the European Union (Article 81 – Regulation n° 2790/1999)

On 22 December 1999, the European Commission enacted Regulation n° 2790/1999 which replaced *inter alia* Regulation 83/83 and which came into force on 1 June 2000. This Regulation exempts certain vertical agreements from the prohibition of Article 81 (formerly 85) of the EC Treaty.

In principle, agency contracts do not fall under the prohibition of Article 81 since the agent acts in the name and on behalf of a principal. Principal and agent are thus presumed to form one economic unit. However, whenever the agent assumes financial and commercial risks similar to those of the distributor (reseller), the contract may fall within the scope of Article 81 and may need to comply with Regulation n° 2790/1999. In such a case, the parties are recommended to seek expert advice for the drafting of the appropriate clause(s).

5.1.8 The *ICC Model Commercial Agency Contract* (ICC Publication 644)

Scope of application – This ICC Model Contract is meant specifically to apply to international contracts with self–employed commercial agents for the sale of goods. Agency contracts for services, for example, or with agents who are not self–employed (e.g., "salaried commercial representatives"), do not come within the scope of this contract, although it may still be used as a source of inspiration. Similarly, "buying agents" or "purchasing agents" who procure goods for a principal, generate a different set of considerations and the ICC Model was not developed for these situations.

Agents as employees – In the case of agents who may be considered employees of a particular principal, national labour law may override the provisions of the ICC Model Contract. The simplest way to avoid this problem is for principals to contract only with agents which have the legal status of a company or corporation or other "legal person".

5.1.9 Key clauses in agency contracts

The following examination of the key clauses in agency contractsis based on the *ICC Model Commercial Agency Contract*.

1) *Territory and products* – A precise definition of the products is essential because the obligations set out in the contract apply only to products that are clearly covered by the contract. Agents usually desire the right to distribute as many as possible of the principal's current and future products, whereas principals may wish to restrict the agent to only certain products. The contract products can be described specifically or generally. A specific listing is more precise but can result in a contract that must be updated too frequently to accord with a periodically changing product line. An overly general description may bring goods into the contract which the principal would have preferred to distribute through another agent or himself.

   The ICC Model sets forth a compromise solution: the principal must inform the agent of any intention to put new products on the market and must discuss with the agent the possibility of including the new products in the contract.

   The contractual territory should also be described precisely. Generally, this territory is that area where the agent can realistically promote sales, although in some cases a wider territory may be granted as a form of incentive (additional territories may be permitted, for example, on a non–exclusive basis).

2) *Good faith and fair dealing* – This clause sets forth the parties' commitment to abide by standards of decency, fairness and reasonableness.

3) *Agent's functions* – This clause states the duty of the agent to actively and competently promote the contract goods, and to follow reasonable directions made by the principal. The ICC Model works on the assumption that the agent is independent and not an employee of the principal. This

distinction can be significant, because in many countries an employee's contract cannot be submitted to arbitration, which would defeat one of the essential premises of the ICC Model.

The ICC Model also includes a provision that the agent has no express authority to bind the principal toward third parties, nor to vary the terms and conditions of the principal's standard sales contract. Note, however, that the principal cannot completely remove the possibility that the agent will act with "apparent" authority, the only solution being practical supervision and vigilance.

Note further that there may be tax consequences in allowing an agent to enter into contracts which bind the principal. Such acts may be considered for tax purposes as sufficient to indicate a "permanent establishment" of the principal in the given jurisdiction.

4) *Acceptance of orders by the principal* – It is important for the agent to contractually oblige the principal to inform the agent rapidly and in good faith whether an order has been accepted or rejected. The principal should not arbitrarily refuse orders. A principal unhappy with an agent but lacking objective or contractual justification for terminating the contract, might be tempted to "freeze" the agent out of business by arbitrarily refusing orders. Under the ICC Model, such "freezing out" would constitute a breach of contract.

5) *Undertaking not to compete* – The agent must not sell products which compete with those of the principal. It may not always be easy to determine exactly what constitutes a "competing product", so it may be advisable to provide for a precise definition of "competing products".

Under the ICC Model, the agent is free to represent non–competing products, provided that he informs the principal in advance. He does not have to inform the principal if the products are so obviously non–competitive that it would be unreasonable to expect him to do so. However, an exception to this latter rule is made for the products of a competitor of the principal. If an agent worked for competing principals this could easily give rise to conflicts of interest, which could impair the necessary trust between principal and agent.

6) *Sales organization* – A good agency contract will balance the principal's right to set standards of quality with the agent's freedom to design his own internal organization:

- SERVICING OR WAREHOUSING – If these are an important competitive feature, the principal should contractually provide for minimum service standards or warehousing capacity. The parties should determine whether the stock should be owned by the agent (which may entail changing the legal status to that of distributor) or by the principal (in which case it would be consignment stock).

- CONSIGNMENT AGREEMENTS – A consignment agreement should make clear which of the parties will be liable for the cost of storage and maintenance of the stock. Specific clauses should cover handling, safeguarding, insurance, and procedures for inventorying the stock.

  In some countries, special laws apply to consignments, making recognition of the principal's ownership of the stock conditional on the stock being appropriately identified and even stored physically apart from other goods. This is especially important in the event of the insolvency of the agent, in which case the agent's creditors may seize the agent's stock. The principal must have precisely followed the legal provisions in order to be able to assert control over the goods.

- STOCK OWNED BY THE AGENT – The parties may want the agent to hold stock on his account, so that he is able to rapidly effect delivery. This brings up issues of whether or not the relationship is really one of principal and exclusive distributor. In the European Union, this raises the question of whether competition and cartel regulations may apply. Presumption of distributorship may also arise if the agent is contractually required to effect after–sales servicing activities free of charge, without receiving any compensation from the principal.

- AFTER–SALES SERVICE – If service is under the principal's guarantee, it is usually free (for the agent as well as for the ultimate customer) and in some way reimbursed by the principal. Also, if the after–sales service is judged as "necessary", the agent can ask the principal for compensation for costs. After–sales service may in some cases be a cost or burden for the agent, but in other cases it can be a primary source of revenue. For example, it would appear that in the elevator business the agent may earn more from the service contract than the sale contract.

  The parties should calculate the probable costs associated with after–sales service, and then decide whether these costs should be covered by the agent's commission, or whether extra compensation will be granted for service. The parties should specify whether the agent will be required to stock spare parts.

- ADVERTISING – Agents usually are not responsible for advertising, but the principal may wish to allow it in particular cases. The agent's knowledge of the local market may enable him to suggest necessary adaptations to the principal's advertising materials. Sometimes the agent is reimbursed for a percentage of advertising costs incurred, as an incentive for the agent to invest in the product, and as an encouragement to use his best efforts to sell the product.

- FAIRS AND EXHIBITIONS – Presence at trade fairs and exhibitions may be important. If so, the parties should develop a team approach with shared responsibilities.

7) *Guaranteed minimum target* – Under the ICC Model, the parties can set either an ordinary sales target or a guaranteed minimum target. An ordinary sales target is a "soft" target, indicating a sales figure that the parties believe is possible, but fixing no direct consequence from a failure to reach the target. Especially in new markets with no previous experience with the principal's product, it may be unreasonable to set a guaranteed minimum target. A guaranteed minimum target is a "hard" minimum. It can be calculated in terms of money, amount of products sold, or percentage of the general sales target. Failure to reach the target constitutes a breach of contract allowing the principal to terminate the contract. However, the principal might take steps less drastic than terminating the contract, i.e., eliminating the agent's exclusivity, or reducing the size of the agent's territory.

The agent may, therefore, wish to negotiate for a clause excusing non–attainment of the minimum when such failure was caused by conditions beyond his control (such as an economic decline, new import restrictions, the arrival of new competitors, etc.).

Since it may be difficult to estimate a suitable minimum target, the parties may provide an alternative incentive, by requiring the agent to spend a minimum amount of money on advertising, sales promotions and participation in trade fairs. Under this option, the agent is given an incentive to recover his investment, but he does not bear the risk of termination of the contract based on limited sales, which may be beyond his control.

8) *Sub–agents* – Either the matter will be completely left up to the agent ("Alternative A" in the ICC Model), or the principal will require that the agent, for example, notify her before the engagement of any sub–agent

("Alternative B" in the ICC Model). The employment of sub–agents is most commonly left to the agent, because of the basic principle that the agent is independent and should be free to organize his activities. However, in some cases the principal may have entered into the agency contract specifically because of the personal reputation of a particular agent. In this case the principal may justifiably refuse to allow the agent to delegate his responsibilities to a sub–agent.

9) *Principal to be kept informed* – The agent should report back to the principal on market conditions, and answer any reasonable request for information from the principal. Under the ICC Model, the agent must also keep the principal informed on regulations such as those involving labelling and technical specifications.

10) *Financial responsibility* – The agent must generally take a certain level of care in checking the solvency of potential customers. Although, under the ICC Model, the agent is not required to perform an exhaustive credit check on the potential customers, he must not pass on an order to the principal if he has any reason to doubt the solvency of the customer. If the principal wants the agent to perform a credit check on all new customers, then this should be included in the contract.

Del credere contracts – The ICC Model spells out the possibility of a *del credere* contract, under which the agent agrees to reimburse the principal for any loss the principal may suffer from non–payment by the customer. Because the potential exposure of the agent under such an agreement is great, these agreements are frequently subject to legal limitations on the extent to which the agent must indemnify the principal. There are two basic possibilities:

i. 100% reimbursement – the agent agrees to reimburse the principal for 100% of the loss he may suffer, in which case it may be advisable for the agent to limit this exposure to certain types of business or certain sectors. Under this option, the parties will usually agree on an increased commission for the agent; or

ii. limited percentage reimbursement – the parties limit the agent's exposure to a certain percentage of the loss (i.e., 15%) suffered by the principal. The primary goal under this option is to provide a strong incentive for the agent to do a thorough job in verifying the credit of potential customers.

Because the *del credere* clause can have a large financial impact on the agent, the ICC Model requires that the Del Credere Annex be signed by both parties. Since many national laws limit the agent's power to subject himself to *del credere* exposure, parties should seek to arrive at a balanced solution which does not impose undue liability on the agent (a rule of thumb is to limit the percentage to that of the agent's commission).

11) *Principal's trademarks and symbols* – Both principal and agent have an interest in protecting the principal's intellectual property rights in the contract products: infringement will cost both parties money. Thus, agency contracts often require the principal to protect his intellectual property interests in trademarks, trade names and corporate symbols (although this is not the ICC approach). Similarly, the agent is often contractually required to share the obligation of protecting such property, as by initiating legal procedures – though this is not required under the ICC Model.

In the absence of any contractual provisions on intellectual property, an unscrupulous agent might be able to register the principal's trade names or symbols under his own name, and retain the rights to these names after the termination of the contract. The consequences could be serious if the principal had allowed the agent to use the principal's name or symbols in the agent's corporate name – after termination of the contract the principal might not be able to prevent the agent from continuing to use a name which could easily be confused with the principal's.

The ICC Model therefore expressly prohibits the agent from registering the principal's marks in his own name. After the termination of the contract, the agent must immediately and clearly stop associating himself with the principal's trademarks. The agent must also inform the principal of any possible infringements of the principal's trademarks. However, since a defence of these trademarks may be quite expensive and prove unsuccessful, *there is no obligation in the ICC Model for either party to undertake such a defence*.

12) *Complaints by customers* – Under the ICC Model, the agent has no authority to commit the principal to take back allegedly defective goods or to compensate the buyer for any alleged breach. In many cases, however, the principal and agent will agree on the need to quickly respond to customer complaints. If it is anticipated that such a quick response will be necessary, the principal should give the agent specific written authorization to respond to the complaints.

13) *Exclusivity* – Agency agreements may provide for total exclusivity in the territory to the agent, or for no exclusivity whatsoever. Generally, the principal will grant exclusivity only if he is convinced that the agent will do a good job of promoting the goods throughout the territory. Many agents will refuse to undertake investments in promoting the principal's products in the territory unless assured of exclusivity.

The ICC Model seeks to strike a balance. The agent is granted exclusivity in the territory, with the exception that the principal himself can make sales into the territory (provided that he informs the agent and pays the agent's commission on these sales). If the principal already has large customers or prospects in the territory, there is not much reason for him to grant full commission to the agent on sales made to these parties. Therefore, the ICC Model provides for an Annex in which these customers can be listed, and allows the principal to pay reduced commission for these sales. Where the agent is in a strong negotiating position, he may obtain full exclusivity: even if a customer within the territory contacts the principal directly and without intervention by the agent, the principal must pay commission to the agent.

14) *Agent to be kept informed* – The agent should be kept continually informed on developments involving the products, their technical features and their competitive position against the prices and technical characteristics of rival products. The agent should also be fully briefed on the principal's operations, because clients may ask for details. For example, the agent should know the principal's financial status, growth projections, factory specifications, number of employees, capital reserves, research plans, export strategy, etc. Ideally, the agent will have a permanently accessible interlocutor at the principal's home office.

The ICC Model's clause does not prevent the principal from carrying on business according to his own strategic interests. He may decide to rank the territory as a low priority in terms of marketing or promotional investments. However, he may not act so as to harm the interests of the agent, as by refusing to make deliveries when a credit–worthy customer places an order, or by making late deliveries or deliveries of defective products.

15) *Commission* – The agent's commission is usually expressed as a percentage of the value of sales made during the life of the contract. The commission may be a simple set percentage, or there may be a variable commission depending on the size of a particular sale or on the total volume of sales.

Under the ICC Model, the agent is entitled to a commission an all sales made in the territory, even if the agent did not actually do any of the work required to approach a particular customer. This provision was drafted so as to accord with Art. 7.2 of the European Directive on Agency.

Exceptions to the rule (entitling the agent to payment of a reduced commission) are allowed for:
• sales made by the principal himself;
• orders placed outside the territory, but owing to the agent's work, or placed within the territory, but not owing to the agent's efforts;
• sales on reduced price terms;
• commissions where the customer turns out to be insolvent but the principal is reimbursed for her loss by insurance.

The above rules avoid the problem of two agents from different national territories claiming commission for the same sale, by encouraging agents to try to make sales even if it appears that the ultimate order will be placed from outside the territory. Agents are often willing to make sales at reduced prices even if it means giving up part of the commission; the ICC Model therefore allows for such a practice if expressly agreed to by the parties.

The agent will not be reimbursed for any expenses incurred in fulfilling the contract (such as telephone or travel expenses). It is expected that the commission paid will allow the agent to cover these expenses and still earn some profit. However, the ICC Model allows the parties to provide otherwise with a specific agreement in writing.

16) *Method of calculating commission and payment* – The calculation of the commission payable to the agent is not unfrequently the source of disagreement between the parties. The ICC Model seeks to set out a clear scheme by calculating the commission on the net amount of the invoice. An alternative would be to agree on a fixed lump–sum commission per item sold.

Since the calculation is based on the net invoice price, any reductions granted by the agent to the customer will reduce the commission owed. If the principal grants any additional price reductions after sending the invoice, such as a discount for payments made in cash, these will not affect the commission. Additional expenses for packaging, carriage, or taxes, are excluded from the calculation when they appear separately on the invoice, which is generally the case. However, if the additional expenses and taxes are included in the net invoice price, they must be included in calculating the commission.

Time of payment of commission – If the agent has been given the authority to represent the principal, then it may be reasonable to allow him to claim the commission as soon as the customer has agreed to place an order. If the agent lacks the authority to bind the principal, several options are possible – the commission may become payable when:
- the order is placed (very favourable for the agent – he may even claim commission on orders ultimately rejected by the principal);
- the order is accepted by the principal – here the commission will remain due even if the order is ultimately not executed or the customer fails to pay;
- the goods are delivered by the principal;
- the customer pays for the goods (most favourable for the principal).

The ICC Model has chosen the latter of the above possibilities – commission is payable when the principal receives payment from the customer for the goods. The agent is allowed partial payment only in proportion to partial payments made by the buyer. The commission must be paid not later than the last day of the month following the quarter in which it became due (this rule is required under the EC Directive).

17) *Unconcluded business* – The ICC Model clause strikes a balance as regards allocating liability for the principal's failure to conclude a contract with a customer. If the principal does not conclude the sale because of, for example, insolvency of the buyer, strikes, natural disasters or other factors beyond her control, she will not have to pay commission. If the non–performance, however, is the principal's fault, then the commission will still be owed to the agent.

18) *Term of the contract* – The ICC Model provides for two alternatives:
- a contract for an indefinite period (which can be terminated at any time upon sufficient notice by either of the parties); or
- a contract for a fixed period which is automatically renewable for successive one–year periods (which can be terminated at the end of the fixed period, provided sufficient notice has been given).

In either case, if the contract has lasted less than five years, a minimum of four months' notice is required by either party to terminate the contract; if the contract has lasted more than five years, the minimum notice is six months.

Typically, the principal and agent will have opposing perspectives as regards the term of the contract. The agent, called upon to invest time and energy in marketing the principal's products, wants to be assured of a long duration. The principal, on the other hand, would like to be free to move to another system of distribution, as by opening a subsidiary himself, and therefore prefers a shorter term. A common compromise is for parties to agree to an indefinite term but to specifically enumerate the conditions under which each party is allowed to terminate the contract. The parties should always keep in mind that the applicable national law may require certain minimum conditions concerning termination, rendering invalid any contractual provisions to the contrary.

19) *Unfinished business* – Under the ICC Model, if the agent's efforts result in orders being placed before the termination of the contract but only concluded after termination, a commission shall be payable to the agent.

20) *Earlier termination* – Notwithstanding the basic termination provisions, an earlier termination is possible if either of the parties is guilty of a substantial breach of contract. Moreover, the parties may indicate specific conditions which they would consider as constituting a substantial breach. Certain specific situations automatically give rise to the termination right: bankruptcy, liquidation, receivership, etc.

21) *Indemnity in case of termination* – In many countries there is a legal right on behalf of the agent to claim compensation for the goodwill that the agent has built up for the principal in the event of termination of the contract. Therefore, the ICC Model provides for two possible alternatives:
   i.   A termination indemnity equal to a maximum of one year of an agent's average remuneration;
   ii. No indemnity.

However, in many jurisdictions it will not be possible to choose the second alternative.

Clearly, agents will prefer to stipulate an indemnity in the contract, whereas principals will be reluctant to agree. However, the principal should be aware that regardless of the contract drafting, national law in certain countries (particularly in Latin America and the Middle East) imposes certain restrictions on principals and protection for agents. Even where an indemnity is made available by law, an agent generally cannot benefit from the indemnity if in fact the principal has not derived any substantial revenues from customers introduced by the agent.

22) *Arbitration – applicable law* – In the ICC Model, dispute resolution is by arbitration under the *Rules of Arbitration* of the International Chamber of Commerce. Arbitration was chosen because arbitration proceedings are confidential, and are often faster and cheaper than litigation in state courts.

Two alternatives are provided in the event that the arbitrators are not able to find the solution by looking to explicit contractual provisions. Under the first alternative, the arbitrators will refer to the *lex mercatoria*, which are the principles of law generally recognized in international trade as applicable to agency contracts. The second alternative is to specifically make the contract subject to a particular national law.

If the agent is established in a country where mandatory legal rules are in force with respect to agency contracts, these mandatory rules will be applied regardless of the choice of *lex mercatoria* as the legal foundation for dispute resolution.

23) *Previous agreements; modifications in writing* – The ICC Model is presumed to supersede all previous agreements between the parties. Modifications to the contract must be in writing.

5.2 Distributorship contracts – the ICC Model Distributorship Contract

5.2.1 Characteristics of exclusive distributorship contracts

The *ICC Model Distributorship Contract* refers to "exclusivity" of representation. In practice, a distinction is sometimes made between what is referred to as a "sole" distributorship and an "exclusive" one, to the effect that with a "sole" distributorship the supplier (or the seller) himself may make sales into the territory, whereas with an "exclusive" distributorship not even the supplier may compete with the distributor in the territory. However, this distinction is not always supported by the law.

Because the distributorship contract contains many of the same elements as the agency contract, we will not repeat the same detailed analysis here as above. However, the following points concerning the characteristics of the distributorship relation should be noted.

Generally speaking, a sole distributorship agreement provides that a supplier grants a foreign party the sole trading rights within a particular territory with respect to the supplier's goods. This agreement is commonly completed by a reciprocal provision that the buyer will rely on the supplier as sole source of supply.

Note that the sole distribution agreement is not itself a contract of sale – rather, it sets out the general framework for later individual contracts of sale between the manufacturer and distributor, and further sales to end customers. Where the contract includes exclusive buying provisions, and the buyer resides in either the European Union or the United States, which have strict competition laws, the parties should be careful to avoid violating the law.

Although distributors are often loosely referred to as agents, a sole distributor does not – as opposed to an agent – act on behalf of the principal in dealing with the end customer. Rather, the distributor resells the goods in his own name and his profit is derived from the difference between his buying price from the supplier and his selling price to the customer, and this difference is, in principle, left to his discretion.

An important advantage of the distributor agreement for the exporter is that he does not have to worry about the credit–worthiness of the ultimate customers – he only sells to the distributor, whose credit he will have fully investigated before signing the distributorship agreement.

5.2.2 Key clauses in distributorship agreements

Because many of the legal issues covered by distributorship agreements are similar to those covered in agency contracts (discussed above), our examination of distributorship agreements is somewhat briefer.

a. TERRITORY

The geographical extent of the territory should be precisely described. In some cases, the parties may wish to provide that when sales reach a certain level, the distributor will be entitled to a larger territory. The supplier will often be required to pass on direct inquiries from consumers in the territory to the distributor, and the distributor may also be required to pass on enquiries from outside the territory to the supplier. The supplier will often require the distributor to keep lists of customers and to supply them to the supplier. Within the European Union, a supplier may not prohibit a distributor from accepting orders emanating from another exclusive distributor's territory. So long as the distributor does not actively solicit such customers, no further restrictions are allowable.

b. PRICE

The competition laws of many countries prohibit principals from requiring distributors to adhere to certain, fixed prices. Distributors must therefore be allowed freedom to set their own resale prices. Manufacturers may, however, provide suggested prices and price ranges.

As for the price of the goods to the distributor, this provision is tricky in the same way as any other long–term supply contract. Obviously, the prices of most goods will vary according to economic or strategic developments. One solution is to peg the contract price to a publicly available market price on a specific date. Another solution is to grant the distributor a price equal to the best price quoted by the supplier to any customer which is not a subsidiary or associated company of the supplier. In order to avoid contravention of antitrust rules, the exporter must avoid trying to set the distributor's prices precisely or to control them.

c. SOLE BUYING OR SELLING RIGHTS

While it is common for the supplier and distributor to exchange reciprocal agreements for sole buying and selling rights, this is not necessary. The supplier may be wise to specifically provide that the distributor will undertake positive and energetic efforts to offer the supplier's goods in the market. Otherwise, the distributor would be free to ignore the distributorship contract after having signed it, although he would be able to prevent the supplier from selling into the territory through any other intermediary. Along these lines, the supplier may wish to provide for a minimum target, giving the supplier the option of terminating the contract if the orders placed by the distributor do not represent a minimum value during a trial period.

d. ADVERTISING; MARKET INFORMATION; PROTECTION OF INTELLECTUAL PROPERTY

The seller commonly requires the distributor to undertake certain minimum obligations with respect to the advertising of the goods, as well as to provide him with basic commercial and market information, and moreover to help protect his intellectual property rights in trademarks or patents.

5.2.3 EU competition law

An *Addendum* to the ICC Model Contract has been drafted to take into account EC Regulation n° 2790/1999 which replaced *inter alia* Regulation 1983/83 and which came into force on 1 June 2000.

Some amendments have been proposed, to the extent that EU competition law is applicable, i.e., with respect to distribution contracts that may affect trade with the European Union.

Article 12 has been amended to take into account the prohibition under Regulation n° 2790/1999 for the distributor to actively sell in exclusive territories reserved by the supplier for himself or allocated by the supplier to other exclusive distributors or buyers.

In Article 18, the parties are recommended to limit the contract duration to five years to take into account the requirement made under Regulation n° 2790/1999 that the non–competition clause must not last more than five years.

5.3 ICC Short Form Model Contracts – International Commercial Agency/International Distributorship

In 2001, ICC published a *Short Form Model Contracts on Commercial Agency and Distributorship* (ICC Publication 634) which only provides the essential clauses for the drafting of straightforward transactions. For more complicated transactions, the parties should refer to the long version of the *ICC Model Contracts on Commercial Agency and Distributorship* which contain more sophisticated alternatives.

Since the Short Forms contain many of the same elements as the long versions (see *supra* 5.1 and 5.2), detailed analysis is not provided here. It is, however, worth noting the following essential issues considered in the Short Forms:

■ FOR THE INTERNATIONAL AGENCY CONTRACT:

- The products,
- Territory,
- Commission,
- Termination,
- Goodwill indemnity,
- Applicable law,
- Resolution of disputes, and
- EU competition rules.

■ FOR THE INTERNATIONAL DISTRIBUTORSHIP CONTRACT:

- The products,
- Territory,
- Termination,
- Goodwill indemnity,
- Applicable law and law governing sales to the distributor,
- Resolution of disputes,
- Reservation of title, and
- EU competition rules.

5.4　International franchising

The basics: Franchising is a form of shared investment in the expansion and replication of successful business systems. International franchising allows franchisors to grow rapidly in foreign markets with minimum capital investments. "Unit" franchises confer the right to exploit a single operation, while "master franchises" and "area development" agreements confer the right to sub–develop and/or grant sub–franchises in a particular territory. Master franchises are particularly suitable internationally because they permit local supervision of networks. Franchising contracts can be complex and in some jurisdictions are subject to local laws for the protection of franchisees.

5.4.1　Introduction

Franchising is based on the attractive notion of replicating success. The origin of most franchises is in the development of a business system so efficient and competitive that it that has superior chances of succeeding in new territories. However, in order to grow rapidly, business networks need large infusions of capital. Rather than invest his own capital, the franchisor enters into agreements with (usually) local entrepreneurs – the franchisees. The franchisor grants to each franchisee the right to exploit all or part of the franchisor's business system, including trademarks, logo and distinctive signs, intellectual property, technical know–how and processes. In return, the franchisee usually makes a "front money" payment in order to enter the franchise network, invests a minimum amount in setting up and operating the business, pays the franchisor fees and royalties, and adheres to the franchisor's standards for quality of services. The combination of the franchisor's reputation and expertise with the franchisee's capital, local knowledge and motivation, can result in explosive growth.

Well–known examples of franchising success are McDonald's, Holiday Inn, Yves Rocher and Hertz, but there are countless others. Franchising has become one of the primary distribution channels for products and services in developed economies, where image and service reputation can determine market share. Franchising is found in industries as diverse as fast food chains, computer retail sales, real estate services, automobile rental and service stations, to name but a few. According to the International Franchise Association, more than one–third of all retail sales in the United States are conducted through franchises, accounting for hundreds of millions of dollars in annual sales and hundreds of thousands of jobs. Even outside the top franchise markets of the United States, Canada and the United Kingdom, franchising is becoming one of the most popular methods for business expansion.

In addition to the advantages described above, franchising can offer cost savings from the decentralization of management and financial controls. A further attraction for the franchisor is that franchisees are usually familiar with national labour, safety, health and technical standards. However, one of the corresponding risks for the franchisor is that the franchisee may eventually set up his own firm and become a competitor of the original franchise. Therefore, franchising contracts often contain special non–competition clauses.

Franchising, like agency, has in some countries raised political sensitivities. Some organizations have expressed concern that local franchisees, like agents, have little bargaining power against large franchisors and therefore require mandatory legal protection. Thus, in certain countries there are strict regulations dealing with such things as the amount of disclosure that must be made by franchisors when recruiting franchisees. It does happen that franchisees claim to have been "lured" into franchises by a franchisor's inflated, fraudulent statements as to likely returns on investment.

5.4.2 Different types of franchises and franchising structures

Product (or *trademark*) *franchising* involves granting the right to manufacture and/or market a product under a specific trademark to the franchisee. *Business format franchising* covers a complete system of doing business, including service concepts and operations, in addition to trademark and logo rights. In *production* (or *manufacturing*) *franchises*, the franchisee manufactures according to the franchisor's specifications and sells the goods under the franchisor's trademark. In a *service franchise*, the franchisee provides a service developed by the franchisor under the franchisor's service mark. Under a *distribution franchise arrangement*, the franchisor manufactures the product and sells it to the franchisee for resale to the final consumer.

The franchisor may structure a franchise network in terms of either *unit* or *territorial franchising*. In the case of unit franchising, the franchisor enters into an agreement directly with each franchisee. Under a territorial franchise, an entire geographical area is developed by a *master franchisee* or *area developer* responsible for a number of outlets.

International franchising is generally conducted in the following ways: 1) direct/unit franchises, 2) through franchisor's branch or subsidiary, 3) through a development agreement, 4) through a joint venture, 5) through master franchises. Unit franchising is most common in domestic markets – it facilitates a maximum of control by the franchisor over the individual outlets, with promotion of the franchise system and trademarks usually remaining in the hands of the franchisor. In an international context, however, a unit franchise approach runs counter to one of the underlying business principles of franchising – minimizing costs via decentralization. The costs of supervising an international network from a single headquarters could prove onerous. In the international context, therefore, it is generally only advisable to franchise directly when the target country is geographically, culturally, linguistically and/or legally proximate to the franchisor's country.

Territorial franchises cover multiple outlets in a specified area and may be granted through either a franchise development agreement or a master franchise agreement. Under a typical development agreement, the developer/franchisee is required to open and operate a certain number of units in the assigned geographical area (usually a particular country) within an agreed time frame. The franchisor benefits from dealing with a manageable number of franchisees. Area developers usually have sufficient financial and human resources to manage the set–up and day–to–day operation of the business with a relatively high degree of independence from the franchisor. Training costs can also be reduced, because the franchisor only trains the developer; the developer in turn trains the unit franchisees.

Area developer agreements are also subject to corresponding risks. If the developer fails, all of the outlets in the territory will be affected. On the other hand, if the franchisee does extremely well, he may become uncomfortably indispensable to the franchisor, because the developer may represent so many outlets. Another possible problem is that area developers may employ salaried managers to run the individual shops (as opposed to highly motivated unit franchisees).

Under master franchise agreements the franchisor grants the master franchisee (or sub–franchisor) the right to develop and operate franchise outlets on his own account, as well as – in some cases – the right to sub–franchise outlets to sub–franchisees. Some sub–franchisees may even be allowed to run several units, which may add to the complexity of the system. Decreased control over sub–franchisees is generally to be expected as a corollary to the increased decentralization. Although master franchise agreements commonly include strict provisions regarding the supervision of the system, their enforcement may be difficult in certain countries.

A variety of other legal forms can be chosen for international franchise agreements. One option is to establish an overseas subsidiary in each target territory to act as franchisor. Under this system, the franchisor retains direct control over the foreign franchisees, but still benefits to some extent from local know–how. Alternatively, a joint venture may be set up by the franchisor and a local enterprise. Guidance from an experienced lawyer is essential.

5.4.3 The ICC Model International Franchising Contract

This ICC Model Contract applies to international distribution franchise agreements. The following key elements should be kept in mind by the parties:

a. KNOW–HOW
Know–how consists of all confidential, valuable and proprietary information, experience and operating techniques of the franchisor that would enable the franchisee to reproduce the franchisor's success. This also includes the franchisor's assistance in the operation of the business and training of the franchisee. In return, the franchisee has to respect the franchisor's proprietary rights and take all reasonable steps to protect the confidentiality of the franchisor's training materials and operation manuals.

b. FRANCHISOR'S TRADE NAME, TRADE MARKS AND PATENTS
The franchisee must acknowledge that the franchisor is the owner of all proprietary rights, titles and interest in the systems to ensure a proper protection of the franchisor's rights. Customer recognition and confidence in the products or services are usually linked to the trade mark, which is one of the key elements of a successful franchise system.

c. PRODUCTS AND TERRITORY

A clear definition of the products and the territory is essential to achieve the quality requirements, and also to allow the franchisee to maintain a stock of products to meet the needs of customers and to attain the sales requirements or targets. The granting of an exclusive territory will enable the franchisee, an independent business operator, to prosper. During the term of the contract, the franchisor is not allowed to operate itself or to license any person other than the franchisee to operate the business within the territory.

d. PAYMENT OF FEES AND ROYALITIES

The parties should clearly decide how and when payment shall occur, taking into consideration the fact there are many ways to calculate royalties. Failure to pay royalties may be considered a breach of the contract and result in a right to terminate the contract.

e. TERM AND RENEWAL OF THE CONTRACT

The parties can contract for a definite period or an indefinite period. In the former case, they should bear in mind that the number of years cited in the contract should be tied to the capital investment of the franchisee, which should be reasonably able to recover its investments. Moreover, the relationship may evolve and new products or services may be introduced on the market. The parties should therefore carefully consider the conditions upon which the contract will be renewed, prolonged or terminated (i.e., the grounds for early termination and its effects).

5.5 The ICC Model Occasional Intermediary Contract (Non–circumvention and non–disclosure agreement)

This ICC Model contract completes the set of ICC Model Contracts in the field of international distribution. Given the countless number of intermediary contracts, it is necessary to indicate that an occasional intermediary is an intermediary that occasionally promotes the business of its counterpart, i.e., it may, for example, conclude contracts between a principal and a third party. Contrary to the agent, the intermediary, however, may agree to promote a specific business or to inform its counterpart about business which may come to its notice, without any continuing obligation to develop the market. Moreover, its activities may be limited to the simple supply of information about a possible business, whereas the agent has to negotiate the contract on behalf of the principal.

The parties should clearly define the type of service that the intermediary is to provide, e.g., to supply information about third parties or to put the principal in contact with third parties. They should also agree on the level of exclusivity with respect to the business the intermediary agrees to promote. In return, the intermediary must be assured that it will receive remuneration (commission or lump sum), which is a guarantee that it will not be "circumvented" by its counterpart for the work provided.

As in other ICC Model Contracts, special attention should also be given to the confidentiality of the information provided, and to the non–competition clause – whereby the intermediary can accept or not accept to act for its counterpart's competitors. The term and renewal of the contract is also an important item to consider.

Note

(1) Roger E. Axtell, *The Do's and Taboos of International Trade: A Small Business Primer*, John Wiley & Sons (1991), p. 77–78.

CHAPTER SIX

International Payment Options

The basics: There are a wide variety of payment methods available in international trade, each with particular advantages and disadvantages. In essence, if traders seek to assure a high level of payment security, then payment methods will be relatively more costly. Conversely, if payment security is not a priority, because the parties know or trust each other, then cheaper, simpler payment methods can be used.

The central risks in international trade are the exporter's risk of non–payment and the importer's risk that the goods shipped will not conform to the contract. Both of these risks may be reduced via the documentary safeguards provided by the letter of credit mechanism (commercial letters of credit are referred to by bankers as "documentary credits" – the two terms are hereafter used interchangeably). However, since documentary credits involve relatively higher banking fees and more complex documentary procedures, this option is not always appropriate. Parties with long trading histories or residing in adjacent countries may be willing to make sales on open account or with payment in advance – payment modes which are easier and less expensive, but which do not similarly reduce risk.

Exporters should be aware that *documentary credits require impeccable document–management* on the part of the exporter.

In addition to payment–related risks and safeguards, other transaction risks can be reduced via effective credit investigations and management, exchange rate management, bank guarantees or suretyship bonds and insurance.

Negotiable instruments (like bank drafts and bills of lading), which are at the heart of payment–security systems, can also be used by traders to raise interim finance or receive immediate, discounted payment.

6.1 Overview of payment, finance and security for international transactions

Export payment mechanisms, such as the documentary credit and documentary collection, are flexible systems which can be used as 1) means of payment, 2) security mechanisms, and/or 3) finance devices.

1) *Payment means* – There are simple ways for the importer to effect payment, such as by bank draft or wire transfer, but in an international transaction these alone would leave either the exporter or importer entirely at risk (depending on whether payment was made before or after receipt of the goods). In international trade, bank cheques are uncommon. More common is to find payment effected when the importer (or his bank) accepts or pays the exporter's draft or bill of exchange. Drafts or bills of exchange are in themselves simply payment devices (and when used alone are referred to as clean bills). However, traders have found further protection by requiring the attachment of additional documents to the bills of exchange; these bundles of documents are then processed through banks: hence, documentary bills (a bill of exchange with other documents – such as bill of lading and commercial invoice – attached).

2) *Security mechanism* – With documentary bills, the exporters' goods (represented by the bill of lading or other transport document) and the importer's payment (represented by the importer's acceptance or payment of the bill of exchange) are exchanged through a neutral third party, the bank. This removes the danger that either exporter or importer will unfairly end up with both goods and money. Documentary bills, which are used in both documentary credit and documentary collection operations, therefore represent a linkage of payment and security functions.

Note, in contrast, that standby credits and demand guarantees are meant to be used primarily as security instruments rather than payment devices. Thus, if an exporter agrees to grant the importer 90 days credit, backed by the importer's standby credit (or bank guarantee), the standby credit is not meant to be the primary payment device. Rather, the exporter will submit invoices for payment to the importer at the appropriate time. Only should the importer fail to pay will the exporter seek recourse to the standby credit. Security devices will be looked at in detail in Chapter 8.

Each of the international payment options has different risk–reduction and documentary characteristics. Generally, the reduction of risk is purchased at the cost of greater documentary complexity and higher banking fees or service costs. Parties tend to choose the cheaper and simpler options when they have a great deal of confidence in each other, or when one of the parties has such a strong bargaining position that he is able to force the other to accept somewhat risky terms.

Both export seller and import buyer are exposed to risk. The seller faces the risk of non–payment, the buyer the risk of non–receipt of goods of contract quality in due time. These risks can be reduced or eliminated by selecting wisely amongst the various payment mechanisms.

3) *Finance device* – Finance, in contrast to payment, is related to the need to grant credit to the exporter or importer. Bills of exchange, either alone or in combination with documentary credit or collection operations, can be used as sources of finance. Commonly, importers would like to be granted a credit period (from 30 up to 180 days or more), so that they can re–sell the goods before they have to pay the exporter. Exporters may be willing to grant such terms provided the importer (or the importer's bank) undertakes to pay at the end of the credit period, as by issuing a deferred payment letter of credit or "accepting" a term bill of exchange. Exporters are able to discount the accepted bills for ready payment. Discounting practices, such as "forfaiting", are covered along with factoring and other short–term finance devices in Chapter 7.

6.2 Credit management and export credit insurance

6.2.1 Credit management

Credit management begins with the firm's realization that delayed payment, non–payment or difficulties with collection can become extremely costly. Proper credit management is one of the distinguishing characteristics of highly professional export firms. Firms that understand the importance of credit management seek to integrate it throughout the entire export process, from quotation to final receipt of payment. Sales personnel are not allowed to conclude contracts without a credit manager's approval of the payment method and terms. Customers are thoroughly investigated for credit–worthiness, and penalty schedules are established for customers who pay late or exceed their allotted credit limit.

Most professionally managed enterprises have developed systems for dealing with domestic credit risk. However, it is not sufficient for the exporter simply to translate domestic procedures into the international arena. The exporter should set up specific systems for dealing with risks not found in domestic trade. International transactions by their nature involve countries with differing politico–economic environments, thus, the element of country risk. In addition, exporters should not assume that security mechanisms which are effective in the home market will necessarily be effective abroad. Legal remedies, in particular, may prove surprisingly weak or difficult to apply.

Although small exporters may wish to avoid these complexities by simply turning the entire process over to an export credit insurer, international factor or other service provider, a basic familiarity with the issues will allow the exporter to better oversee the work of these agents. Export credit management can be summarized as follows:

a. CREATION OF AN EXPORT CREDIT MANAGEMENT SYSTEM AND CREDIT POLICY

If the exporter has a domestic credit manager, he should set down on paper the specific additional steps that will be required for international transactions. These should be communicated to export marketing, sales and shipping personnel. Standard contracts and conditions of sale may need to be adjusted accordingly. It may be useful to consult with a specialized credit insurer, the trade finance department of a bank, or an export consultant or management company.

b. ASSESSMENT OF THE RISKS ASSOCIATED WITH POTENTIAL CUSTOMERS

For many countries, ample credit information will be available, especially as regards larger customers. Highly detailed analyses are provided by credit ratings companies such as Dun & Bradstreet. At the very least a credit history or a reference from the customer's bank may be available. These services can be expensive, so the need for them should be balanced against the size of the sale and the payment mechanisms that the customer is willing to accept. For a buyer willing to pay cash in advance or by confirmed letter of credit, extensive credit checking may not be worth the expense (unless the goods are made to order or require specific preparation).

Despite the foregoing, the exporter's credit analysts should understand that other countries have different accounting systems and business practices. A comparatively high level of late payment or a low level of working capital may be considered acceptable in the importer's country, and the exporter who is too risk–averse may find himself shut out of these markets. In some of these cases, informal measures of credit–worthiness, such as general and personal impressions gained on business trips, may significantly supplement the data available to the credit analyst (although such informal indicators should never substitute for rigorous credit investigation).

c. CHOICE OF THE APPROPRIATE PAYMENT MECHANISM OR OTHER SECURITY

The exporter's credit policy should specify appropriate payment methods for different transaction amounts and customer risk profiles. Let us briefly list the key payment options from the point of view of the exporter (each of these will be examined in greater detail in the following chapter sections):

1) *Cash in advance* – Obviously the safest for the exporter, this is generally unavailable in competitive markets. A partial advance payment (e.g., 20–30%) may be more acceptable to the importer and therefore more realistic, but leaves the exporter exposed to risk on the balance. Despite the great risks to the importer of payment by cash in advance, some importers may find they have no choice. It does happen, for example, that importers from certain developing countries find it necessary to pay in advance in order to obtain high–demand goods from developed countries.

2) *Documentary credit or "D/C" (also known as a "letter of credit" or "L/C")* – After cash in advance, this is usually considered the next safest method for the exporter. However, because of its complex documentary nature, the documentary credit can be relatively expensive in terms of banking fees; moreover, the exporter must have a rigorous document–preparation system in place so as to avoid the risk of non–payment due to non–conforming documents being presented to the bank.

3) *Documentary collection* – Not as safe as a letter of credit, but significantly cheaper; the seller must be willing to take the risk that the importer will not pay or accept the documents.

4) *Open account* – The least safe method, to be used when the importer is fully trusted and creditworthy. The exporter should consider the need for protection with credit insurance.

d. MANAGEMENT OF EXCHANGE RATE RISKS

The easiest way for the exporter to avoid exchange rate risk is to only accept payment in his own currency. However, in competitive markets exporters must often be prepared to accept payment in a foreign currency, thereby exposing themselves to exchange rate fluctuations. The various mechanisms for dealing with exchange and currency risk are summarized in the last section of this chapter.

e. INSTALLING DOCUMENT–PROCESSING SYSTEMS

Most export transactions today are still based to some extent on paper documents. Increasingly, as use of the Internet expands, export–related "documents" are being transmitted electronically; for more on this see Chapter 10 on e–commerce. Indeed, as discussed later in this chapter, ICC has already developed rules for the presentation of electronic documents.

When documents are processed behind schedule, or contain erroneous information, or are incomplete, the exporter risks delayed payment or non–payment. Export documentary systems should combine checklists of necessary documents with time–schedules for issuing or receiving them. Export software and electronic document–management systems can greatly simplify these tasks. Another alternative is to turn over certain document–processing responsibilities to a reputable freight forwarder or export management company. Specialized documentary credit consultants are available in some countries to take over a trader's documentary credit processes.

f. OBTAINING EXPORT INSURANCE

This is a basic safeguard which does not, however, cover all risks or for an unlimited time. Moreover, this protection comes at a price. It is explored in the section below.

g. COLLECTION OF OVERDUE ACCOUNTS

Late payment penalties may dissuade importers from tardiness in settling accounts, but if the exporter has not arranged for a payment security, he may need to implement a collection procedure. Of course, any legal recourse should be preceded by informal persuasion. The exporter may then wish to turn the account over to an international collection agent or factor. In large transactions, a legal action for non–payment may be commenced; for more detail on this latter course, see Chapter 3 on international dispute resolution.

6.2.2 Export credit insurance (or "trade credit insurance")

As we have seen in other sections, the major distinction between domestic and international sales is that the latter involve higher risk. In this chapter we focus on payment–related risks, which leads us to consider the possibility of insuring against payment default. This type of insurance is indeed quite common, and is referred to as "export credit" insurance or "trade credit" insurance. Since this form of insurance is one of the key security devices employed by export firms, we will deal with it in detail in Chapter 8 on "Security for International Transactions" (see Chapter 8, section 8.2).

6.3 Documentary sales and payment: shipping documents

Because of the central role of documents in our discussion of payment mechanisms, we will briefly summarize the characteristics of the principal documents here:

6.3.1 The key documents

a. THE BILL OF EXCHANGE

A draft or bill of exchange ("B/E") is a negotiable instrument which represents an unconditional demand for payment. Together with the bill of lading, it forms the basis for documentary collections procedures. Together with the exporter's commercial invoice (see below), the B/E can be used to charge the importer for the goods. Bills of exchange are defined as follows: "An unconditional order in writing addressed by one person to another signed by the person giving it requiring the person to whom it is addressed to pay on demand or at a fixed or determinable future time a sum certain in money to or to the order of a specified person or bearer."

Thus, the draft is written by the drawer (export seller) to the drawee (import buyer), requiring payment of a fixed amount at a specific time. A draft payable upon presentation is called a sight draft, while a draft payable at a future time is called a usance (or time) draft. The draft is legally accepted when a bank or the buyer writes "accepted", the date, and a signature on the face of a time draft. A draft accepted by a bank is called a banker's acceptance, while a draft accepted by a buyer is called a trade acceptance.

When the seller attaches the bill of lading or other transport document to a bill of exchange, the bill of exchange is called a documentary bill. By doing this, the seller ensures that the buyer will not obtain any rights to the goods (via the bill of lading) before having accepted or paid the bill of exchange. Since they are negotiable, drafts may be transferred by endorsement to a third party, who may become a holder in due course.

EXPORT DOCUMENTS – DRAFT (BILL OF EXCHANGE)

Exchange for US$100,00   Austin, May 25, 2001

At sight of the bill of exchange pay to the order of ourselves
One hundred thousand and 00/000 US dollars

Drawn under Banco Mexicano, Mexico, D.F., Documentary Credit N°.12345

Value received and charge same to account of

TO: Banco Mexicano S.A.,
           Ave. Insurgentes 1910
           Mexico, D.F., Mexico
                                        _____
                                        Acme Exports, Inc.

UNCITRAL bill of exchange format

Austin, May 25, 2001
US$100,000
**At sixty days after sight for values received,
pay against this bill of echange to the order
of ourselves**
the sum of US dollars one
hundred thousand
**effective payment to be made in US dollars
only without deduction for and free of any
tax, import levy or duty**
**present or future of any nature under the
laws of the United States or any political
subdivision thereof or therein.**
This bill of exchange is payable at
The First Bank of Texas in Austin

Drawn on The First Bank of Texas, Austin

Accepted ....

            _____
            **For and on behalf of
            Acme Exports, Inc.
            Austin, Texas**

EXPORT DOCUMENTS – BILL OF LADING

Hapag-Lloyd Aktiengesellschaft, Hamburg/Bremen

MULTIMODAL TRANSPORT OR PORT TO PORT SHIPMENT		PAGE 2

SHIPPER:

VOYAGE-NO.	B/L-NO.

SHIPPER'S REFERENCE

CARRIER:

Hapag-Lloyd

STATUS*:

CONSIGNEE OR ORDER:

NOTIFY ADDRESS (Carrier not responsible for failure to notify; see clause 20 [1] hereof):

Place of Receipt:

PRECARRYING VESSEL:

Place of Delivery:

OCEAN VESSEL(S):

PORT OF LOADING:	PORT OF DISCHARGE:

PORT(S) OF TRANSHIPMENT:

Container Nos, Seal Nos; Marks and Nos.	Number and kind of packages; description of goods	Gross weight	Measurement

Bill of Lading ORIGINAL

SHIPPED ON BOARD

DATE:

NVOCC-F.M.C.-NO.:

Shipper's declared value:
(see clause 7(1))

Above Particulars as declared by shipper:
Without responsibility or warranty as to correctness by carrier (see clause 11(1) and (2))

Total No. of Containers received by the Carrier:	Packages received by the Carrier:

Movement:

RECEIVED by the Carrier from the Shipper in apparent good order and condition (unless otherwise noted herein) the total number or quantity of Containers or other packages or units indicated in the box opposite entitled ""Total No. of Containers/Packages received by the Carrier" for Carriage subject to all the terms and conditions hereof (INCLUDING THE TERMS AND CONDITIONS ON THE REVERSE HEREOF AND THE TERMS AND CONDITIONS OF THE CARRIER'S APPLICABLE TARIFF) from the Place of Receipt or the Port of Loading, whichever is applicable, to the Port of Discharge or the Place of Delivery, whichever is applicable. One original Bill of Lading, duly endorsed, must be surrendered by the Merchant to the Carrier in exchange for the Goods or a delivery order. In accepting this Bill of Lading the Merchant expressly accepts and agrees to all its terms and conditions whether printed, stamped or written, or otherwise incorporated, notwithstanding the non-signing of this Bill of Lading by the Merchant.
IN WITNESS WHEREOF the number of original Bills of Lading stated below all of this tenor and date has been signed, one of which being accomplished the others to stand void.

Freight and Charges:	Prepaid	Collect
Origin Land Freight / Transp. Add'l		
Origin THC / LCL Charge		
Sea Freight		
Destination THC / LCL Charge		
Destination Land Freight / Transp. Add'l		

Freight payable at:

Place and date of issue:

Number of original Bs/L:

Commodity Code:

Appropriate columns to be marked with "X"

*e.g. owner of the cargo, freight forwarder, NVOCC or other classification

90112361

EXPORT DOCUMENTS – FIATA BILL OF LADING

EXPORT DOCUMENTS – COMMERCIAL INVOICE

Copyright © 1996 **UNZ & CO.**

SHIPPER/EXPORTER Glotz Industries 1492 Columbus Blvd. Fort Wayne, IN 12345-6789	**COMMERCIAL INVOICE NO.** TO-02 / **DATE** July/16/96 **CUSTOMER PURCHASE ORDER NO.** 193 / **B/L, AWB NO.** AA 2977321 **COUNTRY OF ORIGIN** USA / **DATE OF EXPORT** July/16/96
CONSIGNEE Widgets by Otto Rudiger Paschold Strasse Baden-Baden, Germany	**TERMS** Sale: FCA Chicago (O'Hare Airport) Payment: Net 30 days
	EXPORT REFERENCES Currency: U. S. Dollars
NOTIFY Zoll Clearance 6 Haberkamp Strasse Stuttgart, Germany	
FORWARDING AGENT A. N. Deringer 29320 Goddard Rd. Romulus, MI 48174	**AIR/OCEAN PORT OF EMBARKATION** Chicago **EXPORTING CARRIER/ROUTE** Air Everywhere Flt 102 Frankfurt

Terms of sale and terms of payment are governed by Incoterms 1990 (ICC 460), UCP 500 for letters of credit, and URC 522 for documentary collections.

PKGS.	QUANTITY	NET WT. (Kilos)	GROSS WT. (Kilos)	DESCRIPTION OF MERCHANDISE	UNIT PRICE	TOTAL VALUE
5	50 ea	153.7	160.8	Blue Widgets (HS# 123456)	$ 5.00	$ 250.00
				TOTAL EXW FORT WAYNE, IN		$ 250.00

PACKAGE MARKS:
Otto
Baden-Baden
1/5 - 5/5
MADE WITH PRIDE IN USA

MISC. CHARGES (Packing, Insurance, etc.)	
Pre-Carriage	$ 34.50
FCA Chicago	**INVOICE TOTAL** $ 284.50

CERTIFICATIONS

We certify that this invoice is true and correct, and that the origin of these goods is the United States of America. These goods licensed by the U.S. for ultimate destination Germany. Diversion contrary to U.S. law is prohibited. License G-Dest.

AUTHORIZED SIGNATURE

Printed and sold by *UNZ&CO* 700 Central Avenue, New Providence, NJ 07974 (800) 631-3098

EXPORT DOCUMENTS – INSURANCE CERTIFICATE

GERLING-KONZERN

ALLGEMEINE VERSICHERUNGS-AKTIENGESELLSCHAFT
Otto-Beck-Str. 36
D-68165 Mannheim

Insurance cover is granted to/ Versicherungsschutz besteht gegenüber:	

to order of
Smith & Co.
P.O.Box 650

Mogaro/Tanzania

~~for account of whom it may concern/für Rechnung wen es angeht~~

Certificate of Insurance
Versicherungs-Zertifikat

Date of Issue/Ausfertigungstag
20.03.1996

Cover No./Vertrags-Nr
28-434854

Certificate No./Zertifikat Nr.
2

Number of Originals/Anzahl der Originale
337

Sum Insured/Versicherungssumme
16.940,-- US-$ US-Dollars sixteen
thousand nine hundred forty------

In case of loss or damage exceeding 2.000 DM immediately contact/Bei Schäden über 2.000 DM sofort benachrichtigen:

Toplis and Harding (Tanzania) Ltd
P.O.Box 799   Tel. (51) 25508
1 st Floor Dsm Bookshop Bldg. Fax (51) 39881
Indira Gandhi Street
Dar es Saalam/Tansania

Insured Voyage/Versicherte Reise

Place of commencement of insurance/Ort des Beginns der Versicherung
Ladenburg/Germany

Means of transport/Transportmittel
truck, rail

Oversaa vessel/Seeschiff
M/S "Nedlloyd Asia"

Port of loading/Verladehafen
Bremen

Port of destination/Bestimmungshafen
Dar es Salam

Place of termination of insurance/Ort des Endes der Versicherung
Mogaro/Tanzania

Insured Goods (Marks. Nos: number, kind of packages)/**Versicherte Güter** (Markierung. Nr.; Anzahl, Art der Packstücke)

Marks:
MUSTERMAN BARIUM GMBH
STRONTOUM CARBONAT 'A'
MADE IN GERMANY = EINECS-NO: 216
EINECS-NO: 216-643-7 = H-O

Goods:
oone 20' container
STRONTIUM CARBONATE A TYPE
ORIGIN GERMANY, CREDIT NUMBER M02
gross: 17,710 to Net: 17,500 to

Conditions (to be followed overleaf)/**Bedingungen** (Fortsetzung umseitig)

1. German General Rules of Marine Insurance (ADS). Special Conditions for Cargo (ADS Cargo 1973-Edition 1984)/
   Allgemeine Deutsche Seeversicherungsbedingungen (ADS). Besondere Bestimmungen für die Güterversicherung
   (ADS Güterversicherung 1973 in der Fassung 1984).
2. Conditions of the above mentioned Cover/Bedingungen des oben genannten Vertrages.
3. Types of Cover, Conditions or Clauses (as printed overleaf)/Deckungsformen, Bedingungen oder Klauseln (wie umseitig)

13	16	17	--	--	--

Premium paid/Prämie bezahlt

4. In addition/Ferner

including rain and fresh water damages as in the above mentioned
conditions and clauses. Claims are payable in US-Dollars.

GERLING-KONZERN
ALLGEMEINE VERSICHERUNGS-AKTIENGESELLSCHAFT

Reineke   ppa. Dr. Herold

TR 8/1 - 10. 95 - 20*

EXPORT DOCUMENTS – INSPECTION/QUALITY CERTIFICATE

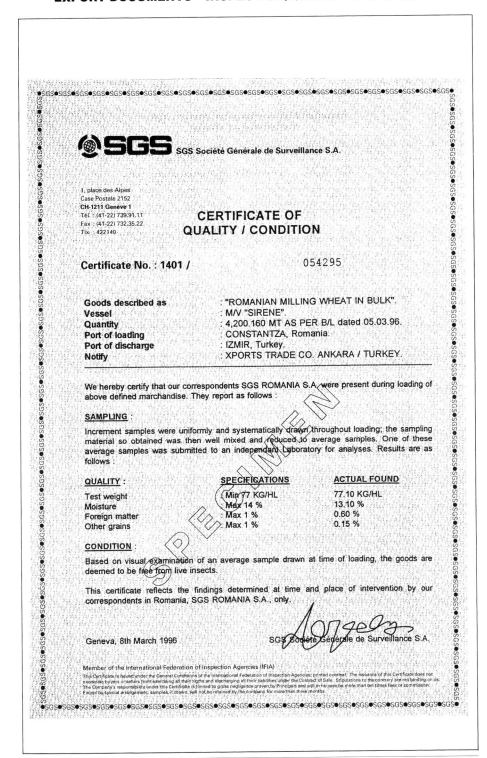

SGS SGS Société Générale de Surveillance S.A.

1, place des Alpes
Case Postale 2152
CH-1211 Genève 1
Tél. : (41-22) 739.91.11
Fax : (41-22) 732.35.22
Tlx : 422140

CERTIFICATE OF
QUALITY / CONDITION

Certificate No. : 1401 /   054295

Goods described as	: "ROMANIAN MILLING WHEAT IN BULK".
Vessel	: M/V "SIRENE".
Quantity	: 4,200.160 MT AS PER B/L dated 05.03.96.
Port of loading	: CONSTANTZA, Romania.
Port of discharge	: IZMIR, Turkey.
Notify	: XPORTS TRADE CO. ANKARA / TURKEY.

We hereby certify that our correspondents SGS ROMANIA S.A. were present during loading of above defined marchandise. They report as follows :

SAMPLING :

Increment samples were uniformly and systematically drawn throughout loading; the sampling material so obtained was then well mixed and reduced to average samples. One of these average samples was submitted to an independant Laboratory for analyses. Results are as follows :

QUALITY :	**SPECIFICATIONS**	**ACTUAL FOUND**
Test weight	Min 77 KG/HL	77.10 KG/HL
Moisture	Max 14 %	13.10 %
Foreign matter	Max 1 %	0.60 %
Other grains	Max 1 %	0.15 %

CONDITION :

Based on visual examination of an average sample drawn at time of loading, the goods are deemed to be free from live insects.

This certificate reflects the findings determined at time and place of intervention by our correspondents in Romania, SGS ROMANIA S.A., only.

Geneva, 8th March 1996   SGS Société Générale de Surveillance S.A.

EXPORT DOCUMENTS – CERTIFICATE OF ORIGIN

(C) SITPRO 1992

Seller (name, address, VAT reg. no.)	**CERTIFICATE OF ORIGIN**
SB SmithKline Beecham International	
SB House, Great West Road, Brentford, Middlesex, TW8 9BD.	
Telephone: 0181 560 5151 FAX: 0181 975 4481	
VAT No. GB 493 9256 01	

Invoice number		Sheet no.
00017989 / 027951	00076163	1
Invoice date (tax point)	**Seller's reference**	
13OCT95		
Buyer's reference	**Other reference**	

Consignee	VAT no.
MAURITIUS PHARMACEUTICAL	
MANUFACTURING CO. LTD.	
P.O. BOX 685	
BELL VILLAGE	
PORT LOUIS, MAURITIUS	

Buyer (if not consignee)	VAT no.
MAURITIUS PHARMACEUTICAL	
MANUFACTURING CO. LTD.	
P.O. BOX 685	
BELL VILLAGE	
PORT LOUIS, MAURITIUS	

UNISON NO 207

Country of origin of goods	**Country of destination**
UNITED KINGDOM	MAURITIUS

Terms of delivery and payment

CIP - PORT LOUIS
180 SIGHT BILLS OF EXCHANGE

Vessel/flight no. and date	**Port/airport of loading**
MSC ROSA M	FELIXSTOWE
Port/airport of discharge	**Place of delivery**
PORT LOUIS	MAURITIUS

VESSEL: MSC ROSA M
ETS: 24.10.95
ETA: 20.11.95
REF: MLCLF 471 1526

Shipping marks; container number	No. and kind of packages; description of goods	Commodity code	Total gross wt (kg)	Total cube (m3)
FULLY ADDRESSED	11 KEGS		387	0.748
	PHARMACEUTICALS			
MPM/139/VA/PS	74022 SB	**Total net weight (kg)** 320		

Item/packages	Gross/net/cube	Description	Quantity	Unit price	Amount
		Invoice Line Item Total GBP			XXXXXXXXXXX

Invoice total	GBP	XXXXXXX
	U.K. POUND STG	

Name of signatory
LISA ABEL

Place and date of issue
BRENTFORD, MIDDX   11OCT95

Signature

V501   SmithKline Beecham p.l.c. Registered in London 2337968 Registered Office: New Horizons Court, Brentford, Middlesex, TW8 9EP   Export Trade Connections. SITPRO approved licensee No 10

b. THE BILL OF LADING

A venerable definition of the bill of lading...

"A cargo at sea while in the hands of the carrier is necessarily incapable of physical delivery. During this period of transit and voyage, the bill of lading...is universally recognized as its symbol, and the endorsement and delivery of the bill of lading operates as a symbolical delivery of the cargo. Property in the goods passes by such endorsement and delivery of the bill of lading...just as under similar circumstances the property would pass by an actual delivery of the goods...[T]he bill of lading is...a key which in the hands of the rightful owner is intended to unlock the door of the warehouse, floating or fixed, in which the goods may chance to be."

Lord Justice Bowen, <u>Sanders Brothers v. Maclean & Co.</u> (1883)

The bill of lading ("B/L") is a central document in the traditional export transaction, linking the contract of sale, the documentary payment contracts, and the contract of carriage. We shall briefly summarize here the function of the classic B/L, the marine (or ocean) bill of lading, which provides the documentary basis for traditional maritime shipments. For a fuller discussion of the bill of lading, see Chapter 9.

The **marine bill of lading** serves three basic functions:

1) *The B/L – at any rate a B/L made out "to order" represents control over – or "stands for" – the goods.* The holder of the B/L can direct the carrier to release the goods. It is sometimes said that the B/L is a document of "title" – a phrase which may give the inaccurate impression that the party who holds the bill of lading also "owns" the goods. As we shall see in chapter 9, the holder of the bill can exercise control over the goods vis–à–vis the carrier: whether she owns the goods or not will depend on the contract of sale and on the law applying to that contract.

2) *The B/L evidences the contract of carriage* – The B/L must contain the terms of the contract of carriage, either explicitly or by reference to another document. Under documentary shipment sales the seller must procure and transfer to the buyer a contract of carriage on "usual" or reasonable terms. Provided, therefore, that the B/L contains no "unusual" term, it will represent the contract of carriage called for by the contract of sale.

3) *The B/L is a receipt* – The B/L is a receipt which evidences the delivery of the goods to the carrier for shipment. The B/L therefore describes the goods and states that in a certain quantity and in apparent good order

they have been loaded on board. If the carrier detects that the goods have been damaged, a notation to that effect will be made on the face of the B/L. The B/L will no longer be considered a "clean" B/L – it is now referred to as a "dirty" or "claused" bill. At that point, the B/L may no longer be acceptable for presentation under a documentary credit.

A B/L may be issued in either negotiable form (often called an "order bill of lading") or non–negotiable form (a "straight bill of lading").

Perhaps the key issue as regards bills of lading in the payment context is their value to the banks as security for the credit amount. This security value will vary depending on whether or not the bill is a negotiable one – in which case possession of it has money value, because the bill can be auctioned off – or whether it is a non–negotiable "waybill" type document, in which case it may have virtually no security value to the bank, unless the bank is named as consignee and steps are taken to ensure that this designation is irrevocable.

c. THE COMMERCIAL INVOICE

This document is prepared by the exporter and includes: identification and addresses of the seller and buyer, a listing and description of the goods (including prices, discounts and quantities), an invoice number, packaging details, marks and numbers, shipping details, and the date and reference number of the buyer's order. Because other documents (such as the documentary credit) will be checked against the commercial invoice, it is of the utmost importance that it be correct and exact in all particulars. An inexact invoice can be fatal to a letter of credit transaction. The buyer will often need the information in the invoice in order to comply with import licenses, customs duties and exchange restrictions. Because of these needs, the buyer will often request an advance form of commercial invoice, called the pro forma invoice.

d. INSURANCE DOCUMENTS

With documentary sales under such trade terms as CIF and CIP Incoterms 2000, the seller must procure and pay for insurance for the benefit of the buyer. A letter of credit application will necessarily reflect this insurance obligation, and an insurance document will have to be presented by the seller in order for them to receive payment. Depending on the case, the document required may be an insurance policy (or facultative policy, for single consignments), an open contract (for continuous or repeated shipments), or a certificate of insurance (indicating cover under an open contract). The Institute of London

Underwriters Clauses specify the coverage required under *Incoterms 2000*; they are generally attached to policies, and indicate precisely the risks covered and exclusions from coverage.

e. OFFICIAL CERTIFICATES AND LICENCES

The most important of these is the certificate of origin, which evidences the origin of the goods and is usually prepared by the seller's local Chamber of Commerce. Inspection certificates, which certify the quality of the goods, are commonly prepared by private inspection agencies; two of the most famous are SGS (Switzerland) and Bureau Veritas (France).

6.4 Method of operation of the basic payment mechanisms

Open Account
Cash in Advance
Collection
Documentary Collection
Clean Collection
Documentary Credit (Letter of Credit) (see §6.5)

6.4.1 Payment on Open Account

With open account payments the exporter ships the goods to the buyer and then, at an agreed–upon future time, transmits an invoice and other shipping documents; i.e., the importer "buys now, pays later". These are sometimes called sales "on credit", because the seller extends credit without documentary security for the buyer's indebtedness. Open account sales are fairly common in domestic sales, but are less common in international transactions because they substantially increase the risk for the seller. An export seller should only agree to open account terms if he has absolute confidence in the import buyer as well as in the stability of the buyer's country and its import regulations. An additional source of security is a stable market in the particular goods, because in unstable markets a sudden drop in prices will often motivate importers to try to escape their contracts.

For the importer, of course, open account terms are quite advantageous, as there is no need to pay for the goods until they have been received and inspected. An importer may even be able to sell the goods and use the proceeds to pay the exporter's commercial invoice when it arrives.

6.4.2 Payment in Advance

As we have seen, payment on open account is used when the trading partners have the utmost confidence in each other. At the other extreme, when the exporter has serious doubts about the creditworthiness of the importer (or doubts about the economic or political stability of the importer's country or that country's banking system), the exporter may demand cash in advance. Here, the seller takes no risk whatsoever. However, the importer is obviously at serious risk, and should never consider cash in advance payment unless full information on the reputation of the seller is available. If advance cash payments are made at all, they are usually only partial payments.

A variation on cash in advance is for an advance payment to be made via some form of documentary instrument, such as under a "red clause" letter of credit.

Many exporters fail to consider that open account payment backed by a standby credit or demand guarantee can be as secure as cash in advance (and even more secure than partial cash in advance). Although the exporter grants the importer credit and expects payment by bank transfer or other similar means upon presentation of commercial invoices, the standby credit or demand guarantee is the best possible payment security. If the importer does not pay the invoice, the exporter can claim the amount of the standby credit or guarantee. The danger here, of course, is for the importer. An unscrupulous exporter could make an unfair or fraudulent claim under the standby credit or bank guarantee.

6.4.3 Collection – Documentary Collection/Clean Collection

While cash in advance represents the ideal option for the exporter, and open account payments represent the ideal for the importer, the next two payment mechanisms we will consider are compromises that offer benefits to both sides: the documentary collection and the documentary credit.

The documentary collection must first be distinguished from the clean collection. A clean collection is essentially an open account payment made via bill of exchange; the exporter ships the goods, then sends the importer a bill of exchange. A documentary collection, on the other hand, allows the exporter to retain control of the goods until he has received payment (or obtained an assurance of receiving payment). Generally, the exporter ships the goods and then assembles the relevant commercial documents, such as the invoice and the bill of lading, then turns them over, along with a draft, to a bank acting as an agent for the exporter. The bank will only release the bill of lading to the importer if the importer pays against the draft or accepts the obligation to do so at a future time. There are two possibilities:

1) *D/P* – *"Cash against documents"* – The importer pays the draft in order to receive the bill of lading (the document which enables the importer to obtain delivery of the goods); hence this form of collection is referred to by banks alternatively as "cash against documents", "documents against payment", "D/P", or "sight D/P".

2) *D/A* – *"Documents against acceptance"* – Here, the importer accepts the draft in order to receive the bill of lading. By accepting the draft, the importer acknowledges an unconditional legal obligation to pay according to the terms of the draft.

The exporter's instructions to present a draft for acceptance or payment will be transmitted through a series of banks. Usually, this will involve at least the exporter's bank (here called the remitting bank) and a bank in the importer's country (called the collecting or presenting bank, because it presents the relevant documents for collection to the drawee). This somewhat long information–chain makes it crucial that the exporter's initial instructions be precise and complete. Thus, the process begins when the exporter fills out a collection form (also called a lodgement form), in which the exporter indicates the instructions which the banks are to follow. On the basis of this information, the remitting bank prepares a collection order which will accompany the documentary collection when it is transmitted to the collecting bank. The banking practice relating to collection arrangements is standardized in ICC's *Uniform Rules for Collections* (ICC Publication 522).

ADVANTAGES AND DISADVANTAGES

Advantages of collections for the exporter are that they are relatively easy and inexpensive, and that control over the transport documents is maintained until the exporter receives assurance of payment. The advantage for the importer is that there is no obligation to pay before having had an opportunity to inspect the documents and in some cases (as by an examination in a bonded warehouse) the goods themselves.

Disadvantages for the exporter are that collections expose the seller to several risks: the risk that the importer will not accept the goods shipped, the credit risk of the importer, the political risk of the importer's country, and the risk that the shipment may fail to clear customs. The prudent exporter will, therefore, have obtained a credit report on the importer as well as an evaluation of country risk. Another disadvantage for the exporter is that collection can be relatively slow. However, the exporter's bank may be willing to provide finance to cover the period during which the exporter is waiting for the funds to clear.

The importer takes only the risk under a D/P collection that the goods shipped may not be as indicated on the invoice and bill of lading. The banks assume no risks for documentary collections (other than that of their own negligence in following directions). This is one reason why collections are generally significantly cheaper, in terms of bank fees, than documentary credits.

During negotiations a documentary collection may be suggested as a helpful compromise. In terms of relative advantages for exporter and importer, it lies mid–way between the sale on open account (advantageous for the importer) and the letter of credit (advantageous for the exporter). Thus, an exporter will prefer the documentary collection as an alternative to a sale on open account proposed by the importer. The importer will prefer a documentary collection as an alternative to a letter of credit proposed by the exporter.

6.5 Documentary credits (letters of credit): An in–depth look

The basics: Documentary credits (also called letters of credit) facilitate international payments, providing security for both export seller and import buyer. The seller is assured of payment upon production of constructive evidence of shipment of the contract merchandise, and the buyer is assured that the bank will not pay unless the seller has met documentary requirements complying with the buyer's instructions. International letter of credit practice is governed by a set of rules produced by ICC, commonly known as the UCP 500 *(Uniform Customs and Practice for Documentary Credits)*.

6.5.1 Introduction

Documentary credits (or "D/C's", also called letters of credit or "L/C's") substantially reduce risks for both exporter and importer. Not surprisingly, therefore, the letter of credit is the classic form of international export payment, especially in trade between distant partners. The letter of credit is essentially a document issued by the importer's bank which undertakes to pay the exporter upon due compliance with documentary requirements. Hence, the term "documentary credit" – payment, acceptance or negotiation of the credit is made upon presentation by the seller of all stipulated documents. These documents (e.g., bill of lading, invoice, inspection certificate) provide a basic level of proof that the right merchandise has been properly sent to the importer – although, of course, there is always the chance that the documents may prove inaccurate or even fraudulent.

Although there are endless variations on the letter of credit, as we shall see below, a typical procedure is as follows. The process begins when the exporter and importer agree on a contract of sale. Typically, it is the exporter who insists on payment by letter of credit – because the exporter does not want to take a credit risk, and cannot get sufficient information on the creditworthiness of the buyer so as to grant another form of payment.

The importer then initiates the letter of credit mechanism by going to her bank and requesting to open a letter of credit. The importer's bank issues the credit (and is hence called the "issuing bank"), under which it agrees to pay according to the importer's instructions. The credit is then sent to the exporter or to a bank in the exporter's country (depending on the type of credit). Commonly, under the sales contract and/or credit application the exporter's bank (or another bank in the exporter's country) will be requested to confirm the documentary credit, thereby committing itself to pay under the terms of the credit. Exporters may insist on confirmed credits when they want to have a trusted local paymaster.

If the exporter agrees with the terms of the credit, the exporter then proceeds to ship the goods. After shipment, the exporter goes to the bank nominated in the credit to effect payment and presents the documents that the importer has asked for. The exporter usually also presents a bill of exchange or bank draft, a document representing the bank's payment obligation (see document definitions above).

The bank examines the documents carefully to ensure that they correspond exactly with the terms of the credit. If the documents do not conform to the letter of credit, the bank observes a documentary discrepancy, notifies the exporter, and refuses to pay the credit. The exporter may then either correct the documents or obtain a waiver of the discrepancy from the importer.

There are benefits for both sides from the banks' examination of the documents. For the buyer, clearly, because payment will only be made against documents in conformity with the precise terms and conditions of the credit. But the exporter may also benefit from an early examination of the documents, since this allows for a possibility of quickly correcting any discrepancy. With documentary collections, discrepancies may remain undetected until much later, when the documents are checked by the buyers themselves.

6.5.2 Rules for Letters of Credit: the UCP 500

International letter of credit practice has been standardized by ICC rules known as the *Uniform Customs and Practice for Documentary Credits* (UCP 500). The UCP is sometimes cited as the foremost example of how international business self–regulation can be more efficient than treaties, government regulation or case law. Indeed, legal commentators have called the UCP the most successful act of commercial harmonization in the history of world trade.

The law governing letters of credit developed substantially around the world as international trade expanded after WWI. However, purely national legal solutions are unsatisfactory in an international business context, because trading partners do not want the burden of having to predict the reasoning of judges and tribunals in distant countries.

Thus, there was a need for international standard rules for letter of credit practice, rules which could be updated in light of changing banking practices. The first adopted version of the UCP dates from 1929; the 1933 revision of this text gained broad acceptance in Europe. The next revision was adopted in 1951 and brought the UCP to truly global scope, being used by banks in Asia, Africa, Latin America, the United States and Europe. The 1962 revision provided a major breakthrough, gaining the acceptance of the influential UK and Commonwealth banking community. Further revisions, adding technical refinements and improvements, were released in 1974 and 1983. The currently valid version, UCP 500, entered into effect on 1 January 1994. At the time of writing, ICC was considering whether to revise UCP 500, a process which, if agreed on by the ICC Banking Commission, is likely to take at least three years to complete. It is generally thought that the next revision will be more of a technical nature than a major overhaul of the rules, as was the case with UCP 500.

The UCP is a more flexible set of rules than any national or international legislation. When the United Nations drafts an international treaty or convention, the entire process, if one includes ratification by the signatory countries, can take decades. The UCP, in contrast, is not binding law, but applies because banks voluntarily incorporate the UCP into the contracts upon which the letter of credit is based. In essence, the UCP is the codification of actual trade practices, based on the experiences of trade banks, exporters and importers. Periodic revisions have allowed the UCP to keep in step with advances in banking practice. As a result, the UCP arguably provides a more practical procedural framework than could an international law or treaty.

With regard to the legal effect around the world of ICC's documentary credit rules, the basic principle is that the UCP rules are creatures of contract, and thus apply principally when they have been voluntarily incorporated by the parties. Thus, documentary credit application forms generally contain a statement to the effect that the credit will be subject to the UCP 500 – this is considered legally to represent the parties' willingness to submit interpretation of the credit to the rules of the UCP.

After more than 70 years of existence, the UCP has achieved such universal effect that in some countries the UCP is recognized as having the force of law, or at least that of a trade custom. However, in other countries, such as the United Kingdom, the UCP does not have formal legislative status, and will only apply when the parties specifically incorporate the UCP into the documentary credit by explicitly invoking the UCP on the credit application forms. In the United States, the Uniform Commercial Code governs the use of letters of credit, but the UCP is considered to govern when the parties have specifically incorporated the UCP or when the UCP is the customary trade practice.

Even where the UCP is applicable, its somewhat general provisions cannot cover all cases. As a result, national courts are often asked to interpret certain provisions. The ICC Banking Commission also regularly issues interpretations of provisions of the UCP based on questions received by ICC, which collects and publishes these opinions every few years, providing a valuable aide for practitioners. The most recent version of ICC opinions, *Collected Opinions of the ICC Banking Commission 1995–2001* (ICC Publication 632), contains seven years of opinions on UCP 500. It is available at www.iccbooksusa.com.

Although it is beyond the scope of this text to go in detail through the numerous refinements and improvements included in UCP 500, the most important ones deserve brief mention here:

- A credit is now deemed to be irrevocable when the credit is silent on whether it is revocable or irrevocable (this reversed the position under the previous version of the rules, the UCP 400).

- The bank examining the documents will have a reasonable time, not to exceed seven banking days following the day of receipt of the documents, to decide whether or not to take up the documents or reject them and inform the beneficiary to that effect (the previous position under UCP 400 did not give a precise maximum time limit for examination of documents). However, note that courts may rule that in particular cases a "reasonable" time is much shorter than seven days.

- *Transport documents* – Articles 23–30 – These provisions have been fundamentally reworked, so that each type of transport document is now covered by a separate Article, thereby rendering the respective requirements for document types somewhat clearer. There has been some criticism from transport circles that UCP 500 went too far in specifying the requirements for transport documents, but on the whole Articles 23–30 have been well received.

- *International banking standard practice* – sub–Article 13(a) sets forth the rule that the compliance of documents with the terms of the credit will be judged according to international standard banking practice "as reflected in these Articles". Because there has been considerable discussion as to what constitutes "international standard banking practice", the ICC Banking Commission has undertaken a multi–year survey of practice worldwide and is publishing its own booklet on the subject, detailing practice as it applies to many of the terms and provisions in the UCP.

6.5.3 Basic Concepts and Terminology

a. THE PARTIES

In documentary credits, the seller/exporter is alternatively referred to as:
- *Beneficiary* – Because it is the seller who receives payment from the letter of credit.
- *Shipper* – Because the seller ships the goods.
- *Consignor* – Again, because the seller ships the goods, sometimes referred to as "consignment" in international transport.

The buyer/importer is alternatively referred to as:

- *Opener* – Because the importer "opens" the credit to begin the process.
- *Applicant* – Because the importer must begin the process by submitting a credit "application" to a bank.
- *Account party* – Because the importer's application to open a credit creates an "account" relationship with the issuing bank, and is supervised by an account officer.

b. THE BANKS AND THEIR ROLES

1) *Issuing (or "opening") bank* – The bank which receives the importer's application and agrees to "issue" the credit. The issuing bank is commonly, but not necessarily, located in the importer's country. By issuing the credit, the bank is making an irrevocable undertaking to pay the beneficiary the value of the draft and/or other documents, provided that the terms and conditions of the credit are complied with.

2) *Nominated bank* – The bank which is stipulated in a credit as authorized to pay, issue a deferred payment undertaking or accept drafts. Unless a credit expressly states that it is available only with the issuing bank, it should nominate some other bank. If the credit is of the "freely negotiable" variety, any bank qualifies as a nominated bank. A nominated bank is not normally bound to pay under the credit, unless it has added its confirmation to the credit and become a confirming bank (see further on).

3) *Advising bank* – The bank which notifies or "advises" the exporter that a credit has been opened in the exporter's favour. By advising a credit, the bank is only acting as a conduit for the issuing bank; the advising bank does not take any further risk, and only has the responsibility of taking reasonable care that the credit is an authentic one. The advising bank is commonly, but not necessarily, located in the exporter's country. An advising bank will frequently perform one or more of the functions of confirming, negotiating, or paying, which are defined further on.

4) *Confirming bank* – The bank (normally also the advising bank) which adds its own irrevocable undertaking (known as "confirmation") in addition to that given by the issuing bank. The confirmation allows the exporter to be paid by a bank in the exporter's own country, or by a bank which the exporter otherwise trusts. The confirming bank irrevocably commits itself to paying the exporter upon presentation of conforming documents. As with the role of paying bank, the bank accepting the role of confirming bank exposes itself to the risk that it will fail to detect a discrepancy in the documents.

5) *Paying (or "paying agent") bank* – The bank which reviews the documents presented by the exporter and, if they conform to the terms and conditions of the credit, arranges payment to the exporter. A paying bank's main risk is of paying against documents that turn out to contain discrepancies, in which case it may not be able to recover the funds from the issuing bank. However, a bank acting as paying agent may refuse to pay the exporter if the issuing bank's account is not sufficient to cover the draft (this applies where the bank has not added its confirmation to the letter of credit).

6) *Negotiating bank* – The bank which examines the documents presented by the exporter, then "negotiates" the credit (i.e., in the case of a usance draft, purchases the draft from the exporter at a discount from the face value). This negotiation, or purchase, is usually done "with recourse", which means that if the issuing bank fails to reimburse the negotiating bank, the negotiating bank will recover the funds advanced to the exporter. This distinguishes the negotiating function from the confirming function. When a confirming bank pays the exporter, it is "without recourse", which means that even if no reimbursement is received from the issuing bank, the confirming bank cannot recover the funds from the exporter.

c. TYPES OF LETTERS OF CREDIT (to some extent also dealt with in definitions of banks)

1) *Irrevocable/revocable* – An irrevocable letter of credit cannot be amended or cancelled without the consent of all parties. This essential undertaking allows the exporter to procure the goods or prepare them for shipment with the assurance that payment will be received if the stipulated documents are presented. A revocable letter of credit provides little if any security for the exporter, and is consequently unusual. The UCP 500 provides that credits will be deemed irrevocable unless explicitly stated as revocable (this reversed the previous position under the UCP 400).

2) *Confirmed* – As stated in the definition of confirming bank above, a credit is confirmed when a bank (usually the advising bank in the exporter's country) adds its own irrevocable undertaking at the request of the issuing bank in addition to that of the issuing bank. Generally, this assures the exporter of payment by a local bank or one which is trusted more than the issuing bank.

3) *Sight/Usance* – Credits may provide for payment at sight (immediately) or for payment at a specified time in the future – a usance credit.

4) *Revolving* – If the importer is a regular customer of the exporter, the parties may wish to arrange for a revolving credit. Under a typical revolving credit, the bank issues a credit for a certain maximum sum which is automatically renewed at certain intervals. Revolving credits save the parties from the administrative tasks of having to repeatedly re–apply and re–issue similar credits. Although revolving credits do have expiry dates, they tend to be valid much longer than normal credits.

5) *Red clause* – A red clause credit allows pre–shipment advances to be made to the exporter at the risk and expense of the applicant. Under a red clause credit the bank will honour the exporter's sight drafts up to a specified percentage of the total credit against production of certain preliminary documents. Originally, the clauses specifying a red clause credit were actually printed or typed in red ink, hence the name. Obviously, such credits should only be used when the importer has great trust in the exporter.

6) *Transferable* – Transferable credits are used in "middleman" situations, where an export merchant or agent plays the role of an intermediary between a supplier and the importer. The middleman–beneficiary transfers all or a portion of its rights to a supplier–beneficiary (called the "second beneficiary" in the UCP). The middleman may not wish to reveal the identity of the ultimate supplier, and may keep this information from the importer by substituting the middleman's invoice for the ultimate supplier's invoice. The various permutations of transferable credits can become exceedingly complex, so that importers should proceed with some caution. In particular, the importer may accept the risk that the ultimate source of the contract goods remains unknown; therefore, it is difficult for the importer to be assured of the ultimate supplier's reputation and reliability.

7) *Back–to–back* – Under a back–to–back credit, the middleman–beneficiary uses the letter of credit as security for a second, separate credit in favour of the ultimate supplier. Whereas under a transferable credit the importer must request the transferable credit in the application, under a back–to–back credit the importer may be ignorant of the back–to–back arrangement. Although the middleman may, therefore, wish to use a back–to–back credit if it wishes to conceal its recourse to an ultimate supplier, the middleman takes an additional risk in doing so. With the back–to–back procedure, the middleman must repay the bank for any valid payment to the ultimate supplier under the second letter of credit regardless of whether or not the middleman receives payment under the first letter of credit. This is a major risk area for banks, which are very cautious as regards back–to–back credits.

8) *Standby* – The standby credit is to be distinguished from the above–defined letters of credit in that the primary function of the standby is to serve as a security or guarantee rather than as a payment mechanism. Under a typical standby, the beneficiary will claim payment in the event that the contract partner has failed to perform or fulfil certain obligations. Standby credit practice has largely developed in the United States, where banking law long forbade banks to issue guarantees (recent changes in the law, however, do not seem to have significantly altered bankers' reliance on the standby). From a legal point of view, standbys are virtually indistinguishable from bank guarantees. In practice, however, standbys appear to be used for a much broader spectrum of uses. Although standby credits are specifically referred to in the UCP 500, the majority of the Articles have no direct bearing on the issuance or handling of this type of credit. In fact, a number of UCP Articles were considered to be inappropriate for standbys, which is one reason why a separate set of rules for standbys, called ISP98, were developed (see 6.7 further on). Note that standbys may also be issued subject to the *ICC Uniform Rules on Demand Guarantees* (ICC Publication 458) (see Chapter 8).

6.5.4 Example: procedure for an irrevocable, confirmed credit

Note: The documentary credit process described below covers the specific case of a confirmed, irrevocable letter of credit. Note that not all credits are confirmed (nor irrevocable), so that the procedure below is not meant to apply to all cases (thus, the example does not apply to cases where a credit is only advised and not confirmed).

a. THE SALE CONTRACT

The sale contract should clearly specify that payment will be by confirmed irrevocable letter of credit if the exporter wishes to insist on this highly secure form of payment. The sale contract is sometimes referred to as the underlying contract in relation to the documentary credit operation. As will be discussed later, it is a fundamental principle that the documentary credit is independent and autonomous of the contract of sale, meaning that disputes under the contract of sale cannot normally prevent payment under the credit. However, the credit must be opened in accordance with the conditions specified in the contract of sale.

The sale contract may or may not provide additional details or conditions with respect to the credit (as, for example, the time of payment, the documents to be presented, etc.). The export seller will normally insist on a confirmed credit whenever he is less than fully confident in the credit risk of the issuing bank, or when he fears that there may be political or foreign exchange risks associated with the buyer's country.

b. THE CREDIT APPLICATION

Assuming that the parties have agreed in the sales contract as to the terms of the documentary credit, the importer (the applicant) will apply for the credit at his bank. The credit application, when accepted, constitutes a contract between the importer–applicant and his bank (the issuing bank). The bank agrees to issue the documentary credit and the buyer agrees to reimburse the bank for payments made under the credit. Since the bank will open a credit which follows the instructions given by the importer, it is up to the importer to make sure that these instructions do not contradict the contract of sale (if there is a contradiction, the importer will be in breach of the contract of sale).

Although the applicant must respect the terms of the contract of sale, it is quite common for the contract of sale to be silent on one or more terms and conditions. In such cases, the applicant may include additional details but the exporter–beneficiary will not be contractually bound to accept them when he reviews the credit.

In some cases the applicant will bring the sales contract in to his bank when she prepares the credit application. The issuing bank may be tempted to simply transpose the conditions of the contract into the credit. However, great care should be taken that the credit does not contain any non–documentary conditions – conditions which cannot be established by a specific document.

Amongst the minimum details that will be specified in the credit application are:

i. *Time of payment* – Specifying whether the credit will be payable at sight or under a usance draft;

ii. *Date and place of expiry of the credit* – These dates should give sufficient time for the beneficiary to prepare and ship the goods;

iii. *Latest date for shipment and presentation of documents* – As above, these time limits should be reasonable in light of circumstances to allow the beneficiary to perform his obligations; in any event, should the credit be silent on the time allowable for presentation of documents after the date of the transport document, the UCP specifies a maximum period of 21 days;

iv. *Beneficiary* – the beneficiary's name and address must be exactly and completely spelled out;

v. *Type of credit* – i.e., irrevocable/revocable, confirmed, transferable, etc.

vi. *Amount* – In some cases, due to uncertainty as to the exact quantities to be shipped or the freight rate, the sales contract will only have contained an approximate price. The credit may, therefore, specify an amount which is "about" or "approximately" a certain sum, in which case a 10% variation will be allowable; alternatively, the credit may specify a maximum amount through the use of such words as "up to";

vii. *Shipment details* – These will specify, inter alia, whether partial shipments or transhipments are allowable. Unless the applicant has strong reasons for disallowing partial shipments, it is better to allow them, as they provide flexibility for the beneficiary. If the goods are of a hazardous or bulky nature which may require carriage on deck, the credit should specifically allow for bills of lading indicating that such carriage has occurred or may occur;

viii. *Goods* – It is important that the goods not be described in excessive detail, which can give rise to disputes later when documents are presented; rather, as is stated in the UCP, the description of the goods should be general and with just–sufficient detail to identify the contract goods. It is advisable for applicants to identify the contract by its reference number; applicants may also wish to require that the beneficiary provide a certificate to the effect that all conditions of the contract have been complied with. In no case should contractual documents (such as pro forma invoices or technical specification sheets) be attached to the letter of credit, as these multiply the opportunities for confusion and mistakes;

ix. *Documents* – The documentary requirements are of the utmost importance and should be carefully thought through by the applicant, as it is likely that they will undergo close scrutiny by the beneficiary when the credit is received. In general, applicants should be discouraged from asking for an excessive number of documents or from insisting on full sets of originals when single documents or photocopies will do. The prudent beneficiary will understand that as the number of documentary requirements increases so does the possibility that a document will contain a discrepancy and therefore block payment under the credit.

The importer makes the credit application by filling in a standard form provided by the bank. On occasion, these forms are based on models proposed by ICC (see ICC Publication 516, *New Standard Documentary Credit Forms for the UCP 500*). The application form has been designed to correspond to the model form for the credit itself, thereby greatly facilitating the transfer of information from the application to the credit.

c. ISSUANCE OF THE CREDIT

The issuing bank will decide whether or not to issue the credit after considering the importer's creditworthiness. From the bank's point of view, the documentary credit amounts to a borrowing request by the importer for the time period dating from the opening of the credit to its expiry date.

The bank issues a documentary credit in favour of the exporter–beneficiary under which the bank agrees to pay the beneficiary, provided that the beneficiary presents documents which conform to the terms and conditions of the credit. It is said that this undertaking constitutes the third "contract" of the documentary credit mechanism (although, strictly, under some systems of law it is not a true contract owing to the unilateral nature of the under-taking), the first contract being the contract of sale between the exporter and buyer, and the second contract being the one formed by the credit application, whereby the bank agrees to issue the credit for a fee and the applicant agrees to reimburse the bank for payments made under the credit).

d. CONFIRMATION

When the credit application specifies a confirmed credit, the issuing bank will request that another bank, usually in the beneficiary's country, confirm the credit. By confirming the credit, the confirming bank adds its irrevocable obligation to that of the issuing bank. The exporter is thus assured of a reliable paymaster in his own country.

The confirming bank's decision to confirm will involve a credit analysis of the issuing bank's credit risk as well as the relevant political and foreign exchange risks. Having confirmed the credit, the confirming bank must pay the beneficiary upon presentation of conforming documents, regardless of the issuing bank's ability to reimburse the confirming bank.

The confirming bank advises the confirmed credit to the beneficiary. The confirming bank's undertaking to pay now constitutes the fourth contract in the chain.

e. RECEIPT AND REVIEW OF CREDIT BY SELLER–BENEFICIARY

When the exporter receives the letter of credit, it is strongly recommended that he immediately review it, carefully checking it against the terms of the contract in light of the anticipated circumstances of the shipment.

A disturbingly high percentage of documentary credit transactions encounter difficulties upon first presentation of documents (as many as 50% – 90%, depending upon the country). One of the reasons for this problem is that sellers so often neglect to review the credit when they receive it. An immediate review allows sellers to detect in due time any inconsistencies with the contract of sale or with their intended means of preparing or shipping the goods.

If the exporter, upon reviewing the credit, realizes that it would be impractical or impossible to comply with its terms, he should immediately notify the importer and request that the credit be amended. The exporter should verify that the credit is actually amended and that he is notified of the amendment – it is unfortunately not unheard of for the exporter and importer to agree to an amendment but neglect to inform the issuing bank, thereby permitting a troublesome discrepancy to arise later.

f. SHIPMENT OF GOODS AND PRESENTATION OF DOCUMENTS

In order to be paid under the credit, the exporter must prepare the goods for shipment in due time, and must assemble all the necessary documents. The exporter is well advised to check the documents himself against the documentary credit specifications before presenting them to the bank.

It is highly recommended that the beneficiary present the documents as early as possible, and at the very least, more than seven working days prior to the expiration of the credit. This is because the bank will take a certain amount of time to check the documents (a period which cannot exceed seven working days under the UCP 500) and, in the event the bank detects a discrepancy which can be corrected, the beneficiary will want to have enough time to correct the discrepancy and re–present the documents before the expiry of the credit.

After shipment, the beneficiary presents the documents (and a draft, in those common cases where the credit calls for a draft) to the confirming bank.

g. EXAMINATION OF DOCUMENTS BY CONFIRMING BANK

The confirming bank will carefully check the documents presented by the beneficiary against those specified in the letter of credit. The bank will note any discrepancies (differences between the documents presented and the terms of the credit), or will observe that the documents are conforming (that they correspond to the requirements of the credit).

Under the UCP, the bank must conduct its examination of the documents within a reasonable time not to exceed seven banking days following the day of receipt of the documents (this is equally true for the issuing bank, confirming bank and/or nominated bank). The bank must notify the beneficiary of a decision to refuse the documents by telecommunications or other expeditious means, in no event later than the maximum period specified above.

If the documents are found to be conforming, the bank will pay, accept or negotiate the credit, according to its terms. A confirming bank's payment to the beneficiary is without recourse, which means that the confirming bank cannot recover the funds from the beneficiary, regardless of the issuing bank's subsequent decision not to reimburse the confirming bank (there may be an exception to this rule in some jurisdictions, with the effect that a bank can recover the funds if it can prove fraud by the already paid beneficiary).

If the documents are discrepant, the exporter may be able to correct the documents if there is still time remaining before the expiration of the credit, and provided that the discrepancies are of a nature that permits correction. Obviously, some kinds of discrepancies cannot be corrected (transport document not as per credit, inspection certificate indicating flawed merchandise, etc.), regardless of the time frame. Should the beneficiary be unable for whatever reason to correct the documents, he may still approach the applicant for a waiver of the discrepancy (the approach may be made directly or via the advising or confirming bank). An applicant may be willing to grant a waiver, especially if the discrepancy appears to be an insignificant one and there are strong commercial reasons for going through with the deal. Unfortunately, however, it is sometimes reported that applicants use discrepancies as an opportunity to bargain for discounts from exporters; all the more reason for beneficiaries to prepare the presentation of documents with great care.

The stages of a documentary credit operation

The case of a confirmed, irrevocable documentary credit:

A. The sale contract; credit application

In documentary credit terminology, the Exporter is called the "Beneficiary", and the Importer is called the "Applicant". Generally, the parties will have concluded a contract of sale with a payment provision stipulating payment by documentary credit. The importer then proceeds to her bank and submits a credit application, which should be in conformity with the contract of sale.

B. Issuance of the credit; confirmation

Provided the bank approves the credit application, it will issue the credit and request that a confirming bank add its own irrevocable commitment to pay under the terms of the credit.

C. Advice of credit; review by beneficiary

Once the Exporter-Beneficiary has received the written notification of the credit from the confirming bank, he should carefully review the provisions of the credit, comparing these with the provision of the contract of sale, and further making sure that he will be in a position to furnish all stipulated documents in due time.

D. Shipment; shipping documents; presentation of documents

6. Goods delivered

EXPORTER Beneficiary

Transport Carrier

Transport document — e.g., bill of lading

7. Presentation of documents
(e.g., B/L also commonly — commercial invoice, bank draft, insurance certificate, certificate of origin, inspection certificate)

Confirming BANK

The Exporter-Beneficary, having delivered the goods to the transport carrier, receives a transport document which, together with the other stipulated documents, is presented to the Confirming Bank for payment.

E. Bank examination of documents; payment; reimbursement

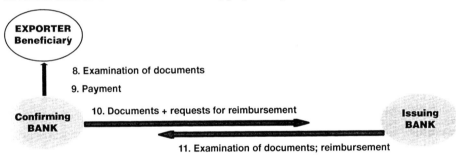

EXPORTER Beneficiary

8. Examination of documents

9. Payment

10. Documents + requests for reimbursement

Confirming BANK

Issuing BANK

11. Examination of documents; reimbursement

The Confirming Bank will closely examine the documents to see if they contain "discrepancies" or conflicts with the credit provisions; if not, the Confirming Bank will pay and will forward the documents to the Issuing Bank, along with a request for reimbursement. The Issuing Bank will also examine the documents and, if it also finds that there are no discrepancies, will reimburse the Confirming Bank.

F. Release of documents; obtaining delivery of goods

13. Bill of Lading

IMPORTER Applicant

14. Delivery of goods

12. Release of documents

Issuing BANK

The Issuing Bank will then release the documents to the Importer-Applicant, who can then use the bill of lading to obtain delivery of the goods from the carrier.

h. ISSUING BANK REVIEW; RELEASE OF THE DOCUMENTS TO THE BUYER

The issuing bank will also review the documents, which it has received from the confirming bank (or, in other cases, the negotiating bank). If, in the judgement of the issuing bank, the documents are discrepant and the confirming bank has made an error in paying under the credit, the issuing bank can recover the funds which it has been debited by the confirming bank. Under Article 13 of UCP 500, the issuing bank must take no more than seven banking days to conduct its examination of the documents and take up or reject them.

If the issuing bank's review indicates that the documents were in fact conforming, then it will debit the account of the applicant and release the documents to her. The documents (particularly the document entitling control of the goods, such as the marine bill of lading), will allow the importer to collect the goods from the carrier. However, the importer is also entitled to conduct his own review of the documents. It is possible that the importer may discover a discrepancy which has been missed or ignored by the banks. In such a case, the buyer can refuse to reimburse the bank and can himself reject the documents. An importer may scrutinize the documents with particular care in cases when the market price for the goods has fallen drastically and it makes commercial sense to escape the transaction if possible. This is why banks conduct such painstaking examinations of the documents – a bank which has paid against discrepant documents may find that it must simply absorb the loss.

6.5.5 The two fundamental principles of documentary credit practice

1) the independence of the credit from the underlying contract and,
2) the requirement that documents strictly comply with the terms of the credit.

a. INDEPENDENCE OF THE DOCUMENTARY CREDIT FROM THE UNDERLYING CONTRACT

The documentary credit is completely independent of the underlying contract. If the exporter fulfils the documentary obligations, payment must be effected according to the terms of the credit, regardless of disputes connected to the underlying contract.

It is essential that all parties remain confident that issuing or confirming banks will respect their payment commitments. The payment obligation of an issuing bank is separate and autonomous from the underlying export contract. Thus, the exporter's breach of a contract condition (i.e., with respect to quantity, quality, delivery date, etc.) is not sufficient to entitle the importer to instruct her bank to stop payment under the credit. The principal exception to this rule has to do with fraud. A bank which receives a clear notification or proof of fraud committed by the beneficiary is not only entitled, but obliged, to withhold payment. However, banks are not required to investigate mere suspicions of fraud.

Courts are quite reluctant to grant injunctions ordering a bank to withhold payment, so clear indications of fraud are generally necessary. Since letter of credit practice has arisen to some extent to avoid risks related to the lack of knowledge or trust between the two trading partners, it is essential that both parties trust the banks. Letters of credit could not function if the parties lacked confidence that the banks would honour their obligations regardless of arguments submitted by the parties. Judges have referred to letters of credit as the "life blood" of international commerce. If banks were allowed to refuse to pay letters of credit whenever trading parties had a dispute, the vital flow of international commerce would soon be blocked.

In some cases, the issuing bank's officers may be obliged to resist pressure from the applicant to bend the principle of absolute neutrality and independence. However, it is unfortunately quite possible for a seller to send bad merchandise (so long as this does not amount to a clear fraud) and yet present good documents. That is one of the reasons that an inspection certificate is so frequently called for. If the importer learns that she may receive an inadequate or late shipment, she may sue for damages for breach of contract.

b. STRICT COMPLIANCE

The terms of the letter of credit must be strictly adhered to: this is known as the doctrine of strict compliance. What this means in everyday practice is that documents presented under the credit must conform very precisely with the terms of the credit.

A court's view of strict compliance...

"There is no room for documents which are almost the same, or which will do just as well."
Equitable Trust Co. of New York v. Dawson Partners Ltd (1927) 27 Ll L Rep 49.

The great majority of letter of credit disputes relate to the issue of discrepancy in the documents, and bankers' decisions as to discrepancies must be based on this doctrine of strict compliance.

In the letter of credit process, the issuing bank acts as an agent of the importer, and as an agent the bank must strictly follow the instructions of the account party.

Example

Strict compliance and falling markets...

An importer contracts for a very large shipment of an agricultural commodity at a price of USD 2000 per container. Then, the international market for that commodity crashes and by the time shipment arrives the price has dropped to USD 1700 per container.

The exporter presents the documents required under the credit, and the bank must normally pay under the credit. However, it is clear that the importer has a strong incentive to refuse to reimburse the bank if it turns out that the documents accepted by the bank were not in fact conforming. The importer is locked into a contract for purchase of goods at far above the market rate; the importer may be unable to re-sell these goods at a profit.

Thus, if the bank makes a mistake and has not strictly followed the instructions given by the importer, the importer may elect to sue to avoid reimbursing the bank. Moreover, if the exporter fails to respect precisely all documentary requirements under the credit (no matter how seemingly trivial), the importer can refuse to authorize an amendment of the credit, thereby avoiding paying the exporter. Although this might seem unethical, in some cases the importer might feel it is the only way to avoid going through with a commercially disastrous deal. Of course, the exporter may still have some legal rights to payment under the contract, but as we have seen in Chapter 3, legal redress can be expensive and risky.

Thus, both exporters and the respective banks must take care that the documents are exactly correct. Exporters sometimes complain that banks go to excessive lengths to make sure that the documents are exactly correct, even down to the spelling of unimportant words. But it should be understood that if the bank pays against even a minor discrepancy, it may find itself faced with an applicant who refuses to reimburse it for that payment. An additional justification for banks' meticulous checking for discrepancies is that banks cannot be expected to be expert in all areas of business. What is clearly a "trivial" discrepancy to an exporter may not be clear at all to the bank. Thus, a bank cannot be expected to know that two different technical words actually mean the same thing.

In one celebrated legal case[1], the letter of credit application specified that the contractual goods were a certain kind of nuts, which were called "Coromandel groundnuts". The bill of lading referred to them, however, as "Machine–shelled groundnut kernels". In reality, these were basically the same kind of nuts, but the bank refused to pay the credit. The court upheld the bank's decision on the grounds that bankers are not required to be experts in the terminology of nuts, nor in the terminology of any of the thousands of trade sectors in which dealings letters of credit are issued. In many legal cases where a bank rejected a credit because of such apparently small discrepancies in the wording on required documents, the bank was found to have acted correctly by courts of law. Unfortunately, it is difficult to derive any universal principle as to just how "big" or "small" an error must be in order to count as a discrepancy. The significance of misspelling and mis–numbering, for example, is an endless source of dispute. As a general rule, exporters should be careful to ensure that spelling and description in the commercial invoice are absolutely perfect and in conformity with the credit.

There is always the possibility that the importer will waive any discrepancies in the documents presented, and this is likely whenever the importer still wants the goods. Thus, a waiver is quite probable if the market is rising and the goods have increased in value, or whenever the buyer desperately needs the goods to fulfil another contract. In any event, the importer must make the decision whether or not to waive discrepancies quickly, so as to avoid exceeding the time limits for review.

6.5.6 Checklist: Recommendations for Letter of Credit Practice

For the exporter/seller
Before beginning to use credits: make sure that you have implemented a rigorous document–management and verification system. Small errors can be extremely costly. Ideally, try to tailor the documentary credit to your commercial context by specifying in the contract of sale precisely the type of credit that you require:
- Carefully evaluate the credit as soon as you receive it – request the buyer to amend the credit if you think you may have any difficulty in complying with its terms.

- Prepare the exact documents called for in the credit – do not volunteer unnecessary information.
- Verify – does the credit call for the requested documents, e.g.:
  - a Marine Insurance Certificate, or
  - a Marine Insurance Policy?
- Present the documents well before the relevant time limits.
- Make sure corrections are authenticated by the issuer.
- Make sure your company is properly listed as the intended beneficiary.
- If possible, ensure that one person in your company is given central responsibility for controlling, co–ordinating, and verifying the progress of the letter of credit.

For the buyer/opener/credit applicant
- Do not include excessive detail; avoid complex, technical specifications.
- Make sure that the credit exactly reflects the contract.
- Do not include non–documentary provisions; for example, any inspection must be evidenced by a document; quality should be evidenced by a certificate.
- Do not call for documents the seller cannot provide; i.e., a marine on board bill of lading when combined or containerized transport will be used.
- Request the issuing bank for advice or assistance in case of any doubt.
- Seriously consider whether you are willing to grant a credit without requiring an inspection certificate. Although many exporters are reluctant to provide such certificates, they are the buyer's best assurance that the goods which were shipped met the contract quality requirements. One compromise is for the buyer to pay for the inspection.

The banks
- Assist the applicant to avoid problems with transport documents, especially if combined transport is called for
  - is transhipment prohibited?
  - is a multi-modal document authorized?
  - is the place of dispatch specified, or a port?
- Counsel inexperienced buyers on the value of inspection certificates.
- Periodically review the wording of the credit application form; ensure that it conforms with *Incoterms 2000, UCP 500*; check it against the model forms provided by ICC.

- Do not exceed a reasonable time for review of documents, even if the applicant is requested to waive possible discrepancies. Understand that the UCP specifies a maximum reasonable time of seven days, but that courts in particular countries may enforce a substantially shorter period.
- As issuing bank, do not unilaterally alter the Incoterm suggested by the applicant if this Incoterm is already incorporated in a sales contract; rather, suggest to the applicant the advisability of contacting the counterparty to have the contract modified before issuing the credit.

6.6 The electronic supplement to UCP 500 (eUCP)

6.6.1 History

With the emergence of electronic documents – shipping records, customs clearance and banking documents, etc. – in the late 1990s, it became clear that ICC, which had developed rules on letters of credit for more than 60 years, would have to adapt the rules to take account of electronic developments. An ICC Banking Commission task force set as one of its goals a greater focus on electronic trade and consequently a need to develop a bridge between UCP 500 and the processing of the electronic equivalent of paper–based documents.

Meeting over a period of 18 months, the task force developed what came to be known as the "*Supplement to UCP 500 for electronic presentation*" (ICC Publication 500/3), termed "eUCP" for short. Consisting of 12 Articles, the eUCP is a supplement to, and not a replacement of, UCP 500, intended to be used in tandem with UCP 500 where part–electronic or all–electronic presentations are made. The eUCP was approved by the ICC Banking Commission and adopted by the ICC Executive Board in late 2001 and came into force on 1 April 2002.

6.6.2 "Presentation", not "issuance"

The eUCP does not address any issues relating to the issuance or advice of credits electronically, since current market practice and the UCP have long allowed this to be done. Consequently, many Articles of the UCP are not impacted by the electronic presentation of the equivalent of paper documents and did not require any changes to accommodate it. This means that a number of UCP Articles – including those on transfer of credits, for example – are affected by the supplement only in relation to presentation. In other words, for any transaction involving all–electronic or part–electronic presentation, if the eUCP is silent regarding an electronic issue, the UCP prevails.

6.6.3 "Part – or all–electronic presentations"

If they are incorporated in the credit, the eUCP can apply to credits involving either part– or all–electronic presentations. The drafters recognized that at this early stage in the use of electronic documents presentations were likely to be mixed – electronic and paper – for some time.

If, in a mixed presentation, paper documents are presented under an eUCP credit, they must identify the credit to which they are linked. Moreover, the eUCP makes clear that if a credit is issued subject to eUCP – and yet contains only paper documents – then only the UCP will apply.

6.6.4 Specific incorporation of the eUCP

The eUCP only come into play when they are specifically incorporated into the credit.

Practically, this means that if the parties incorporate the eUCP, the credit is automatically subject to it and to the UCP as well. But if they only incorporate the UCP, this does not automatically make the credit subject to the eUCP. Until the eUCP are more widely known and used, the drafters did not believe that all parties would be familiar with it, absent specific incorporation.

6.6.5 Other key issues

a. "CORRUPTED" ELECTRONIC RECORDS

The eUCP, in Article e11, addresses the issues that arise when an electronic record is received but which, for technical reasons, is not capable of being read or which may contain a virus rendering it harmful to the recipient's operating system. In such circumstances, the Article leaves the bank/recipient of the electronic record a choice: the bank "may" request that the electronic record be re–presented. If re–presentation does not occur within 30 days, the bank can consider the record to have not been presented. The optional nature of Article e11, i.e., the fact that bank does not have to apply the Article unless it chooses to do so, made it palatable to those believing that this was a field best left to national law.

b. FORMAT

The eUCP does not specify the format in which electronic messages should be sent – for example, in the body of an e–mail or in a text document attached to an e–mail and formatted in one of the various word processing programmes.

It is up to the parties to agree on the forms of electronic messages they can accept. Article e4, which deals with format, says that an eUCP credit "must" specify the formats in which electronic records are to be presented. If it does not, the record can be presented in any format, and the bank/recipient cannot raise objections concerning the nature of the format used (unless the record is "corrupted" (see above)). The eUCP are "technology neutral"; they are broad rules designed to deal with any technology that may be on the market, whether this be electronic imaging techniques, internet transmissions or other any other electronic system

c. AUTHENTICATION

Article e5(f) makes clear that "an electronic record that cannot be authenticated is deemed not to have been presented". However, the rules do not specify what authentication is or how the parties should go about the business of authenticating a presentation. That is because, as in the case of formats, the rules set forth only general principles and leave it to the parties to decide on what means of authentication – whether digital signatures or some other method – they choose to employ.

d. NOTICE OF COMPLETENESS

Where one or more electronic records are to be presented, the eUCP require the beneficiary to provide a notice to the bank to which presentation is to be made, signifying when the presentation is "complete". This differs from UCP, which has no such provision regarding presentation of paper documents. With part–electronic or all–electronic presentations, however, the situation is different: documents may arrive at different times and in different formats, unlike paper documents that usually arrive in a single package. That is the reason that in the eUCP a final act is required to indicate that the presentation is complete.

The eUCP makes clear that this "notice of completeness" can be sent either by electronic communication or by a paper document. This provision was included to take care of cases where, for one reason or another, e.g., the failure of a system, etc., a bank may not be able to receive electronic documents. In such cases, it was deemed unfair to hold up a complete presentation waiting for a notice of completeness which could be blocked by technical problems.

6.6.6 Major elements of the eUCP

The eUCP, as indicated, are a relatively brief supplement to UCP 500. They are issued in version numbers, the first version being termed Version 1.0. Because electronic developments are evolving, it is likely that the eUCP will be revised more often than the UCP. The parties are supposed to refer to the version currently in use. If they do not, the latest version of the supplement will apply.

The 12 Articles of Version 1 of the eUCP are as follows:

- *Article e1 Scope of the eUCP:* (Their use for presentation of part– or all– electronic documents; the need to incorporate the eUCP in a credit; the need to state the version number of the supplement).

- *Article e2 Relationship of the eUCP to the UCP:* (When the eUCP prevails over the UCP; consequences if only paper documents are presented under an eUCP credit).

- *Article e3 Definitions:* (Basic eUCP definitions of key terms, such as "appear on its face", "document", "sign", "electronic record", "format", etc.).

- *Article e4 Format:* (Statement that credit should specify the format in which electronic records will be presented and consequences if it does not).

- *Article e5 Presentation:* (Need to state a place for presentation of electronic records; requirement for a notice of completeness; need to identify the eUCP credit for each presentation, etc.).

- *Article e6 Examination:* (When an electronic record contains a hyperlink; significance of a nominated bank forwarding electronic records; consequences if an issuing or confirming bank is unable to examine an eUCP credit in the format specified).

- *Article e7 Notice of Refusal:* (Time period for examining documents; when the time is extended; consequences if an issuing, confirming or nominated bank does not receive instructions from the party to whom the notice of refusal is sent).

- *Article e8 Originals and Copies:* (Presumption of originality if one electronic record is presented).

- *Article e9 Date of Issuance:* (Implications if an electronic record does not contain a specific date of issuance).

- *Article e10 Transport:* (Consequences when an electronic record does or does not indicate a date of shipment or dispatch).

- *Article e11 Corruption of an Electronic Record after Presentation:* (Steps to take if an electronic record appears to be corrupted; what happens if a bank requests that a corrupted electronic record be re–presented).

- *Article e12 Additional Disclaimer of Liability for Presentation of Electronic Records under eUCP:* (statement indicating that banks, in checking the apparent authenticity of an electronic record, assume no liability for the identity, source of the information; etc.).

6.7 *International Standby Practices* (ISP98)

6.7.1 History

As mentioned, a number of Articles in the UCP were deemed to be inappropriate for standby letters of credit. As a result, the ICC Banking Commission, in April 1998, endorsed and approved a set of rules specifically designed for standbys. These rules, termed *"International Standby Practices"* (ISP98) (ICC Publication 590), were originally developed over a period of five years by a working group under the auspices of the Institute of International Banking Law and Practice, with the cooperation of the International Financial Services Association (IFSA). The widely representative working group who drafted the rules, reflecting the complex nature of standbys, included not only bankers, but also corporate treasurers, credit managers, rating agencies, government agencies and regulators. Drafts of the rules were then reviewed by a working party of the ICC Banking Commission, which made further suggested changes. Eventually, after a spirited debate, they were approved by the Banking Commission and by ICC. They came into effect in January 1999.

6.7.2 Reasons for developing ISP98

Although standbys and commercial letters of credit have features in common, there are important differences which impelled the drafters to develop separate standby rules. As the Preface to ISP98 notes: "Standbys are issued to support payment, when due or after default, of obligations based on money loaned or advanced, or upon the occurrence or non–occurrence of another contingency." As such, they operate in much the same way as guarantees. Moreover, though standbys started as a US product, they are being used more and more worldwide. In recent years, non–US bank transactions have largely exceeded those of US banks in the US. Overall, the value of standbys now dwarfs that of commercial letters of credit.

As far as beneficiaries are concerned, several UCP Articles are inappropriate for standbys. If the credit is an ISP credit, the beneficiary can avoid the need to exclude the inappropriate ICC rules, among which are:

- *UCP Article 17:* (When it is impossible to present documents prior to the expiry because the offices where presentation is to be made are closed due to an event of force majeure (civil strife, earthquake, war, "act of God", etc.), the UCP requires the bank to dishonour documents presented after the expiry. Commercial credit as well as standby credit beneficiaries often modify Article 17).

- *UCP Article 41:* (When the credit provides for instalments and any instalment is not drawn or shipped on schedule, the letter of credit terminates).

- *UCP sub–Article 43(a):* (When the credit stipulates a transport document and the documents are presented later than 21 days or another specified period after the shipment date, the bank must reject the documents even though presented prior to the expiry date).

6.7.3 Incorporating ISP98

As with other ICC contractual rules, ISP98 should be specifically incorporated into the text of the credit, in this case the standby, in order to have legal effect. The drafters suggest wording such as "This undertaking is issued subject to the *International Standby Practices 1998*" or "Subject to ISP98".

6.7.4 Improvements over UCP provisions

Several Rules in ISP98 are said to clarify and/or improve questionable or ambiguous provisions in UCP 500. As such, they could well serve as the basis for a future revision of the relevant Articles in UCP. Among these:

a. PRESUMPTION OF ORIGINALITY

Sub–Article 20(b) of UCP 500, which deals with the question of what is and is not an original document, reads in part as follows: "Unless otherwise stipulated in the Credit, banks will also accept as an original document(s), a document(s) produced or appearing to have been produced:

i.   by reprographic, automated or computerized systems;

ii. as carbon copies;

provided that it is marked as original and, where necessary, appears to be signed."

Some courts, notably in the United Kingdom, interpreted this provision quite strictly and created confusion in the letter of credit community, as banks were increasingly unsure of whether they had to stamp documents "original" or not. The situation became so confused that the ICC Banking Commission had to issue a Decision on original documents, clarifying several issues related to the Article.

Rule 4.15(c) of ISP98, by contrast, states the presumption that a presented document is "deemed to be original unless it appears on its face to have been reproduced from an original", a clear statement that eliminates ambiguity and places the burden of proof on the party claiming that a document is not original.

b. THE PRECLUSION RULE

UCP 500, sub–Article 13(b) sets a maximum time limit for the examination, acceptance and/or refusal of documents, stating: "The Issuing Bank, the Confirming Bank, if any, or a Nominated Bank acting on their behalf, shall each have a reasonable time, not to exceed seven banking days following the day of receipt of the documents, to examine the documents and determine whether to take up or refuse the documents and to inform the party from which it received the documents accordingly." Although this was a distinct improvement over language in UCP 400, which only called for "a reasonable time", without setting time limits, banks too often interpreted the maximum seven–day period to be the norm and delayed their examination of documents until the final days.

ISP98 is more precise and gives a minimum and a maximum time for examining documents. In the ISP, three business days after the receipt of documents is deemed to be a not unreasonable period and more than seven days is deemed to be unreasonable. If the bank fails to honour the presentation or fails to specify a discrepancy within the period allowed, the bank is precluded from asserting the discrepancy or dishonouring the presentation when the period has expired.

c. ELECTRONIC PRESENTATION

UCP 500 is essentially aimed at the presentation of paper documents. There is language in UCP sub–Article 20(b) saying "A document may be signed by handwriting, by facsimile signature, by perforated signature, by stamp, by symbol, or by any other mechanical or electronic method of authentication"; however, the question of electronic presentation is not considered in detail, even though later Banking Commission opinions made clear that so–called "imaging techniques", allowing bills of lading to be reproduced and sent via the Internet, were in accord with the rules. To add precision and to take account of the emergence of more electronic documents, ICC, in 2002, approved a special supplement to UCP (called eUCP) specifically to deal with electronic presentation (see section 6.6.).

ISP98, written several years after UCP 500, when the trend to electronic documentation was coming into its own, takes on the question directly. Rule 1.09(c) defines an "electronic record", "authenticate", "electronic signature", and "receipt" (of an electronic record). The preface to the Rules lays stress on the application of ISP98 to electronic presentations: "Since standbys infrequently require presentation of negotiable documents", it says, "standby practice is currently more conducive to electronic presentations, and the ISP provides definitions and rules encouraging such presentations."

6.7.5 Major elements of ISP98

ISP98 has been criticized as being much more detailed and legalistic than other ICC rules. This is undoubtedly the case; however, it should be noted that standbys involve a wider legal and commercial community than commercial letters of credit, and that they often involve highly detailed provisions. In any case, as the drafters point out, the ISP rules can be varied by the text of a standby and if ISP98 conflicts with mandatory law, applicable law will control.

ISP98 is divided into 10 Rules, each of which has several sub–Rules. An outline of some of the major provisions follows:

- *Rule 1 General Provisions:* (Scope, application, definitions and interpretations).

- *Rule 2 Obligations:* (Obligation of different branches, agencies, and other offices; conditions to issuance; nominations; etc.).

- *Rule 3 Presentation:* (What constitutes a presentation; when timely presentation is made; partial drawing and multiple presentations; extend or pay; etc.).

- *Rule 4 Examination:* (Examination for compliance; required signature on a document; identical wording; non–documentary terms and conditions; standard document types; etc.).

- *Rule 5 Notice, Preclusion, and Disposition of Documents:* (Timely notice of dishonour; notice of expiry; issuer request for applicant waiver with and without a request by the presenter; disposition of documents, etc.).

- *Rule 6 Transfer, Assignment and Transfer by Operation of Law:* (Transfer of drawing rights and conditions thereto; acknowledgement of assignment of proceeds and conditions thereto; rights and obligations of a successor in the event of a transfer by operation of law; etc.).

- *Rule 7 Cancellation:* (Consent of beneficiary required to cancel his rights; issuer's discretion regarding a decision to cancel; etc.).

- *Rule 8 Reimbursement Obligations:* (Right to reimbursement; refund of reimbursement; bank–to–bank reimbursement; etc.).

- *Rule 9 Timing:* (Duration of standby; calculation of time; time and day of expiration; etc.).

- *Rule 10 Syndication/Participation.*

6.8   Managing currency and exchange rate risks

The basics: All firms involved in international trade must face the challenge of managing currency and exchange rate risk. Given the existence of volatility in exchange markets, firms that fail to plan for exchange rate risk are exposing themselves to financial disaster.

Exchange rate risks are necessarily linked to profit opportunities: wherever money can be lost if the exchange rate moves one way, money will certainly be gained if the exchange rate moves the other way. Thus, firms can profit from exchange rate fluctuations as much as they can lose from them.

Beginning and small exporters may prefer simply to avoid exchange rate risk altogether, thereby giving up the possibility of profiting from fluctuations. The most common risk management techniques for simply avoiding exchange rate risk are: 1) insisting that the contractual currency of payment be one's own currency, and, should that fail, 2) using forward or option contracts to hedge against exposure. Larger or more experienced firms may wish to take advantage of the opportunities for profits from exchange rate fluctuations. Once a firm's foreign exchange exposure grows to a certain level, it generally becomes advisable to assign currency management to a single, highly specialized person or department. This will allow the firm to apply a wider range of currency management techniques, which can even generate significant revenues for the firm.

It is generally said that foreign exchange risks fall into three categories: transaction risk, translation risk and economic risk.

6.8.1 Transaction risk

When an international sales transaction involves parties from countries whose currencies are not fixed or pegged, an element of uncertainty is necessarily present. Transaction risk refers to the risk for each of the counterparties that the exchange rate will move in a disadvantageous direction in between the time the price is agreed in the contract and the time payment is made or received. Both parties are always initially exposed to transaction risk.

Example

An American exporter selling to Germany finds himself compelled to quote a price in euros. The contract specifies delivery within 30 days, payment 90 days after receipt of commercial invoice. The contract price is one million euros, and on the date of the signing of the contract this is equal to USD 1,000,000.

Both parties are exposed to transaction risk:

1) If the dollar weakens against the euro in between the time the contract is signed and the time payment is required, the exporter will benefit, because the euros eventually received will buy more dollars than were expected when the contract was negotiated (e.g., the 1 million euros might ultimately yield USD 1,100,000).

---

2) If the dollar strengthens against the euro, the 1 million euros received by the exporter will buy fewer dollars and the exporter will have lost (e.g., the 1M euros finally received by the exporter might, after being exchanged into dollars, yield only USD 900,000).

A conservative or inexperienced exporter will be primarily concerned with avoiding a loss, rather than with potential gain. Therefore, he may wish to use a forward hedge, a foreign exchange contract which locks in the exchange rate in force on the day of the signing of the export contract. The hedge is a contract between the exporter and a bank or intermediary on a foreign exchange market. In the above example, the exporter will conclude a contract to buy USD 1,000,000 in exchange for 1M euros on or after the date payment is due from the importer (in reality, the exporter will receive less than the 1,000,000 USD, because the bank or other party to the foreign exchange contract will charge a commission, for example, 0.9% (USD 9000), leaving the exporter USD 991,000.

The USD 9000 paid to the bank or foreign exchange dealer can be looked at as a sort of insurance policy against currency fluctuation. No matter what happens, the exporter is assured of receiving USD 991,000. He has given up the possibility of gain that would ensue if the dollar weakened, but he has received in exchange the assurance that he will not lose if the dollar strengthens.

6.8.2 Translation risk (also known as balance-sheet exposure)

Translation risk is derived from the periodic nature of accounting report practices. A company will periodically need to state on its balance sheet, in a particular reporting currency, assets and liabilities which may be denominated in another currency. In between two reporting periods, the relative values of the two currencies may have changed. To some extent, the exposure to translation risk can be said to be a strategic risk factor, which should be taken into consideration when weighing the potential costs and benefits associated with a foreign investment decision.

6.8.3 Economic risk

Economic risk is the risk of currency fluctuations over the long term, and is thus also of a strategic order. It arises from a company's commitment over time to a particular set of counterparties and their currencies. Note that this risk cannot be avoided through simple hedging techniques. For example, an exporter may wish to transfer transaction risk to the importer by requiring payment in the exporter's currency. However, over a period of years, if the exporter relies to a great deal on that particular market, he will inevitably be affected by substantial exchange rate fluctuations between the two base currencies.

Note

(1) J.H. Rayner & Co. Ltd v. Hambros Bank Ltd (1943) KB 37.

CHAPTER SEVEN

Short–term Trade Finance: Factoring and Forfaiting

The basics: Both exporters and importers may need short–term financing in order to operate continuously without having to stop and wait for the funds they expect from particular transactions. Cash fuels the engines of trading companies, and a steady flow is essential to keep the motors running. Cash flow problems may in some cases be avoided via the use of short–term finance techniques. When there is some security that the trader will receive funds from trading partners, intermediaries step in on the strength of that security to provide funds. This enables the trader to bridge the time gap between investment and recoupment of profits. Amongst the most common trade finance devices are factoring, forfaiting, discounting of bills of exchange, and letter of credit finance.

7.1 The various forms of short–term trade finance

When an exporter has delivered goods on a contract in which he has been forced to grant credit terms to the importer, he is faced with a gap between the time he has performed the contract and the time he will be paid for it. This may be a problem if that exporter needs to pay off his own suppliers, or if he has the opportunity to make further deals but needs to buy materials in order to perform subsequent contracts. On the one hand, the exporter needs cash, and on the other hand, he is in possession of "accounts receivable" – obligations on the part of his trading partners to make payments to him at specified times in the future. Depending on the legal/financial security of the accounts receivable obligations (i.e., mere contracts, promissory notes, bills of exchange or confirmed letters of credit), the exporter may obtain financing through a variety of different systems.

The easiest, but most limited, solution is for the exporter to rely on overdraft or credit lines with his bank. However, high interest rates make this an expensive alternative which is not suitable for a large volume of transactions. If the export sale is made via a mechanism involving a bank draft or bill of exchange, such as a documentary collection or letter of credit, the exporter can obtain cash by having his bank negotiate or discount the bill. The bank may alternatively be willing to make an 80% or 90% advance against the bill and other shipping documents. The exporter should distinguish between a payment "with recourse" (the bank may charge the exporter if the bill goes unpaid) or "without recourse" (the exporter can retain the finance sums regardless of whether the bank eventually obtains payment under the bill). In the case of confirmed letters of credit and avalised bills of exchange there is not much risk of the bank failing to obtain payment, so financing is generally without recourse.

"Forfaiting" is a variation on the above schemes which is generally used only for larger contracts (e.g., above USD 50,000–USD 100,000), under which the exporter sells the bill of exchange to a third party. Factoring is a broader concept than forfaiting (and may include forfaiting), in which specialized firms offer a range of financing and risk management services to exporters. These two concepts are further explored below.

Like the exporter, the importer may require interim financing. For example, an importer who pays in advance or upon delivery of the goods is faced with a gap between the time she has paid for the goods and the time that this investment is recouped when the goods are sold for a profit. The importer may be able to increase the total number of her transactions if she can obtain an advance upon the revenue she expects from the imported goods, using the advanced funds to pay for further import shipments. The importer may obtain this financing by using a straightforward loan or overdraft facility, but as explained above, this is an expensive and limited option. Often, the importer will pledge the bill of lading of the goods to her bank in exchange for the advanced sums. If the importer subsequently needs to take back the bill of lading to physically obtain the goods, she may contractually guarantee return of the bill of lading to the bank, such as by a "letter of trust" or similar device.

7.2 Factoring

It has been claimed that the origins of factoring date from more than four thousand years ago, when the ancient Mesopotamians exchanged their receivables for cash.(1) "Factoring" is a broad term, covering diverse services offered either separately or in combination by factoring companies (called "*factors*"). The range of basic services offered includes credit risk assessment and protection, collection of overdue accounts, administration of sales accounting ledgers, and financing. An attempt to reach a standard definition of factoring by Unidroit (the International Institute for the Unification of Private Trade Law), concluded that any arrangement which contained at least two of the above services could be considered factoring.

Factoring services are generally called into play by the exporter's need to manage a continuous flow of low average–value invoices to foreign customers. The factor steps in to provide the exporter with one or all of the following facilities:
1) Advance cash payment by the factor to the exporter against sale or assignment of the exporter's receivables.
2) Elimination of the credit risk that the importer may fail to pay.
3) Collection of funds from the importer.

Exporters tend to turn to factors when other means of short–term trade finance are unavailable or inappropriate. Thus, an exporter may be faced with the type of cash–flow problems indicated above, but find that the services offered by banks are too expensive or are based only on negotiable instruments (i.e., bills of exchange) which do not cover a large part of the exporter's accounts receivables. Moreover, in addition to the financing services which banks also offer, factors can provide overall management of the export accounting process. Thus, just as small exporters can virtually sub–contract the entire transport function to freight forwarders, they can also turn over the whole financial side to factors.

Factoring arrangements can be generally divided into two–factor and single–factor schemes. Under a two–factor system, the exporter enters into a contract with a factor in the exporter's country, called the *export factor*. The export factor in turn will establish an agreement with a correspondent factor in the importer's country, called the *import factor*. The two factors may belong to the same company or may simply establish a contractual relationship.

The import factor will prove especially helpful in performing a credit check on a prospective customer in the importing country. When the exporter has delivered the goods or otherwise performed under the contract, he will issue an invoice to the importer, with a copy to the export factor. The export factor will then make an immediate partial cash payment (commonly up to 80%)

available to the exporter. The two factors together will then completely take over the remaining financial and administrative responsibilities. The import factor will chase any overdue accounts and even resort to legal action if necessary. The import factor's knowledge of the importer's local language and customs can make the factor very effective in pursuing recalcitrant payers.

Single–factor or "*direct export*" factoring functions in much the same way as above, except that there is no import factor. In cases where there are long or well–established relationships between the exporter and importer, an import factor's expertise in credit–checking or collections may not be perceived as necessary. Single–factor systems will tend to be cheaper and will also be more exposed to certain risks.

When the exporter is considering making use of the factor's credit protection services, the question arises as to the complementarity of factoring and credit insurance. Factors and credit insurers provide differing benefits depending on the characteristics of the exporter and the transactions concerned. Thus, the factor will often provide a higher level of credit protection (e.g., 100% as opposed to 90%), but will be slower and more exhaustive in conducting its credit evaluation of the prospective customer. The factor's fees are correspondingly higher than those of the credit insurer. In general, beginning exporters may prefer to rely on factors, because of the additional level of service; experienced exporters, with a good understanding of the risks inherent in particular transactions, may prefer the lower cost of credit insurance premiums.

In certain contexts an exporter will not wish importers to know that he is making use of a factor's services, and will require "*undisclosed*" factoring – the factoring is not revealed to the customer. One reason for this is that customers may make certain negative assumptions about the financial status of a company which uses factoring. The key form of undisclosed factoring is "invoice discounting". Under this type of factoring the factor provides financing against the exporter's invoices, but does not provide credit management or accountancy services.

There are four large international groupings of factoring companies. Each of these groups seeks to adhere to standard operational principles, which avoids some of the problems arising from the differing national legal frameworks that govern factoring.

7.3   Forfaiting

Forfaiting is related to factoring in that it provides exporters with a source of trade finance, but there are several important distinctions. First of all, while factoring deals primarily with low–value, short–term accounts receivable (e.g., less than USD 10,000 average invoice, 90–120 day payment terms), forfaiting tends to involve higher–value short–, medium– and long–term obligations (e.g., more than USD 50,000–USD 100,000, up to and above 180 day payment terms). Thus, while factoring contracts tend to involve coverage of a stream of small invoices, forfaiting generally involves a sequence of single, independent transactions.

Since forfaiting only involves the financing related to individual transactions, it does not comprise the additional credit protection and accounting services offered by factoring. Finance payment and costs are different as well. With forfaiting, payment is made on the full value of the invoice price, minus the charge for discounting the bill of exchange. Although there is no discount with factoring, the exporter will only receive a partial advance payment (e.g., 80%) prior to settlement by the customer, and will pay interest on the advanced sum.

In essence, forfaiting can be summarized as the purchase by the forfaiter of an exporter's receivables which are based on negotiable instruments such as bills of exchange and promissory notes. The exporter, in effect, sells the forfaiter a document containing the importer's definite obligation to pay at some future date. Since there will be a ready and liquid market for these bills only if they are "avalized" or guaranteed by a bank, such as the importer's bank, forfaiting is generally limited to bills supported by an aval or bank guarantee.

One of the central benefits to the exporter of forfaiting is that the forfaiter purchases the bills on a non–recourse basis. Thus, even if importer or his bank defaults on payment of the bill, the forfaiter cannot recover the payment to the exporter. The forfaiter therefore assumes both commercial and political risk. Should war break out or the importer's government suddenly impose exchange controls, the forfaiter may not be able to recover payment from the importer or the importer's bank. Interest and currency rate risks on the payment are also assumed by the forfaiter.

Another advantage of forfaiting is that the exporter is quoted a fixed rate for payment against the bill. The discount rate will depend on a variety of elements, including the date of maturity and other risk factors. However, the size of the discount may make the forfaiting option appear relatively expensive (the exporter should remember how much risk is being assumed by the forfaiter). In any event, the cost calculations related to a forfaiting deal can be quite complex and exporters considering forfaiting should seek expert advice. A disadvantage of forfaiting is that strict documentary requirements must be adhered to, which involves obtaining the importer's participation in obtaining the necessary bank guarantee or aval. The importer may be reluctant, for example, to instruct her bank to grant an aval which will count against the importer's credit lines, or to pay a fee for obtaining the aval.

Note
(1) 'Export Factoring and Forfaiting', Horst Ulrich Jaeger, in *The Law of International Trade Finance* (1989), p. 278.

CHAPTER EIGHT

Security for International Transactions

The basics: Many international transactions involve the use of security devices, commonly referred to as "guarantees", "bonds", or "standby credits", designed to protect one of the parties from a breach by its counter–party. Of course, a basic framework of legal security is already provided in the contract underlying the transaction, and additional security can be provided via documentary payment systems such as that of the documentary credit. However, in an international context the judicial enforcement of contractual rights can be slow and expensive, and documentary credits are sometimes felt to provide primary protection for the exporter, leaving the importer at the risk that the exporter will walk away from the contract. International traders, therefore, and particularly importers and employers of foreign contractors, have sought additional means of assuring the performance of their counterparties.

There are two basic kinds of guarantees/bonds in international trade:
1) *demand* guarantees – these represent "instant cash" for the beneficiary – who only has to make a "demand";
2) *suretyship* guarantees – these guarantees are conditional – the beneficiary must prove that he is entitled to the money, as by providing a court judgement.

Parties who remain in unsecured positions or who do not build adequate documentary safeguards into the transaction are particularly exposed to *international fraud*. ICC's Commercial Crime Services provide a variety of publications, information and consulting services to help traders avoid becoming victims of fraud.

8.1 Guarantees and bonds

Historically, the earliest form of international commercial guarantee was the cash deposit. If one party failed to perform under the contract (e.g., the buyer failed to pay for or accept the contract goods, or the supplier failed to provide the contract goods), that party forfeited the deposit. The cash deposit system has many drawbacks. First, the trader must completely immobilize the deposit capital throughout the life of the guarantee. The trader loses the interest that the deposit money could have earned if invested. Moreover, cash deposits can be easily commingled with the counterparty's own funds, creating the risk that the counterparty would be tempted to use the deposited moneys for his own purposes.

These drawbacks were largely overcome with the advent of a system whereby a bank or other financial institution issued a guarantee or bond to the importer in lieu of the cash deposit. Such a guarantee can be "as good as" cash to the importer or other beneficiary in the event of a default, but is much cheaper for the exporter or other counterparty.

The different kinds of guarantee mechanism available are variously referred to as "bonds", "guarantees", "indemnities", "standby letters of credit", "bank guarantees", "suretyship guarantees", "surety undertakings", etc. These security mechanisms may be provided by banks, insurance companies, specialized surety companies, or other financial services firms. It has been reported that there are a growing number of guarantees issued by individuals, including *inter alia* officers in limited liability companies personally guaranteeing the debts of the company. The variety of products and providers is further complicated because different terminology is used in different countries, market sectors, and legal systems.

As we shall see below, ICC has developed three sets of rules to standardize guarantee practice:

- the *ICC Rules for Contract Guarantees* ("URCG 325" – first published in 1978), which are primarily intended for bank guarantees that require documentary proof of default (these rules attempt to prevent unfair calls by beneficiaries by requiring the beneficiary's demand to be accompanied by a court judgement or arbitral award).

- the *ICC Uniform Rules for Demand Guarantees* ("URDG 458" – first published in 1991), which apply to demand guarantees; and,

- the *ICC Rules for Contract Bonds* ("URCB 524" – first published in 1993), which apply to conditional or suretyship guarantees.

In addition, ICC has developed a set of rules for standby letters of credit (standby credits are used in much the same way as demand guarantees):

- The ICC *International Standby Practices* ("ISP98" – adopted by the ICC Banking Commission in 1998). (For more on standby credits, see Chapter 6, section 6.7).

Note also:

- The *ICC Model Guarantee Forms* – ICC has developed model sets of forms for the *URCG* and *URDG* (ICC Publications 406 and 503).

It should be further noted that the United Nations Commission on Trade Law (UNCITRAL) has recently developed a Convention applicable to independent undertakings such as bank guarantees, which, if adopted by a sufficient number of countries, will bring harmonization to the legal framework underlying guarantee practice.

Guarantee/bond terminology

in the discussion below, the terms "demand guarantee" and "suretyship guarantee" will be used to describe two basic but distinct categories of guarantee or bond. However, note that although the word "guarantee" is used here as a general term, there is a lack of international standardization as regards terminology. Although some legal systems distinguish between "guarantees", "bonds", "undertakings" and "indemnities", these terms are often used as synonyms in the everyday language of international traders. It may therefore be necessary to examine the particular characteristics and nature of the guarantee obligation in order to properly classify the guarantee.

8.1.1 The parties

a. BENEFICIARY

The party that receives the benefit of the guarantee in the event of non–performance by the other party. In practice, this is often the buyer or importer. In large construction contracts, the beneficiary is often a government entity.

b. PRINCIPAL/"ACCOUNT PARTY"

The commercial party that issues or directs the issue of the guarantee. Typical examples of principals/account parties include construction companies which guarantee that a construction project will be completed, or large exporters which guarantee that they will re–pay any sums advanced by the importer if the goods are not properly shipped.

c. GUARANTOR

The bank, insurance company or surety company which issues the guarantee on the instructions of the principal, and is responsible for payment of a determined or determinable sum under the guarantee according to its conditions.

8.1.2 Types of guarantee/bond

a. DEMAND VS. SURETYSHIP

Two main categories of guarantee are demand and suretyship. The term "suretyship" is used as an expedient, for lack of a universally accepted term. Some insurance companies prefer terms such as "accessory bond", while legal experts may prefer "conditional" guarantee.

b. DEMAND GUARANTEES

Under a demand guarantee, the guarantor must pay on *first demand* by the beneficiary. The beneficiary only has to demand payment under the guarantee – there is no need to prove that the principal has actually defaulted on a contractual obligation. The beneficiary is assured a speedy and certain monetary guarantee. Conceptually, demand guarantees are thus a substitute for that more ancient system of security, the cash deposit. As a cash substitute, demand guarantees provide readily accessible, trouble–free security for the beneficiary. In most cases, the only documentary requirement for payment is that the beneficiary make a written demand.

Clearly, the principal takes the risk that the beneficiary will unjustifiably make the demand (as with the cash deposit, where the beneficiary could unjustifiably keep the cash). This is sometimes referred to as the problem of the *unfair call*. Although under most legal systems outright fraud or dishonesty by the beneficiary will enable the principal to avoid paying under the guarantee, these legal exceptions vary from country to country and are in any event often difficult to prove. As a result, prudent traders would prefer to avoid granting demand guarantees. In fact, demand guarantees are most commonly used when the beneficiary has great bargaining power and is able to impose the demand guarantee as a "take it or leave it" option. This has often been the case in major construction projects, where many contractors compete for a single contract. When a trader is forced to grant a demand guarantee, the only practical protection against an unfair call may be to obtain insurance against such an eventuality (although there are some procedural safeguards provided, for example, in Article 20 of the URDG). Export insurers in some countries will provide insurance against unfair calls, provided that the commercial context meets certain requirements. The cost of this insurance can then be factored into the exporter's price tender.

Another difficulty inherent in the demand guarantee is that of setting an assured expiry date for the guarantee. Although guarantees are subject to an expiry date as a matter of routine, in practice the beneficiary may be able to force an extension of the validity period with a so–called "extend or pay" or "pay or extend" demand. The principal has no more protection available against such a demand than against an unfair call. In the absence of established fraud enabling the guarantor to refuse payment, the principal will have little practical alternative but to agree to the extension (note again, however, that some protection is provided in the procedural safeguards of the URDG). In some countries, the "pay or extend" practice is not at all uncommon, and can result in repeated forced extensions of the guarantee period.

However, it is certainly possible that a call for an extension may have some legitimate commercial purpose. Thus, such a call can serve as a second chance granted to the contractor by the employer to perform according to contractual obligations. In such cases, it would be unfair to deprive the employer of recourse to a "pay or extend" statement.

From a legal perspective, demand guarantees are said to be *independent undertakings*. The obligation runs directly from the guarantor to the beneficiary and becomes binding upon the guarantor once issued, regardless of the principal's subsequent ability or inability to reimburse the guarantor. Thus, the insolvency of the principal will not free the guarantor from its obligation to pay under the guarantee. The payment obligation is unaffected by the state of affairs under the underlying contract. Even if the principal should claim that the demand is in bad faith because the principal is not in fact in default under the underlying contract, the guarantor will still have to pay against the beneficiary's demand (so long as there is no established fraud on behalf of the beneficiary).

Although a demand guarantee can be fixed for any percentage of the value of the underlying contract, because of its unconditional nature it is rare for principals to agree to demand guarantees for more than a small fraction of the total contract value, e.g., in the 5% to 10% range.

ICC has sought to standardize demand guarantee practice through the URDG, which were adopted in 1991. The URDG grew out of the perceived failure of an earlier set of rules (the *ICC Uniform Rules for Contract Guarantees* – "URCG") to gain market acceptance. The URCG represented an attempt to provide an alternative to the strict demand guarantee, in view of the danger of unfair calls. Thus, the URCG required the beneficiary's demand for payment to be accompanied by a court judgement or arbitral award establishing the fact of default. The approach of the URCG ran counter to the market reality of the frequently superior bargaining power of beneficiaries. Despite its drawbacks, the demand guarantee continued to be widely used internationally and is now clearly here to stay. Employers/importers who are in the stronger bargaining position may see no reason to agree to the kind of conditional guarantee covered by the URCG's provisions. Of course, the URCG may still be used for those contexts where the exporter–principal has been able to negotiate a conditional guarantee to be issued by a bank.

The URDG thus reflect the market reality of the continued broad use of demand guarantees. As with the UCP, the URDG apply when they have been incorporated by a specific reference (as by a mention at the bottom of a bank's guarantee application form). The scope of the URDG is limited to demand guarantees that are themselves in writing and that provide for payment on written demand. Although, technically, standby letters of credit are legally indistinguishable from demand guarantees and therefore fall within the scope of the URDG, the introduction to the URDG observes that standby credit banking practice is more akin to documentary credit practice than it is to demand guarantee practice, and it is therefore expected that standby credits will continue to be issued subject to the UCP for documentary credits.

As has been noted above, an instrument which is very similar in principal to the demand guarantee is the *standby credit*. Standby credits developed largely in the US during a period in which US regulations did not allow banks to issue bank guarantees. However, standby credit practice spread internationally and standby credits are now issued throughout the world. ICC has also adopted international standard rules for standby credits, known as ISP98 *(International Standby Practices)*. These are covered in detail in Chapter 6, section 6.7.

Article 2 (b) of the URDG enumerates the three basic principles of demand guarantee law:
- the independence of the guarantee from the underlying transaction;

- the documentary nature of the guarantee; and

- the limitation of the guarantor's duty to review the written demand to an examination of whether the demand and any accompanying documents conform *on their face* to the terms of the guarantee (this is further spelled out in Article 9).

Article 20 of the URDG sets forth the formal requirements for a demand. Significantly, not only must the demand be in writing and in conformity with the express terms of the guarantee, *it must also be supported by a statement of breach by the beneficiary*. This statement must set forth the nature of the breach. Note that the statement of breach does not have to be provided by a neutral third party (unless expressly stipulated in the guarantee), such as an independent engineer or arbitrator — the beneficiary's own statement is acceptable. The intent of this provision is to discourage unjustified recourse to the guarantee, without going so far as to fundamentally alter the "on demand" nature of the guarantee. The drafters of the URDG felt that this provision would give pause to a beneficiary who might have the intention of making an unfair call, because he would first have to make a deliberately false statement of breach. However, wary of making the URDG unacceptable to beneficiaries, the drafters included a provision allowing the parties to exclude the requirement of a statement of breach; any such exclusion must be explicitly made within the terms of the guarantee.

c. SURETYSHIP OR CONDITIONAL GUARANTEES (E.G., INSURANCE BONDS)

Under a *suretyship* or *conditional* guarantee, the obligation of the guarantor is triggered by the *actual default* or contractual breach of the principal, as evidenced in a document such as a court judgement or arbitral award against the principal. Thus, in order to claim under a conditional guarantee, the beneficiary must first be able to prove in documentary fashion that the principal has failed to meet its contractual obligations.

In contrast to demand guarantees, conditional guarantees are said to be *secondary* or *accessory* obligations, because the guarantor's obligations are dependent on the principal's actual default in performance of the underlying contract. Moreover, the guarantor is only obliged to pay (or to perform the principal's obligations) to the extent of the principal's liability. The guarantor, in a sense, "steps into the shoes" of the principal, in order to fulfil the principal's obligations. Consequently, the guarantor may make use of any defences available to the principal.

Conditional guarantees eliminate the problem of unfair calls and are therefore, from the principal's point of view, preferable to demand guarantees. Since a principal is assured under a conditional guarantee that there will be no payment or performance by the guarantor unless there is a proven default, the principal may be willing to stipulate that the conditional guarantee cover a larger percentage of the total contract value. Thus, it is not unusual for conditional guarantees to be set at 30% or 40% of the contract value. Because of this higher percentage of coverage, a conditional guarantee may be attractive to the beneficiary as well. It is moreover possible to use the two forms of guarantee in tandem on the same contract, the demand guarantee for a small percentage and the conditional guarantee for a larger percentage of the contract value.

As stated above, ICC has issued two sets of rules which apply to conditional guarantees, one of which was drafted primarily for guarantees issued by insurance and specialized surety companies, while the other is more general in application but was designed primarily with banks in mind as guarantors:

- *ICC Uniform Rules for Contract Bonds* (1993)
- *ICC Uniform Rules for Contract Guarantees* (1978) – for conditional bank guarantees.

A potential disadvantage of the conditional guarantee for the beneficiary is that it may take quite some time to obtain the court judgement or arbitral reward specified in the guarantee as triggering the guarantor's obligation. In the interest of assuring a quick remedy for the beneficiary, the *ICC Uniform Rules for Contract Bonds* provide for the possibility of alternative documentary measures. Thus, the parties may agree that the guarantee obligation will be triggered by presentation of a "certificate of default" issued by an independent architect, engineer or ICC pre–arbitral referee. Another alternative is that the guarantor, upon its own investigation, may issue a certificate of default.

Because conditional guarantees require the guarantor to ascertainthe factual details of alleged defaults by the principals, banks have traditionally been reluctant to issue them. From the banks' perspective, demand guarantees are preferable because their operation is simple and straightforward for the bank. Insurance companies, which have great experience in the investigation of the contingencies surrounding defaults, are more willing to issue conditional guarantees. Surety companies are in the market niche specialized in the management of conditional guarantees. However, there are no hard and fast rules; insurance companies and other firms may also be willing to issue demand guarantees, and banks may issue conditional guarantees.

8.1.3 Main uses of guarantees

a. PERFORMANCE BONDS/GUARANTEES

These guarantees cover the risk that the exporter or contractor will fail to adequately perform the contract, or fail to perform in due time. The guarantee amount is generally a stated percentage of the contract price, commonly up to 10%.

b. BID (OR TENDER) BONDS/GUARANTEES

These guarantees are used to secure performance in contracts awarded by competitive bidding. For example, a governmental entity will solicit competitive tenders or bids for a procurement or construction contract; the tenderers will be required to issue a guarantee in favour of the governmental entity. The purpose of the guarantee is to ensure that the bidder chosen by the beneficiary actually accepts and signs the contract according to the terms of the bid (and also that the bidder provides a performance bond if one is required). Failure to take up the contract will result in payment of the guarantee amount, which is commonly set at from 2% to 5% of the contract value.

c. ADVANCE PAYMENT OR REPAYMENT BONDS/GUARANTEES

These guarantees are intended to ensure the return of thebeneficiary's advance payments in case of non–performance by the principal. Typically, an importer who allows an exporter to draw a cash advance will require that exporter to issue a repayment guarantee in the event that the exporter does not actually ship the contract goods in due time.

d. RETENTION BONDS/GUARANTEES

These guarantees are commonly used in contracts involving goods and services. For example, the employer in a construction project may negotiate to retain a certain percentage of the contract price as a sort of insurance against defects which are not immediately apparent. Rather than lose the use of the retained funds, the contractor will prefer to issue a retention guarantee for payment of a specified sum in the event that building defects are eventually discovered.

e. MAINTENANCE (OR WARRANTY) BONDS/GUARANTEES

These guarantees typically secure the warranty obligations of equipment suppliers throughout the period of the supplier's liability for defects.

A demand guarantee operation

Sometimes referred to loosely as a "bank guarantee", the guarantee on first demand is an essential and basic security device for international transactions.

I. Underlying commercial transaction

As part of an international commercial transaction, an importer may require an exporter to issue a demand guarantee (in such a case, the **EXPORTER** is the **principal** and the **IMPORTER** the **beneficiary**).

2. Issuance of the guarantee

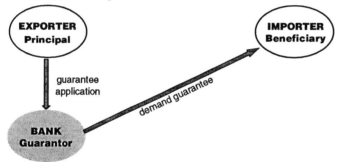

The exporter requests his bank to issue the guarantee in favour of the importer beneficiary.

3. The demand

The importer, should she feel justified in doing so, will made a written demand for payment under the guarantee. Regardless of any allegations by the principal that the demand is unjustified under the contractual provisions of the underlying transaction, the bank must pay (unless there is proof of fraud by the beneficiary): the guarantee is said to be independent of the underlying transaction.

8.1.4 Demand guarantee operation and procedure – direct vs. indirect

a. DIRECT (THREE–PARTY) GUARANTEE

Three–party guarantees, which involve the principal, the beneficiary, and a guarantor (a bank or other trusted third party). Typically, the exporter–principal will instruct its bank to issue the demand guarantee in favour of the importer–beneficiary. The bank will require the principal to enter into a reimbursement contract (called a "counter–indemnity"), obliging the principal to repay any sums paid out under the guarantee to the beneficiary. If the beneficiary believes that the principal has failed to fulfil the contract, the beneficiary will present a written demand for payment to guarantor. The guarantor will pay regardless of any information it may receive concerning the underlying contract. The guarantor will then claim reimbursement from the principal under the counter–indemnity.

b. INDIRECT (FOUR–PARTY) GUARANTEE

This guarantee is similar to the direct guarantee except that a bank in the beneficiary's country is added to the guarantee–chain. Here, the principal's bank instructs a bank in the beneficiary's country to issue the guarantee in favour of the beneficiary. The principal's bank must itself agree to reimburse the beneficiary's bank via a "counter–guarantee". In some countries the local banking authorities may issue administrative rules which have the practical effect of requiring that demand guarantees be in the indirect form. The indirect structure poses certain disadvantages for the principal. First of all, since two banks are involved, the charges will be higher. Second, the guarantee issued by the bank in the beneficiary's country may be subject to the law of the beneficiary's country. The application of local law may preclude certain defences against fraudulent or abusive calls which might be available under the law of the principal's country.

8.2 Export Credit (Trade Credit) Insurance

8.2.1 Introductory

As has been observed elsewhere, the principal difference between international and domestic trade is that international trade entails greater levels of risk and complexity. It is therefore not surprising that insurance companies have seen the opportunity to provide essential services to the international trade market.

Trade credit insurance plays a basic and vital role in international trade. The credit insurer's support is often essential to both supplier and buyer. In the absence of the credit insurer, many trade transactions would have to be done on a cash basis — or not at all. The credit insurer is both a "protector" and an agent for growth:a protector of profit, cash flow, balance sheet and the customer base; an agent for growth in developing trade with existing or new buyers markets. The credit industry's presence in many countries, its trade sector expertise and experience, and its knowledge of a vast number of companies, ensure its continuing role in international trade.

Let us first consider the range of risks the exporter may wish to insure himself against:

■ *Currency risks*
  • exchange rate fluctuations
  • imposition of foreign exchange controls

■ *Business risks*
  • the importer refuses to pay for whatever reason
  • the importer goes bankrupt
  • the exporter fails to adequately perform the contract
  • the exporter or importer's performance is blocked by a "force majeure" event, such as a natural disaster

■ *Political risks*
  • political "force majeure" event, such as revolution or outbreak of war
  • confiscation or expropriation
  • enactment of new regulations which prevent performance of the contract

a. INSURANCE PROVIDERS: PUBLIC V. PRIVATE

There are two basic types of international credit insurers: public and private. Examples of well–known public insurers include the US Eximbank, Canada's Export Development Corporation, the UK Export Credits Guarantee Department, and France's COFACE. The provision of publicly financed export insurance has become the object of international political sensitivity, because such insurance can be considered as an indirect export subsidy which can unfairly distort international markets. As a result, an international agreement has been implemented – the OECD Consensus on Export Credits – with rules on minimum interest rates and down payments and maximum lengths of credits. Especially with regard to short–term coverage, public sector insurers have been scaling down their operations in favour of private insurers. Public sector insurers, unlike private insurers, generally do not offer the exporter the ability to cover both domestic and international risks.

Private insurers frequently market their services through the intermediary of specialized credit insurance brokers. These brokers advise exporters on how to choose from amongst the wealth of insurance services and policies available. In the event of a claim, the broker may assist the exporter in preparing necessary documentation and dealing with the insurance company.

Credit insurers help exporters, not only by reimbursing them for losses sustained from non–payment, but also by helping them set up proper credit management procedures. Insurers may provide exporters with credit data on prospective customers, suggest appropriate credit levels, and supply information on a foreign country's economic and political risk. Some insurers offer collections services for overdue accounts.

b. TYPES OF POLICIES

Different kinds of insurance policies will provide protection against certain of the above risks. Export "credit insurance" is perhaps the most common variety, covering the exporter against non–payment or default by the importer. A "comprehensive policy" may cover the exporter against currency, business and political risks. Various combinations are possible depending on the specific risks the exporter wishes to cover. An example of a useful combined policy is one that covers both domestic and international credit risk.

Exporters who wish to self–insure or handle credit management by themselves (this may be the case with certain large companies) may nonetheless wish to take out a catastrophic loss or "excess of loss" policy. These policies provide total coverage for any losses in excess of a certain threshold, leaving the company to self–insure for losses below that amount.

c. COVERAGE

As with other forms of insurance, coverage extends only to risks specifically named in the policy. Thus, non–payment caused by the exporter's own default is normally excluded from coverage. This can lead to delays in the payment of a claim in cases where the importer alleges that the exporter is guilty of late delivery or of supplying goods which are not of contractually specified quality. In such cases, the exporter may need to prove that he was not in default. Coverage of currency risk is exceptional, especially as the term of coverage increases, and may require a separate policy or premium.

The amount of coverage is commonly in the 80–90% range, although greater or lesser coverage may be possible in particular cases. The cost of coverage is commonly in the range of less than 1% to 2% of the contract price, plus a base fee and the insurer's minimum processing charges.

8.2.2 Basic form and content of the insurance protection

A credit insurance policy insures a supplier (policy holder) against the risk of monetary loss in respect of goods or services sold on credit to another party (the "buyer"), in the event of that buyer's insolvency or default. "Default" (also termed "protracted default") is held to occur when a valid debt remains unpaid after a specified period commencing from the due date for payment. This period varies as between different credit insurance companies but generally ranges from 6 to 12 months after the due date for payment.

In trade between developed nations the risk of non–payment of a debt, due to reasons other than the above mentioned "commercial/insolvency" risks, is relatively minor. It needs to be observed, however, that cover is also available for the "political risk" element. The main significance of this is that by and large, transactions involving a "public buyer" (state or quasi–state entities that are not subject to the normal laws of insolvency), are covered against the risk of payment default. Credit insurance policies normally cover between 80% to 90% of the insured debt – the balance being for the policy holder's own account. (This principle is designed to encourage prudence on the part of the insured as well as to exclude a transaction's profit margin from cover.)

Credit insurance policies invariably cover most, if not all, of the policy holder's credit transactions (whole credit turnover or multiple account) with his numerous buyers.

8.2.3 Discretionary limits

It is general practice to give the policy holder a "limit of discretion", a maximum amount outstanding in respect of any particular debtor, below which amount the insured is free to transact business without contacting the insurer. However, in credit transactions with buyers that exceed the discretionary limit, the policy holder is obliged to obtain the prior consent of the credit insurer.

8.2.4 Credit information

The ability of the credit insurer to underwrite the risks in question (i.e., the default by and insolvency of the various buyers), rests upon the availability of specialized information. This includes up–to–date, reliable and comprehensive financial data about the buyers, as well as information about the various trades/ industrial sectors and about general economic, monetary and fiscal developments in the buyers' market(s).

Credit information on buyers is partly obtained from sources such as professional information agencies. In addition to using such sources, most credit insurers have found it necessary to build up and maintain their own data on buyers.

It will be appreciated that the above–mentioned system of credit limit approval and the subsequent monitoring of the obligations in question, constitutes an important and dynamic credit control instrument in favour of the insured. This service is reinforced throughout the lifetime of the policy, by debt collection and recovery action in respect of seriously overdue accounts and in respect of unpaid debts in an insolvency. The availability of these specialized services – notably in markets outside that in which the policy holder is "at home", constitutes a very valuable management tool for business in general – but especially so in the case of SME's.

8.2.5 Length of credit term / Maximum credit term

Credit insurance policies generally specify a maximum credit term for transactions with a particular buyer. This credit term is normally considered to commence from the date of delivery of the goods or performance of a service contracted for, until the due date for payment. The maximum credit term varies quite substantially between different trades/sectors and markets. In particular,there is a fundamental distinction between short–term credit – where the credit term is only exceptionally longer than 180 days – and medium– or long–term business transactions conducted on credit. The latter are usually regarded as falling within a term of between 3–5 years or longer and normally relate to capital goods and works contracts.

The maximum credit term specified in a policy is usually established in consultation with the policy holder. As has already been mentioned, the term is always market related.

It is not uncommon that a prospective insured or a policy holder may approach the credit insurer for authorization of credit terms which the underwriter considers too long. In extreme cases, this may lead to a refusal to cover the intended transaction; in other cases, the underwriter will usually draw attention to the fact that the premium cost of cover will be higher. The underwriter may seek to persuade the parties to trade within established credit terms and to avoid escalation of these norms. Thus, credit insurance often plays animportant role in discouraging the escalation of credit terms.

8.2.6 Maximum extension period

Credit insurance policies usually provide for a "maximum extension period" for the payment of insured debt. This period is intended to provide reasonable flexibility in the commercial relations between the policyholder and his clientele, when for one reason or another it is pragmatic and reasonable to allow the buyer some latitude in effecting payment beyond the original/specified due date. Any further extensions must be previously approved by the credit insurer.

The "maximum extension period" generally varies between 30 to 90 days, depending on the original credit term. Thus, for example, in the fresh produce sector, where in most cases, the original credit term is currently a maximum of 30 days, it is unlikely that any "maximum extension period" will be more than 30 days.

8.2.7 Collection of insured debts

In the event that an insured debt remains unpaid — generally for more than 30 days after its original (or postponed) due date, the policy holder is required to immediately notify the credit insurer. From that point onwards, the debt in question becomes the subject of a cooperative collection procedure in which the credit insurer may also enlist the assistance of other ICIA (International Credit Insurance Association) colleagues operating in the market concerned. These efforts will be intensified as circumstances warrant Particularly in the case of significant amounts, the credit insurer may be involved in the negotiation of legal arrangements — including corporate financial reconstruction plans and arrangements of compromise — extending to final insolvency proceedings. These actions often extend well beyond the stage when the credit insurer has paid a claim to its policy holder in respect of the insured debt.

CHAPTER NINE

International Transport

The basics: Transport in international transactions has a direct impact on such key sale contract elements as price, speed of delivery and the risk of loss or damage. While large traders may have well–staffed logistics departments, smaller traders often rely on international freight forwarders. It is essential that the freight forwarder receive all possible relevant information about the sale contract, and that the directions to the freight forwarder be as precise as possible, especially with regard to such items as place of pickup, place of delivery, costs for handling and loading, and amount of required packaging.

The choice of sea, air, or ground transport may appear to be dictated by the type of product, destination or buyer, but exporters should take care not to underestimate the competitiveness of alternative means. Air freight can be surprisingly competitive if one factors in cost savings related to lower insurance rates and the increased speed and security of shipment.

Each of the main transport methods has a corresponding legal and documentary framework with which traders must be familiar. Above all, traders should seek to ensure that transport considerations are integrated into overall export management, with sufficient communication between sales, marketing, purchasing and logistics personnel.

9.1 Transport management

Choosing the optimal mode of transport can mean the difference between export success and failure. Consequently, some form of systematic evaluation of the different transport modes available is advisable; this discipline is sometimes called "physical distribution management" or "logistics analysis". Small traders may prefer to delegate this analysis to a freight forwarder, but the trader should have sufficient in–house understanding of transport to be able to supervise and evaluate the performance of forwarders. Regardless of company size or type of management structure chosen, traders must take into consideration the following basic elements of transport management:

a. THE FUNDAMENTAL COST PRINCIPLE: VOLUME DISCOUNTS

Transport service providers charge lower freight rates (or offer rebates or discounts) for large or regular cargo shipments. Consequently, exporters and importers should seek, whenever possible, to ship larger volumes. This can be done by:

- consolidating several different sales into a single shipment;
- arranging for "door to door" shipment; and,
- organizing shippers' clubs or councils for collective bargaining of freight rates.

b. TRANSPORT COSTS' IMPACT ON THE PRICE OF GOODS

Transport costs may account for a significant part of the total cost of the product, especially in the case of commodities or relatively low–value products. The price that the exporter quotes to the importer is inevitably linked to the particular Incoterm chosen and to how much of the corresponding transport required must be covered by the exporter. Small and beginning exporters may prefer to choose the Ex Works Incoterm (EXW), under which all transport responsibilities are entirely the buyer's affair, or FCA or FOB, which place the cost of international transport on the buyer.

However, in choosing Incoterms which place few transport obligations on the seller, such as EXW, FCA or FOB, the exporter may neglect an important profit centre: the exporter could manage the transport operation himself and charge a commission to the buyer for services rendered. An exporter who can competently negotiate and oversee the transport chain can earn money by quoting prices CIF, CIP or DDU/DDP, handling the transport himself, and billing the buyer a commission for these services.

Optimal transport economy will logically result when either the exporter or importer wholly undertakes the transport obligations. This is because the total amount of transport services purchased will be larger, as it will not be divided between two parties. Since a basic transport principle is that larger shipment volumes command proportionately lower prices, it would seem that the choice of Incoterms at either "extreme" of the range would result in economies. These terms are Ex Works or FCA on the one hand (buyer is responsible for transport), and DDU or DDP on the other (seller is responsible for transport). In fact, in many countries DDU and DDP have become increasingly popular with exporters.

c. SPEED OF DELIVERY

In many markets, speed of delivery is a crucial competitive factor. In addition to speed, traders must pay attention to reliability: how common are late or delayed shipments? Since delays may result when a shipment is transferred from one transport provider to another, this is another reason for exporters to consider managing the entire transport chain. For some parties, reliability may prove to be a higher priority than speed. Regardless of which party is at fault for a delayed shipment, the exporter may risk breaching a contractual deadline or otherwise losing the customer by projecting an image of unreliability.

Long transit times also increase total costs owing to the payment of interest rates on working capital throughout the period the goods are inaccessible. For this reason, air transport is sometimes a surprisingly competitive alternative to sea transport.

d. STOCK AND INVENTORY MANAGEMENT

In recent years many companies have identified stock and inventory management as a means for cutting costs and increasing efficiency. A prime example is Japan's renowned "just–in–time" (JIT) manufacturing systems, which can virtually eliminate the need for a manufacturer to maintain large warehouses at the factory, because all necessary supplies are delivered daily. JIT systems are now common around the world.

Stock reduction depends on sophisticated transport management, generally involving a higher frequency of shipments of lower unit volume. The increased transport costs may well be offset by increased efficiencies from smaller warehouses, fewer obsolescent parts and more rapid customer service. JIT systems are often based on sophisticated electronic data interchange (EDI) networks which link the manufacturer to its suppliers.

e. PACKAGING

Packing and packaging costs vary substantially according to the mode of transport. Improper or insufficient packaging results in a higher rate of damage to goods in transit. Consequently, traders should take care not to evaluate different modes of transport purely according to freight rates. A transport mode with cheap freight may require a more expensive packaging and/or have a high frequency of lost or damaged goods. Thus, door–to–door shipments by full container load, which require minimal packaging, are often very competitive even against alternatives with apparently cheaper freight rates.

If the importer is arranging for transport, he should inform the exporter as early as possible of the nature of that transport, and particularly as it may alter the type or amount of packaging required.

f. CUSTOMS

The various transport modes entail different procedures for customs clearance, which may have an incidence on transit time. Thus, the simplified customs procedures available for air and postal shipments, and under certain regimes for road and rail shipments, can increase the competitiveness of these modes as against sea transport.

g. PAYMENT SYSTEMS

Certain payment systems will influence the mode of shipment. Thus, payments by documentary credit may in certain cases require the presentation of an on board marine bill of lading. If the seller stipulates, in the sales contract for example, a different transport document requirement under the credit, such as a multimodal transport document or an air waybill, it may be possible for the exporter to trigger the payment mechanism at a much earlier date, because the transport document will be received as soon as the goods are delivered into the transport chain.

h. COLLABORATION VS. COMPETITION

Whenever possible, shippers in a particular sector should consider forming collaborative groups enabling them to jointly negotiate lower rates and better service from transport providers. Often, competitive postures prevent shippers from working together, which can lower the international competitiveness of the entire sector vis–à–vis other countries.

9.2 International treaties and conventions

There are several different international treaties that apply to the various modes of transport. These treaties are of interest to exporters and importers because they state the extent and limitations of the carrier's liability for goods which are lost or damaged in transit.

a. SEA TRANSPORT

- *The Hague Rules (1924)* – The International Convention for the Unification of Certain Rules relating to Bills of Lading (also known as the Brussels Convention). Signed by approximately 80 contracting countries, this treaty was subsequently criticized for setting liability limits for shipowners too low and for providing a multitude of exemptions and exclusions from liability. The Hague Rules apply to goods carried by sea under a bill of lading drawn up in one of the contracting countries.

- *The Hague–Visby Rules (1968)* – A Protocol amending the Hague Rules, and referred to as the Hague–Visby Rules, was signed in Brussels in 1968 and has to date been ratified by 32 countries. The Hague–Visby Rules generally raised the exposure to liability of the shipowners.

- *Hamburg Rules (1978)* – The UN Convention on the Carriage of Goods by Sea, signed in Hamburg in 1978, was intended to remedy some of the defects of the rules produced by the earlier two Conventions. The Hamburg Rules have found little favour in shipping circles, and although they went into force in 1992, many of the major trading nations have not signed the treaty, and there is some doubt as to whether it will be signed by enough of the trading powers to provide truly global harmonization.

b. AIR TRANSPORT

- *Montreal Convention for the Uniformity of Certain Rules of International Carriage by Air (1999)* – This Convention was adopted on 31 May 1999 and will enter into force when 30 countries have ratified it. It establishes a comprehensive and up–to–date set of uniform rules defining and governing the liability of carriers in relation to passengers, baggage and cargo. It will eventually replace the 1929 Warsaw Convention, as amended by various supplementary conventions and protocols.

- *Warsaw System (1929)* – Until the Montreal Convention comes into force, the Warsaw liability system is in force. The Warsaw Convention; was signed in 1929 and subsequently supplemented by the Hague Protocol (1929), Guadalajara Supplementary Convention (1961), Guatemala City Protocol (1971) and the Montreal Protocol (1975).

c. RAIL TRANSPORT

- *COTIF (1980)* – Since rail transport does not link the continents, it is not surprising that rail transport lacks a global legal framework. Nonetheless, in Europe at least, and in certain contiguous countries linked to the European rail network, rail transport is governed by the 1980 Convention concerning International Carriage by Rail (COTIF), which entered into force in 1985 and applies in approximately 41 countries.

d. ROAD TRANSPORT

- *CMR (Convention Internationale pour le transport des Marchandises par la Route) (1956)* – The situation in road transport is similar to that of rail transport. Approximately 44 countries – mostly European – have signed the Convention on the Contract for the International Carriage of Goods by Road.

e. MULTIMODAL TRANSPORT

- *UN Convention on the International Multimodal Transport of Goods (1980)* – This Convention will enter into force when it has been signed by 30 countries.

9.3 The UNCTAD/ICC Rules for Multimodal Transport Documents

Given the absence of an international treaty effectively covering multimodal transport, freight forwarders have sought to establish and abide by standard rules and documents which would put documents issued by freight forwarders on a similar footing with those issued directly by sea carriers. The *UNCTAD/ ICC Rules for Multimodal Transport Documents* (ICC Publication 481), effective from 1 January 1992, evidence a movement towards the liability regime of the Hamburg Rules, and a rejection of the loophole–filled approach of the Hague–Visby Rules. The UNCTAD/ICC Rules are reflected in standard industry documents, such as the FIATA Multimodal Transport Bill of Lading and the MULTIDOC 95 bill of lading issued by the Baltic and International Maritime Council (BIMCO). Through the wide use by carriers and freight forwarders of these documents, it would seem that the UNCTAD/ICC Rules will have a certain level of international applicability in the foreseeable future. The UNCTAD/ICC Rules were meant to replace the prior ICC Uniform Rules for a Combined Transport Bill of Lading.

9.4 Carrier's liability

As can be seen from the above, there are a number of different legal conventions that can define the extent of the carrier's duties and liabilities in the international carriage of goods. Adding to the complexity of the matter, these treaties do not all have global coverage.

While the rules related to carrier liability can go into fine detail, the following general principles are useful:

- *Money limit to liability claim* – Under each of the conventions, there is a monetary maximum that can be claimed for loss of a cargo, and this is usually expressed in terms of a fixed amount of money per unit of weight or per package.

- *Carrier's responsibility* – Under the Hague and Hague–Visby Rules, the carrier must exercise "due diligence" as regards the seaworthiness of the vessel, its state of fitness for handling the goods, and proper loading, storage or discharging procedures.

- *Carrier's immunities* – Again, under the Hague and Hague–Visby Rules, there is a long list of carrier's exemptions from liability, including:
  - **force majeure or fortuitous acts**, such as earthquakes, tidal waves, fires, perils of the sea, wars, strikes, accidents;
  - **defects in the goods/packaging** causing the damage – if the goods or packaging contain a defect which itself causes the damage, the carrier is exempt;
  - **negligence of employees** – the carrier is not liable for the negligence in the navigation or operation of the vessel by the master, pilot or crew.
  - **procedural limitations** – Normally, any action against a carrier must be brought within a certain time limit, defined by the applicable conventions or law. A buyer receiving visibly damaged goods should make an immediate written, specific notation on the delivery note. This note should be addressed immediately to the carrier or his agent as well as the insurer.

The extent of these carrier's immunities and protections should make it clear why it is so important for international traders to obtain sufficient insurance coverage.

9.5 Charter parties

a. INTRODUCTORY

A buyer or seller may wish to transport certain merchandise by chartering, or hiring, an entire vessel or part of a vessel. The contract for the lease of the vessel is known as the *charter party*. Charters are generally classified as:

- *voyage charters* – the shipowner runs the ship and crew; the charterer merely "hires" the ship, or part of it, for one voyage;
- *time charters* – the shipowner runs the ship and crew, but the charterer handles sales and bookings of the cargo;
- *bare boat* – the charterer runs the ship and crew.

The charterer may himself sub–charter the vessel. Whether or not he does, bills of lading for goods shipped on the chartered vessel will be issued to particular shippers, who may or may not themselves be sub–charterers. These bills of lading are said to be issued "subject" to the charter party. In essence, the charterer becomes a commercial intermediary between the shipowner and the ultimate receiver of the bill of lading. The holder of the bill of lading in such cases needs to know who to sue if the goods are delivered in damaged condition or have been lost.

b. REQUIREMENT OF TENDER OF CHARTER PARTY ALONG WITH BILL OF LADING

Whether or not a bill of lading is an ordinary one or is one which is subject to a charter party and incorporates terms of the charter party can be of major significance for buyers as well as for the banks involved. As a result, under CIF Incoterms the seller in such a case is required to tender a copy of the charter party along with the bill of lading. Such a tender enables the buyers to compare the contract of carriage with the contract of sale to see if they are in conformity. For example, if the contract of sale specified delivery in the port of Marseilles, but the charter party actually only obligated the shipowner to go as far as Barcelona, then the buyer who had not seen the charter party would not have known of the inconsistency of the two contracts. Under CIF Incoterms, the seller would have had to tender both contracts at the same time, enabling the buyer to compare the two documents in due course.

Note that the UCP 500 does not set a requirement of tender of the charter party along with any bill of lading that refers to it, although if the letter of credit expressly calls for such tender, then the exporter must tender the charter party with the bill of lading for payment.

c. DISTINCTION BETWEEN BILL OF LADING AND CHARTER PARTY

The charter party contract is only a contract of carriage, and is thus distinct from a bill of lading, which is also a receipt for the goods and to some extent a *document of title*. A charter party is merely a contract between the *shipowner* and the *charterer*, setting forth the price of the freight and the other conditions of hire. Charter party contracts cannot, therefore, be endorsed and negotiated as can bills of lading.

In many jurisdictions charter parties are allowed greater freedom of contracting than is available for bills of lading, which may be governed by one of the international treaties. Thus, a shipowner may contract with a charterer under terms of lower shipowner's liability than would be possible with an ordinary shipper under a bill of lading.

There may be two kinds of bill of lading in charter parties: the shipowner's bill of lading to the charterer, for the whole of the goods received on board, and the charterer's separate bills covering parts of the shipment.

The fact that a particular bill of lading is issued in connection with a charter party has a definite impact on the interests of the cargo owner, at least by making his rights much more complicated to ascertain. Thus, the purchaser or endorsee of a bill of lading issued under a charter party will have to ask himself certain questions, as for example:

- *whom to sue* – if the goods are damaged or lost, who should the buyer sue, the shipowner or the charterer? Under which contract will the suit be made, the charter party or the bill of lading?
- *acceptability* – are bills of lading referring to charter parties acceptable under the terms of shipment sales and letters of credit?

d. INCORPORATING THE TERMS OF THE CHARTER PARTY INTO THE B/L; ARBITRATION CLAUSES

The bills of lading issued by the charterer may seek to "incorporate" the terms of the charter party contract. It is understandable that the charterer would want the two contracts to accord with each other, so that he would not expose himself to any liability beyond that entailed in the charter party.

If the charterer transfers the bill of lading received from the shipowner to a third party, the contract between the shipowner and the third party will be covered by the bill of lading.

If the bill of lading incorporates a charter party, and if, for example, the charter party specifies that dispute resolution will be by arbitration, then any litigation by a third party buyer against the shipowner would have to be dismissed, because the appropriate forum would be an arbitral one.

However, to incorporate the terms of a charter party, the bill of lading must do so conspicuously and clearly, and in any event the terms of the charter party must not contradict the bill of lading itself, nor the provisions of any international convention applicable to the bill of lading.

9.6 Freight forwarders

9.6.1 Introductory

An indispensable member of the international trade community, the freight forwarder generally acts as an agent for the exporter or importer in shipping cargo internationally. Like travel agents – but dealing with cargo rather than passengers – freight forwarders use their knowledge of varying freight rates to offer the customer the best "package deal".

Amongst the many additional services offered by freight forwarders are the handling of export and customs documentation, insurance, and port and terminal charges. Small exporters will therefore often consult with their freight forwarder before quoting a price in a tender for a particular international transaction.

Traders should understand that the terms "freight forwarder" and "forwarding agent" are generic terms and that there are a variety of specialized functions within the profession. Some forwarders offer a wide range of these functions, whereas others restrict themselves to a single speciality or particular geographical coverage. These various functions are summarized below. In addition, it is important for traders to understand that forwarders may act as either agents or principals, with differing legal consequences.

Freight forwarders as agents or principals – A freight forwarder acts as an agent when he performs functions on behalf of, and under the instructions of, the principal (the exporter or importer). As an *agent*, the forwarder will procure the services of third parties who will perform the packing, storage, transport, handling and customs clearance of the goods. The agent thus acts as an intermediary, "introducing", in a manner of speaking, the principal to the service providers. The principal then enters into direct contractual relations with the service providers. Consequently, the forwarder is generally *not liable* for the errors or breaches of the service providers. As with other agents, the forwarder owes the principal various duties, including the duty to inform and the duty of diligence (see Chapter 5 on agency law).

When the forwarder acts as a *principal*, he contracts directly with the exporter or importer (the "customer"). The customer will deal only with the forwarder, who will issue a single bill to the customer for the total amount of services rendered. As a principal, the forwarder is generally liable for the errors or breaches of the sub–contracted service providers.

It is also possible for a forwarder to enter into "hybrid" arrangements, acting as agent for certain functions and as principal for others.

9.6.2 Different functions and types of forwarders

a. CONSOLIDATORS/NVOCC (NON–VESSEL OPERATING COMMON CARRIERS)
This function involves grouping or assembling diverse shipments from various customers so as to make up full container loads, thus obtaining lower freight rates. Some consolidators offer regular shipments on seagoing vessels that they do not own; these are referred to as NVOCC's.

b. MULTIMODAL (OR INTERMODAL) TRANSPORT OPERATORS (MTO'S)
A multimodal transport operator offers "one–stop shopping" for traders. This enables traders to completely outsource or sub–contract their export logistics to a single service provider. Multimodal transport operators typically offer "door to door" transport, with coverage of all related functions such as insurance, customs, warehousing, etc.

c. CUSTOMS BROKERS
These parties act as the agents of exporters and importers in order to process customs declarations and other formalities and pay duties and taxes. Because they may be liable for very large payments of duties or fines, customs brokers are usually bonded by banks or insurance companies. Traders should take care to give precise directions and limits to customs brokers to avoid incurring liability in the event that an unexpectedly high tariff or fine makes it uneconomical to process a particular shipment.

d. PORT (SEA PORT, AIRPORT OR CARGO TERMINAL) AGENT

This agent represents the shipper at the point where the goods are transferred from one transport mode (typically, from a truck or lorry) to another (as to a seagoing vessel or airplane).

e. AIR FREIGHT AGENT (AIR WAYBILL AGENT)

These agents process shipments for airlines and may have the authority to issue air waybills. Frequently, the air freight agent also handles customs clearance.

f. ROAD HAULAGE BROKERS

Road transport is characterized in many countries by the proliferation of small service providers. Road haulage brokers act as intermediaries between road carriers and shippers and are usually paid by commission.

g. LOADING BROKERS

These brokers act as the agents of shipowners to obtain and process cargo shipments. Commonly, a freight forwarder will represent the shipper while a loading broker represents the shipowner, so that there are two intermediaries between the customer and the transport provider.

9.7 Shipping documents

9.7.1 Miscellaneous documents

The documents associated with international transport frequently also play a key role in the payment mechanism and the underlying sales contract. Consequently, certain of these documents have been treated elsewhere in the sections on legal and payment aspects.

The most important transport document is the *bill of lading* (or one of its many variants); because of its central role, it will be presented in some detail below. First, however, let us summarize some of the other documents commonly encountered.

a. COMMERCIAL INVOICE

This is essentially a bill for the goods sold. It should comprise all essential information concerning the sale, including a precise description of the goods, address and identity of exporter and importer, and delivery and payment details. In many countries, customs authorities use the commercial invoice as the basis for calculating import duties. Unscrupulous traders have been known to prepare a separate, deliberately understated invoice for submission to customs authorities so as to reduce the amount of duty paid; this fraudulent practice is known as "double–invoicing" and, when detected, can result in substantial penalties.

b. INSPECTION CERTIFICATE

A certificate generally issued by a respected independent agency, it verifies that the quality, quantity or specifications of the goods shipped are in conformity with the sales contract.

c. CERTIFICATE OF ORIGIN

A certificate, usually issued by a local chamber of commerce, establishing the country where the merchandise was produced or manufactured. This may be required, for example, for exports from developing countries to benefit from preferential tariff treatment.

d. INSURANCE CERTIFICATE

Proof of type and amount of insurance coverage, generally required for payment by letter of credit (especially under CIF and CIP Incoterms).

e. PACKING LIST

A highly detailed list describing the weight, volume, content and packaging for each separate export package.

f. EXPORT LICENSE

An official permit issued by an agency of the exporter's government, without which the goods cannot be exported. Some countries require all exporters to obtain an official government export license. Hazardous items (e.g., toxic chemicals) or politically sensitive goods (e.g., weapons) often require special export licenses and may in addition be subject to quotas or ceilings.

g. CONSULAR INVOICE

Some countries require an invoice on an official form for all imported goods; these invoices are generally purchased from that country's local consulate in the exporter's country.

9.7.2 The bill of lading

The bill of lading (the "B/L") is a central document in the traditional export transaction, linking the contract of sale, the documentary payment contracts, and the contract of carriage. We shall first consider the classic B/L, the marine (or ocean) bill of lading, which provides the documentary basis for traditional maritime shipments.

a. THE MARINE BILL OF LADING

The *marine bill of lading* is issued by the transport carrier (or its agent, such as a freight forwarder). This B/L serves 3 basic functions:

1) **The B/L represents the right to physical delivery of the goods** – Or, as is sometimes said, the B/L "stands for" the goods. The legal holder of the B/L is solely entitled to take delivery of the goods. Moreover, the B/L is a "negotiable instrument", because the B/L itself can be sold or transferred ("negotiated"), thereby transferring control over the goods. The goods may thus be sold repeatedly even while they are in transit, by mere transfer of the B/L. The negotiable status of the B/L makes it useful to banks as a security device; a bank that has been pledged a B/L may be willing to extend credit or additional credit on the presumed collateral value of that B/L. Under an order B/L, the shipper consigns the shipment "to the order of" a named party, who may be the shipper himself, the buyer or a bank, depending on the level of trust existing between those parties and the banks involved in the financing of the letter of credit. The export seller can transfer the B/L by endorsing it and delivering it to the buyer or to a bank where payment is organized through the banking system.

2) **The B/L evidences the contract of carriage** – The B/L must contain the terms of the contract of carriage, either explicitly or by reference to another document. Under documentary shipment sales the seller must procure and transfer to the buyer a contract of carriage on "usual" or reasonable terms; as between the buyer and the carrier, the B/L is that necessary contract of carriage.

3) **The B/L is a receipt** – The B/L is a receipt that evidences the delivery of the goods for shipment. As such, it describes the goods and states that in a certain quantity and in apparent good order they have been loaded *on board*. If there is a notation that the goods have been in any way damaged, this will be made on the face of the B/L and it will no longer be considered

"*clean*". In some cases, a carrier will issue a B/L as soon as the goods are received, but before they are loaded – this is a "received for shipment" B/L, which will not be acceptable for documentary sales until, after loading, it is converted by the carrier into a "clean on board" B/L (also called a "shipped" B/L).

i. *Uses and advantages of the clean on board B/L* – In light of the above, we can discern certain useful advantages of the *clean on board B/L* (a B/L which shows the goods have been loaded on board, and which is "clean" – e.g., which does not contain any markings or notations indicating damage to the goods). For the buyer, the clean on board B/L provides a valuable bundle of rights. It provides evidence that the seller has performed his contract obligations, by shipping goods that at least appear to conform to the contract of sale (otherwise, the buyer could hardly be expected to allow her bank to make payment against the B/L).

Moreover, the B/L gives the buyer important rights against the carrier of the goods:
- the right to *demand delivery* of the goods when they arrive in the port of discharge, and
- the right to *sue the carrier* for lost or damaged goods.

The B/L also allows the buyer to speculate on the market, selling the goods in transit by transferring the B/L via endorsement. Finally, the B/L allows the buyer (and the seller) to raise finance on the strength of the document's value as the key to the goods.

Because the B/L provides the above benefits to the buyer, it has corresponding benefits for the seller: the seller can get paid as soon as the goods are properly shipped, by presenting the B/L to an authorized bank. Thus, the *seller avoids the risk of non–payment*. The B/L generally benefits international trade, especially in commodities, by reducing risk and enabling markets to speculate on goods while they are in transit. Trade is also facilitated because banks are willing to extend credit on the strength of the value of the goods represented by the B/L.

ii. *Disadvantages of the negotiable marine B/L* – Despite the foregoing, there are significant disadvantages associated with the use of the traditional negotiable marine B/L. The most common of these arises when the ship arrives at the port of discharge before the B/L. Today, with the vastly increased efficiency of marine shipment, particularly in the case of container vessels, a large cargo shipment may cross the Atlantic faster than the related documents. In the oil trade in particular, it is common for the cargo to arrive before the documents. Because the negotiable B/L is a document of title, a carrier takes a grave risk in delivering to anyone other than the holder of an original B/L. If a carrier does so, it is liable to the true holder for the value of the cargo wrongly delivered. The most common solution for this problem is for the receiver of the goods to obtain a bank guarantee or letter of indemnity which protects the shipowner from liability for delivery to wrong person.

Another disadvantage of the marine B/L is that is not well suited to multimodal or combined transport, where the ocean shipment is only one leg of a chain of transport operations. Frequently, the entire operation will consist of a land leg from the seller's premises to the port of shipment, a sea leg to the port of discharge, and then another land leg to the buyer's premises. Only a multimodal transport document or B/L (discussed further on) can cover all three legs.

b. MULTIMODAL TRANSPORT B/L

The *multimodal transport B/L* has very similar characteristics to the marine B/L, except that the multimodal B/L is used for carriage whenever there are at least two different forms of transport. Although the multimodal B/L also serves as a receipt for delivery of the goods, it does not necessarily evidence that they have been shipped "on board" an ocean–going vessel. Receipt in this case may refer to receipt of a container in a container handling terminal.

c. NON–NEGOTIABLE BILLS AND WAYBILLS

A shipment sent under a *straight B/L* is consigned to a specific party, usually the importer. The consignee does not need an actual B/L to receive shipment; adequate identification will do. Unless the choice of consignee is made irrevocable, the shipper remains free to change the consignee any time before the importer pays or accepts the obligation to pay. For this reason, the straight B/L does not provide banks with the security of an order B/L for the purposes of documentary sales. Straight B/Ls may be used when the exporter is confident that the importer will pay, as in open account contexts, or when the importer has already paid, as with cash in advance sales.

Another variation on the non–negotiable B/L is the *sea waybill*. The sea waybill (which comes under a variety of different names, as for example, *data freight receipt*) serves as evidence of the contract of carriage and as a receipt for the goods, but is not a document of title. Consequently, it should not be used whenever the importer wishes to sell the goods in transit, or when the bank requires the bill to provide collateral security. The sea waybill can be advantageous in that an original is not required to take delivery. This is useful whenever it is likely that the goods will arrive in the port of destination before the relevant documents – a common occurrence in international trade, especially on short ocean routes.

For air shipments, the transport document is the *air waybill* (or "AWB"), for which the standard form is the IATA air waybill (International Air Transport Association). The air waybill is frequently issued by freight forwarders acting as agents of the air freight carrier. Generally, the seller chooses the forwarder and has it clear the goods for export. The AWBs that forwarders issue are known as "*house air waybills*" (HAWB), while the airlines themselves issue "*master air waybills*" (MAWB).

For rail shipments, the transport document is the *railway consignment note*. In Europe, this document is governed by the CIM Convention (Convention Internationale pour le transport des Marchandises par voie ferrée).

For road shipments, a *road consignment note* is used, governed in Europe by the CMR Convention (Convention internationale pour le transport des Marchandises par Route).

9.8   Sea transport

9.8.1   Overview of basic commercial practice

Worldwide, maritime transport carries over 90% of international trade. Much of international transport law and practice, even with regard to other modes of transport, is derived from long–standing practices in the carriage of goods by sea. Traders should therefore have a basic familiarity with sea transport.

A typical process begins when the shipper (in CIF contracts, for example, this means the exporter) concludes a contract with the consignee (importer). The shipper contacts a freight forwarder to arrange the transport. The forwarder will make enquiries to determine the dates and places of sailing of suitable ships. Frequently the forwarder will do this by contacting loading brokers, who are agents of shipowners, and who market the shipowners' available space.

Loading brokers handle logistics from the carrier's side. They advertise the dates of sailings, supervise loading, and consult with shipowner's cargo superintendent with regard to the stowage (packing of goods in the ship's hold). In practice, it is not uncommon for a single forwarding firm to act as both forwarding agent and loading broker, although these tasks are usually handled by separate departments.

Commonly, the forwarder will reserve space on a particular vessel, then will appropriately fill in a set of pre–printed bills of lading (a "set" comprises from two to four identical originals). Most shipowners or carriers print their own bills of lading and make these freely available. The forwarder will indicate on the draft bill of lading all necessary information, including the identity of the consignee, a description of the goods which includes shipping marks (visible identification markings on the packages), and details regarding the payment of freight.

The shipper, with the forwarder's assistance, will make sure that the goods are either delivered alongside the ship or into the care of a port terminal, storage shed or warehouse. When the goods are delivered, the shipper will customarily receive a receipt document such as *a mate's receipt, dock receipt, cargo quay receipt* or *wharfinger's note*.

The shipowner will record the details of the goods received, as well as any important defects or damages, on the mate's receipt. This is important, because the bill of lading will be based on information from the mate's receipt. If the mate's receipt indicates damaged goods, then the shipowner will not issue a "clean" bill of lading, which as we have seen is generally necessary for the shipper to obtain payment under a letter of credit.

The shipowner will compare the details of the goods as loaded (recorded by the shipowner's clerks) with the draft bills of lading that the forwarder or shipper has provided. Provided the details match and the goods do not exhibit damage or defects, the shipowner will issue the completed and signed clean bills of lading. The information from the bills of lading is also recorded on a register carried by the ship itself, called the ship's manifest.

Once the goods have been loaded, and the shipper has in addition obtained a marine insurance policy (in CIF shipments, with buyer as policy–holder) and prepared a bank draft, the shipper is able to assemble *a set of shipping documents*. This bundle of documents serves as the hub of many international payment and finance mechanisms. Control over the goods can be freely transferred by *endorsement* of the bill of lading. Endorsement is effected when the party holding the bill of lading and wishing to make the transfer signs the back of the bill of lading. The signature may also be accompanied by directions to deliver to a specific person.

When the goods arrive at the port of destination, the ship's master will deliver the goods to the first party who presents an *original* bill of lading. Commonly, the importer will present the bill of lading to the ship's agent, who will then issue a delivery order; the importer then uses the delivery order to obtain release of the goods.

It is not uncommon for the goods to arrive before the bills of lading have been processed through the payment system and received by the importer (the consignee). Since a delay in receiving the goods may result in penalties or storage charges, the consignee may ask his bank to issue a letter of indemnity ("LOI") to the shipowner, which will protect the shipowner in the event that he incurs liability for delivery to the wrong person. The shipowner will then release the goods against the letter of indemnity. In some sectors, such as the oil trade, this practice is common.

9.8.2 Sea freight

a. CONFERENCES, TRAMPS AND OUTSIDERS

Conferences are groups of shipping companies serving specific ocean routes and ports. They fix and publish common freight rates and adhere to quality standards and regular shipping schedules. Because they function much like cartels, which are prohibited by the antitrust or competition law of many countries, conferences have obtained specific exemptions from such laws.

Shipping companies that are not members of conferences are called *outsiders*. Outsiders are not obliged to adhere to conference freight rates nor observe their quality standards and shipping schedules. However, certain large outsiders are able match the quality and regularity offered by the conferences. Outsiders tend to offer lower freight rates than conference members.

Conference freight rates are normally not negotiable. However, conferences offer rebates to loyal customers, as well as discounts to freight forwarders. Rebates are calculated on either a deferred or immediate payment basis. Thus, the deferred rebate may be 10% (to be returned to the shipper if he remains loyal for a period of 6 months), or 9.5% payable immediately.

Tramps are vessels for hire. Their services are marketed through brokers, and freight is negotiated on a case–by–case basis.

b. FREIGHT CHARGES

Freight is the price the carrier charges for carrying the goods to destination. The amount of freight is most commonly calculated according to either the weight or volume (e.g., per ton or cubic metre), of the cargo, whichever is most favourable for the carrier. Commonly, the carrier will provide alternative freight rates based on a standard ratio between volume and weight. If the goods exceed the ratio of volume to weight, the freight is charged according to volume; otherwise, freight is charged according to weight. Other possibilities are for the freight to be calculated per unit or parcel, or relative to the value of the cargo.

c. SURCHARGES (BAF AND CAF)

Sea carriers commonly levy certain surcharges on the basic freight. The most common surcharges are the Bunker Adjustment Factor (BAF), which allows the carrier to adjust freight according to fuel price fluctuations, and Currency Adjustment Factor (CAF), for fluctuations in the exchange rate of the currency in which the freight is quoted. While the basic freight is usually fixed for periods up to six months or one year, the CAF and BAF are subject to overnight revisions. Consequently, exporters should consider including price adaptation clauses in their sales contracts for CAF and BAF adjustments. Other common surcharges are levied for cargo which is exceptionally long or heavy.

d. FREIGHT PREPAID AND FREIGHT COLLECT

Under CIF contracts the price includes carriage to the port of destination. The freight may either be prepaid by the seller or paid by the buyer on arrival under a "freight collect" bill of lading. Under freight collect terms the seller deducts the freight from the price on the commercial invoice.

e. CARGO HANDLING

Charges will commonly arise when goods arriving in the port area by truck or lorry are unloaded and transferred to storage sheds or brought alongside the ship. These charges are generally not included in the freight and will therefore be paid either by the exporter or importer according to the Incoterm selected (see section on Incoterms).

f. LINER TERMS

Before agreeing to a given freight rate, the shipper will want to know whether the loading and unloading of the goods is included in the freight. The answer will depend on the particular "liner term" offered by the shipping line. Again, since Incoterms such as FOB, CFR and CIF divide the costs and risks of loading at the ship's rail, it is important that the Incoterm chosen in the contract of sale accord with the liner term specified in the contract of carriage (see section on Incoterms). It is crucial that traders understand the distinction between liner terms, as part of the contract of carriage, and Incoterms, which are part of the contract of sale. Liner terms govern the contractual relations between shipper and carrier, whereas Incoterms govern the relationship between seller and buyer. A trader who has the responsibility for carriage should look first to the contract of sale to see whether the chosen Incoterm sets a clear rule with regard to loading or unloading. The trader, acting as shipper, should then make sure when procuring a contract of carriage that any liner terms in it do not conflict with the contract of sale's Incoterm.

There are many variations for quoting liner term freight rates (see § 9.8.3 as regards a new ICC attempt to introduce standard terminology). Commonly, however, particular liner terms correspond to freight which covers transport beginning and/or ending 1) on the quay, 2) under ship's tackle, and 3) on board the vessel. Each of these three variations can be found upon both loading and unloading (since these can be freely combined, there are at least nine basic variations; moreover, since port and conference customs vary widely, the practical number of variations is very high):

1) *ex quay*
   - **loading** – the carrier's responsibility extends to loading goods brought anywhere within the area alongside the ship. What exactly is meant by "alongside the ship" may vary according to port custom.
   - **unloading** – carrier's responsibility includes lowering the goods to the quay, sorting the goods into different consignments, and in some cases, storage under cover or in shed.

2) *under ship's tackle*
   - **loading** – the shipper must bring the goods directly under the crane or derrick which will hoist the goods on board; in particular, the goods must be taken out of any storage shed on the quay.
   - **unloading** – the carrier will unstow the goods and place them on the ship's deck; all other operations, including lowering the goods to the quay and sorting them, are for the shipper or consignee.

3) *on board – also called "free in", "free out", or "free in and out"*
- **loading – "free in"** – the carrier only makes the ship available; the shipper must hoist the goods on board and stow them in the ship's hold.
- **unloading – "free out"** – the carrier only brings the ship alongside the quay; the shipper or consignee pay for having the goods unstowed and lowered to the quay.
- **"free in and out"** – under this variation, the carrier will handle only the stowing and unstowing of the goods.

g. STEVEDORING

In many cases, private contractors called stevedores will take care of all cargo handling operations and will bill them, according to the particular shipment, to either the carrier, the shipper or the consignee. Stevedores will not normally split the charges between shipper and consignee. This has caused problems in the past with respect to the FOB, CFR and CIF Incoterms, which require that costs be divided at the ship's rail. This is one of the reasons that many shippers have moved away from these Incoterms to the corresponding newer Incoterms specifically developed for modern transport techniques, FCA, CPT and CIP.

9.8.3 Standard shipping terms – ICC Finland

The ICC Commission on Maritime Transport has undertaken a study to determine the feasibility of establishing standard shipping terms, which in essence would amount to a set of standard liner terms. This study is based on standard terms which are in actual practice in Finland, developed by ICC Finland. The purpose of the terms is to define the obligations of the contracting shipper and the carrier in marine transportation of break bulk goods. While it may be premature to question whether or not such terms can achieve wide or universal international usage, they are of interest for the light they shed on the basic range of shipping options.

> Note that each of these terms has both a loading and a discharging component. Thus, traders could agree on a combination of any of the two. For example, a contract could be concluded as follows: Loading – ICC Finland Gate Term; Discharge – ICC Finland Ship term.

a. GATE TERM

The term which imposes the least obligations on the contracting shipper: he merely delivers the goods on a means of transport to the unloading point.

Discharging is by delivery on the loading bay of a warehouse, or loaded on to a further means of transport (Gate term, loaded).

b. WAREHOUSE TERM

The contracting shipper delivers the goods in a warehouse in the port. At discharge, carrier delivers the goods to the consignees in a warehouse in the port of destination.

c. TACKLE TERM

The contracting shipper delivers the goods to the carrier on the quay in the port of loading. In the port of discharge, the carrier delivers the goods to the consignee on the quay, unloaded from the vessel. The tackle term is meant for use with convention handling techniques, and should not be used with Ro–Ro transport.

d. SHIP TERM (FREE IN)

The contracting shipper delivers the goods on board the vessel. At discharge, goods are delivered on board the vessel in the port of destination.

9.9 Containerized and multimodal transport

Although not all containerized transport is multimodal, and vice versa, they are so often inter–related that it is useful to consider these two concepts together. When, as is common in international trade, goods move from seller to buyer through two land legs and one sea leg, the advantages of using the container become evident. Not only is the container transferred with ease from one leg to the next, the risks of damage and theft are greatly reduced.

Containers are basically large boxes, 8 x 8 feet in cross–section, and either 10, 20 or 40 feet long. The first all–container ship came into operation in the Pacific in 1956. In 1965, the first container vessel docked in Europe. The spread of containerization throughout the world over the next decades progressed with breathtaking speed. Today, each of the world's major ports handles millions of containers per year.

Container volumes are measured in TEU's (Twenty–foot Equivalent Units). The first container ships carried 500 TEU, with the most recent generation in the 3000 – 4000 TEU range. The standardization of containers allows for great automation of loading and transhipment, so that port operations that used to take days are now completed in hours.

Shippers should always be careful to demand the *internal measurements* of the type of container they plan to use, so that the packaged or unitized goods can be prepared so as to properly fit the container.

9.9.1 Containers and Incoterms

In light of the tremendous importance of containerized shipment in international trade, ICC has seen fit to adapt its Incoterms to container traffic. Thus, it has introduced terms which are specifically appropriate to containerized and multimodal transport:

- **FCA** *(Free Carrier)*, which can be thought of as the containerized/ multimodal equivalent of FOB;
- **CPT** *(Carriage Paid To)*, which can be thought of as the containerized/ multimodal equivalent of CFR; and
- **CIP** *(Carriage and Insurance Paid to)*, which can be thought of as the containerized/multimodal equivalent of CIF.

The importance of using these newer Incoterms is linked to questions of insurance cover and division of costs. Since container shipments are frequently taken over by the carrier at the shipper's premises or at container terminals which are remote from the port of departure, it does not make sense to divide risk (and therefore, insurance coverage) at the ship's side, as is done under FOB, CFR and CIF.

If a shipper uses FOB or CIF for containerized shipments delivered to an inland transport terminal, he will have to be careful to provide for insurance cover for transport from the inland terminal to the ship's side. It may happen that the goods are damaged or lost after delivery to the inland terminal and before loading in the port of departure. In such a case, a shipper who has only insured transport up to the inland terminal could find himself without possible recourse via an insurance claim.

Moreover, with regard to costs, a shipper who hands the goods over to the carrier at the shipper's premises will prefer not to absorb the costs all the way to the ship's side, and will therefore prefer FCA to FOB.

9.9.2 Overview of basic commercial procedure

As with traditional cargo shipments, container shipments are frequently arranged by freight forwarders. There is a basic distinction between shipments that fill a full container load (*FCL*) and shipments for less than a full container load (*LCL*).

a. FULL CONTAINER LOADS

FCL – In the case of FCL shipments, an empty container is taken out of a stack in a container park and sent to the exporter's premises, where it is loaded or *"stuffed"* with the goods. After the container has been stuffed, it is closed with the carrier's seal. Theft or pilferage of the goods in transit will normally be indicated by a broken seal. Sophisticated electronic seals have become available to help protect valuable goods.

b. LESS THAN FULL CONTAINER LOADS

LCL – In the case of LCL shipments, the exporter delivers the goods to a container terminal, where the cargo is grouped together with other cargo sufficient to stuff a container. At a terminal near the destination point, the cargo is unloaded from the container and broken down into separate consignments.

c. CONTAINER FREIGHT

There are two separate cost elements – the rental of the container, and the freight. Frequently, the rental of containers provided by the carrier is included in the freight. In other cases, however, the shipper will lease the container. Shippers are advised to take care as to the time period allowed under the lease contract, because these contracts often provide for liquidated damages in the case of containers returned late.

Container freight charged by shipping lines in conferences is generally linked to the type of goods shipped, whereas outsiders tend to charge a flat rate per box.

Containers are usually delivered in the port area to a terminal which charges a fixed amount for handling the container and moving it to the ship's side. At the port of departure the terminal charges are often referred to as *container service charges*, whereas at the port of destination the charges may be called *terminal handling charges*; in practice, the terms are employed *interchangeably*.

9.10 Air transport

9.10.1 Introductory

Air transport has profoundly accelerated the pace of international business. Indeed, international trade in certain kinds of merchandise would not exist were it not for the rapidity of air transport. Highly time–sensitive goods, such as newspapers and magazines, or highly perishable goods, such as fresh flowers or seafood, would not be available at all in many markets if it were not for air transport. The speed of air transport also reduces exposure to risk so substantially that goods of great value, such as jewellery, pharmaceuticals and medical supplies, prize livestock, art works or manuscripts, will usually move by air. Thus, air freight has been said to account for only 1% by weight, but 10% by value, of all goods transported. However, even with regard to products for which distribution is not so time–sensitive, air transport is deceptively competitive.

Although air freight rates are much higher than ocean rates, air shipments can provide savings with respect to other crucial costs:

1) *Insurance* – premiums are generally less than half those for sea transport (e.g., 0.3% of cargo value as opposed to 0.7%);

2) *Customs duties* – may be charged on gross weight, which is generally lower for air shipments (less packaging) than for sea shipments;

3) *Packaging* – much lighter and cheaper for air transport;

4) *Inventory costs* – in many cases air transport can greatly reduce and even eliminate the need for warehousing which would be necessary with sea transport; since warehousing costs include not only the leasing of warehouse space at either end of transit, but also related tax and insurance costs, as well as the cost of goods which become obsolescent while stored in the warehouse, this cost factor can be decisive in favour of air transport;

5) *Financing costs* – for shipments in which the buyer's payment obligation is triggered by delivery to the buyer's premises, the seller will receive payment much sooner with air transport.

Even in those cases where the cost of sea transport is lower, the seller may prefer to use air transport for competitive reasons. Thus, an export seller of spare parts may find that he cannot compete against domestic sellers unless he matches their delivery speeds, which can only be done with air transport.

9.10.2 Overview of air transport procedures

Air freight is either shipped:
- along with luggage in passenger planes,
- in hybrid aircraft with special compartments for cargo, known as combis, or
- in cargo aircraft.

Specialized cargo craft, such as the Boeing 747F freighter, can now carry payloads in excess of 100,000 kg, but combis and passenger planes remain more profitable for airlines than cargo freighters. Thus, shippers have in the past complained that airlines did not pay enough attention to the cargo business. However, with some airlines today generating close to half of their revenues from cargo, shippers can now expect a competitive air freight market.

a. AIR TRANSPORT AND INCOTERMS

In the past, many shippers quoted "FOB Airport" prices for air shipments. This caused many misunderstandings with respect to airport handling charges and extent of insurance coverage. The FOB (free on board) term was developed in maritime trade, where the ship's rail was the traditional point for the division of costs and risks. Obviously, an airplane does not have a "ship's rail" and goods are not delivered "alongside the plane". Thus, the application of FOB principles derived from sea transport was not appropriate. Consequently, ICC discontinued the FOB Airport term in its most recent revisions of Incoterms. ICC recommends that shippers use the FCA Incoterm instead, with the specified point of delivery being the named air freight or consolidator's terminal.

b. FREIGHT FORWARDERS/CONSOLIDATORS

Air transport gave many freight forwarders an entire new line of business. Air carriers, through the International Air Transport Association (IATA), oversee a worldwide cargo agents' organization, to which many forwarders adhere. Appointment as an IATA air cargo agent allows a forwarder to market air cargo services knowing that IATA airlines will carry the goods for a fixed price and with a commission for the forwarder. IATA agents must demonstrate certain financial and cargo–handling resources, and must agree to remit to the air carrier freight billings according to fixed schedules.

Air carriers may provide forwarders with air waybills (AWBs) featuring the airline's logo. As with other non–negotiable transport documents, the AWB is both a receipt for the goods and a contract of carriage. In some countries the AWB system is computerized and the air carriers only issue AWB numbers to the forwarders, leaving the forwarder to print out the AWB number and airline logo on a forms known as the Neutral AWB.

Forwarders acting as consolidators may issue AWBs in their own name as carriers, in which case their role can be likened to that of NVOCCs (Non–Vessel Operating Common Carriers) in sea transport. By consolidating –

grouping – several consignments together, forwarders are able to obtain the lower freight rates offered by carriers for large shipments. In this, the air consolidators perform a groupage function like that of container shipping terminals. Consolidators may provide highly efficient warehouse services upon departure, and upon arrival may handle the notification of the consignee by telephone. In addition, consolidators often offer a door–to–door service, which includes customs clearance and insurance coverage.

c. CARGO HANDLING

Air cargo containers corresponding to the shape of the plane's cabin are known as *unit load devices* (ULDs). There are various shapes and sizes of ULDs (some are called "*igloos*"), each designed to be stored in a different part of the airplane. Cargo is handled primarily by pushing or pulling of pallets and ULDs, which move over systems of rollers. Since ULDs are usually stuffed in terminals at or near the airport, it is possible for cargo delivered to an air terminal to be shipped on a departing flight within two hours. The actual loading or unloading of cargo can take less than one hour.

d. GUARANTEED SHIPMENT TIME

Some airlines offer guaranteed shipment times or dates, which eliminates the risk to the shipper that his cargo will be delayed as a result of being forced off a particular flight to make room for special high–priority items. Although the extent of the guarantee values from airline to airline, it is generally useful for the shipper to request one, in particular because some airlines make such guarantees at no extra charge.

e. HAZARDOUS GOODS

Since shipments of hazardous goods can in some cases jeopardize the safety of the entire aircraft, regulations on restricted articles are strictly enforced. IATA publishes an annual update of such regulations. In many cases, cargo is allowed provided that it is appropriately packaged and "hazard" labels are affixed. Both shippers and forwarders must be quite careful in assuring that all declarations relating to potentially hazardous cargo are complete and correct; failure to do so can result in the application of heavy penalties.

f. AIR FREIGHT

Under IATA schedules, freight rates decrease according to the weight bracket of the shipment. The basic weight brackets are: 0 – 45 kg, 45 – 100 kg, 100 – 300 kg, 300 – 500 kg, 500 kg – 1 ton, and above 1 ton. The benefits of *consolidation* are apparent. Rather than send five 25 kg shipments on 5 separate flights over a period of days, it will be much cheaper to group the five shipments into one 100 kg consignment. Preferential rates (sometimes called "corates") are available for certain commodities shipped in bulk.

As with sea freight, rates are also subject to a volume–weight ratio. Extremely light, low–density products will therefore pay freight based on a "theoretical weight" which is calculated as a fraction of their volume.

Cargo handling charges in airports can be relatively expensive. Shippers are therefore advised to have these specified in advance.

9.11 Road and rail transport

9.11.1 Road haulage

The total number of vehicles engaged in road haulage worldwide, more than *80 million*, dwarfs the number for any other transport method. The great advantage of international road haulage is that it offers the possibility of true door–to–door service with no transhipment whatsoever. Moreover, loading at point of departure and unloading at destination require relatively little in the way of specialized equipment – a loading platform and a steel sheet "bridge" are often all that is needed. Articulated vehicles (a lorry or truck which pulls a container–trailer) are particularly well–suited to *roll–on roll–off* (Ro–Ro) ships, which allow for safe and simple transfer from land to sea and back again to land. In addition to this great flexibility, road vehicles can carry as much as 45 tons, although national regulations may set a maximum limit.

As with sea and air transport, specialized forwarders offer consolidation services for road transport. Their services can involve grouping small consignments, warehousing, and integrating several modes of shipment so as to offer a door–to–door price. Sophisticated integrators today offer many computerized services, including monitoring of the progress of the shipment from departure to destination. In addition, many of these integrators offer express services featuring guaranteed delivery dates.

a. ROAD HAULAGE RATES

Rates vary widely from country to country. One reason for this is that labour rates for drivers will correspond to the prevailing wages in the particular country. As with sea and air transport, road freight is generally calculated by weight but subject to a volume–weight ratio. For road transport this ratio falls between the ratios for sea (1.33 to 1) and air transport (6 to 1), and is generally in the area of 3. Thus, if the volume in cubic metres is more than three times the weight in kg, freight will be set according to a "theoretical weight" in kg calculated by dividing the total volume in cubic metres by three.

b. TIR CARNET SYSTEM

International customs carnet for road haulage – The TIR (Transport International Routier) Carnet is very similar in function to the ATA Carnet discussed earlier, except that the TIR Carnet was created to allow trucks or lorries carrying international cargos to pass through intervening countries (provided they are signatories to the TIR Convention) without having to go through customs control procedures.

9.11.2 Rail transport

Just as road and air transport have boomed for half a century, rail transport has declined. As compared with road transport, rail transport is much less flexible in terms of the total number of shippers and consignees that can be directly reached, and loading is generally not so easy. Since different countries may use different rail widths or gauges, as well as different tunnel clearances, international consignments can be complicated and require transhipment.

However, for certain classes of shippers or cargo, rail remains the indicated transport choice. Railway wagons can carry cargo of tremendous weight. Certain special flat–bed rail trucks can carry up to 500 tons. Rail is thus often the preferred choice for bulk transport of industrial ore and liquids. Moreover, when both shipper and consignee have private rail sidings (direct connections from warehouses to rail lines) rail shipments can provide the most straight–forward door–to–door service. Additional flexibility has resulted from the development of road–rail schemes, under which, for example, a road trailer arriving from a roll–on roll–off ship is placed on a rail wagon and transported to destination by rail.

Railway freight – In contrast to other modes of transport, freight is generally not subject to a volume–weight ratio. Railways generally offer two sets of rates for full wagons, one for express service and one for slow goods service. In terms of price per unit of weight, railway freight is quite competitive.

9.12 Cargo insurance

International trade shipments are almost without exception insured against damage or loss in transit by some form of cargo insurance. Depending on the Incoterm chosen and any express insurance provisions in the contract of sale, either the exporter or importer may have the primary responsibility to insure. In some cases, both parties will have the cargo insured to varying extents. The variety and complexity of possible permutations is such that no exporter or importer should do without the counsel of an insurance agent or broker.

Many small traders have insurance cover arranged by their freight forwarder. Alternatively, the trader may have a long–term "open" or "floating" cover with the insurance company, which will cover a number of shipments over a given period of time. In other cases, the trader will directly insure a particular shipment via a marine, aviation, or overland insurance policy. Despite their names, such insurance policies are generally not limited to insurance for only the marine, air, or land legs of transit, but can each be extended to cover the goods "warehouse to warehouse".

a. DUTY TO INSURE VS. COMMERCIAL NEED TO INSURE

An initial distinction must be made between the contractual duty to insure and the commercial need to insure. Thus, under CIF and CIP Incoterms, the exporter has a contractual duty to the importer to provide a minimum level of insurance to cover the goods during international transit. Under all other Incoterms, there is no contractual duty for either side to provide insurance (although the parties may freely stipulate any additional insurance require-ments in the sale contract).

However, the absence of a contractual duty to insure does not remove the obvious practical need to obtain insurance in most cases. The parties will normally obtain insurance coverage to protect themselves as a matter of ordinary commercial prudence. At a minimum, the parties will wish to be insured during that part of transit in which they are at risk. Each Incoterm fixes a point for the transfer of risk from seller to buyer; before that point, the seller is at risk and will wish to be insured; after that point, the buyer is at risk and will wish to be insured.

b. SPLITTING OF INSURANCE COVER ACCORDING TO DIVISION OF RISK

It might therefore seem reasonable that parties would only wish to pay for insurance coverage for that part of the transit in which they were at risk. Thus, if we take the example of an FOB shipment, transfer of risk is at the ship's side. Since the seller is at risk up to that point, he might reasonably wish the cargo to be insured by himself up to the ship's rail, and no further. He has no contractual duty at all to insure the goods up to the ship's side, but he will normally do so out of self–interest. Likewise, the buyer might desire that his insurance coverage should begin at the ship's rail, and no earlier.

However, since insurance coverage is most often warehouse–to–warehouse, it is not a common practice to split insurance coverage at the transfer of risk point. Splitting insurance coverage, each side seeking only to insure its own interest for its leg of the transport, has several disadvantages. First of all, there is the risk that the two insurance covers will not match up exactly, leaving a gap – a portion of the transport chain where there is no insurance cover. Second, if loss or damage is only discovered upon arrival, it may be difficult to prove where the loss or damage occurred (and therefore, under which policy), with the result that both insurers may be able to avoid payment. Finally, two separate partial insurance covers are generally more expensive than a single warehouse–to–warehouse cover for the entire transit.

Example

Consider an FOB or CFR seller on open account terms, who will only be paid after the goods are received by the buyer. Such a seller would be unwise to only insure the transit leg prior to the transfer of risk point (the ship's rail). If the goods are lost or damaged after the transfer point, the buyer may refuse to effect payment, leaving the seller without coverage. The seller would have to file a lawsuit rather than a somewhat simpler insurance claim.

It would therefore seem preferable that one of the parties obtain continuous coverage for the entire transit, warehouse–to–warehouse, from a single insurer. However, this is not always possible. Many countries require by law that their importers and exporters insure transport risks with domestic insurers. Also, many traders already have long–term marine cargo insurance under a floating policy or open cover (discussed further on). Moreover, some traders may be reckless enough to wish to do without insurance cover for their leg of transport.

Even in those cases where the other party has taken out a warehouse to warehouse policy, the coverage may be for an insufficient amount, or may exclude certain likely risks. The trading partner in such a case may wish to take out supplementary *"difference in conditions"* or *"contingency"* insurance.

As can be seen from the foregoing, traders should consider carefully how much insurance coverage they need, and for what portion of the transit they need coverage. They should consider whether insurance coverage provided under minimum standard terms such as the Institute Cargo Clauses is sufficient for their purposes, and if not, they should consider amplifying or increasing the coverage. If the other party has procured insurance, they should also consider whether it is sufficient, or whether it should be complemented with contingency insurance.

They should review with their insurance agent or broker, as well as their trading partners, the various options for obtaining such coverage. Finally, they should stipulate precisely in the contract of sale the desired level of coverage and who must pay for it.

c. INSURABLE INTEREST

Regardless of who takes out the insurance policy, a party can only recover under a claim on that policy if he has an "insurable interest" in the goods at the time they were damaged or lost. Roughly, this means that a party must have ownership or some other interest (including risk) in the goods in order to claim under the policy. Generally speaking, the seller will have an insurable interest in the goods up to the transfer of risk point, and the buyer will have an insurable interest thereafter. However, there are exceptions to this rule, and in some cases one of the parties will assign his rights under the policy to the other party.

d. "OPEN" COVER OR "FLOATING" POLICIES

"Open" cover and *"floating"* policies are intended to cover multiple shipments over a period of time, and therefore only state the general conditions of the insurance contract. In each case, the insured party notifies the insurer of the specific voyages to be covered under the policy. Open cover may also be taken out by forwarders or carriers, who then use it to cover specific consignments for their clients.

Under a *floating policy*, the value of the risk insured on each voyage is deducted from the total value of the insurance contracted. Under an open policy, the insurance limit is automatically renewed after each voyage.

In some cases, such as those involving payment under a letter of credit, the shipper will need to have an insurance document included in the set of shipping documents. Under an open policy, this is accomplished by the use of "insurance certificates", which are issued by the insurers at the instruction of the insured party. Traders should take care, because a letter of credit that explicitly requires submission of an insurance policy will not allow an insurance certificate as a substitute.

e. COST OF INSURANCE

Insurance premiums vary widely according to the mode of transport and the nature of the goods. Premiums for air shipment are generally the lowest, in the area of 0.3% of the value of the goods, while the highest are for long road or rail transport legs (especially in developing countries), which in exceptional cases may be up to 2%. Sea transport premiums are commonly in the range of 0.6% – 0.7%.

f. INCOTERMS AND INSURANCE

Only two Incoterms, CIF and CIP, specifically require insurance. Under these terms, the seller must take out an insurance policy for the buyer. The minimum amount of coverage is set at 110% of the value of the goods, and the conditions of the coverage are specifically those set out in the Institute of London Underwriters Cargo Clauses. The Institute of London Underwriters is a professional association of insurance companies; there are three standard clauses, known respectively as Institute Cargo Clauses A, B and C. These clauses define the risks covered by the insurance policy, and were intended to replace and improve the previously common clauses known as "all risks", "with average" (WA), and "free of particular average" (FPA).

Institute Cargo Clause A provides the broadest coverage and is therefore sometimes considered to provide "all risks" cover. However, such terminology is deceptive, because several important risks are not covered by Clause A, notably the risks of strikes or war, as well as damage resulting from insufficient packing, delay, ordinary wear and tear of transport, or the insolvency of the carrier, amongst others.

Clauses B and C are even more restrictive, covering only risks which are specifically referred to.

Under Incoterms, the seller may choose Clause C, which provides the least coverage. Importers should therefore be forewarned that in cases where such minimum coverage is insufficient, they will need to specify in the contract the level of additional insurance they require. For example, if the importer expects to earn a high profit margin on the goods, coverage of 110% of the value of the goods may be insufficient; 120% or 130% may be advisable (although this will obviously raise the cost of the premium).

One solution is to provide a specific clause in the contract of sale setting out the scope, time and extent of insurance coverage, and particularly whether coverage will extend to risks of strikes, riots and civil commotion (called "SRCC" coverage; an example of such a clause is set out in the Chapter 4 on Incoterms).

9.13 Customs

Case Example – Non–human, all–too non–human?

The European Union imposed a quota on the importation of "non–human" dolls from China. This left EU customs officials with the sometimes difficult task of determining what exactly constituted a non–human doll. Thus, in 1994, imports of dolls resembling Captain Kirk, a character in the popular Star Trek television and cinema series, were allowed into the UK under the quota, but similar courtesy was not extended to dolls based on Captain Kirk's on–screen partner, Mr Spock. UK customs officials apparently reached their conclusion on the observation that the Mr Spock dolls featured "pointy ears". The case attracted media attention and the ire of fans of the Star Trek series (known as "trekkies"), who protested that according to Star Trek lore, Mr Spock was actually half–human (although admittedly half–"Vulcan" on his father's side; hence the ears).

Comment: In large transactions involving goods with novel characteristics, prudent traders are advised to seek an advance ruling from the relevant customs authorities.

International trade transactions always involve at least two customs clearances, one upon export and one upon import. Upon export, an export license may or may not be required. Export licenses are most commonly required in the case of sales of politically or strategically sensitive goods, such as exports of arms or weaponry, chemicals or high–technology goods.

Upon import, duties and taxes will be payable. The choice of Incoterm will determine who, as between exporter and importer, has the responsibility of export or import clearance. The clearance responsibility has 3 components:

- the responsibility to obtain necessary *licenses* and fill out *forms and declarations*;
- the responsibility to pay official *duties* and *taxes*; and
- assumption of the *risk* that customs clearance may be physically or legally impossible.

The World Customs Organization (WCO), an intergovernmental organization based in Brussels, promotes the standardization of customs procedures; it has 158 member countries. ICC has issued a set of International Customs Guidelines for efficient customs services, which are intended to help customs authorities set clear goals and benchmarks for improving customs control and trade facilitation.

Traders generally rely on *customs brokers* (also known as "customs house brokers" or "CHB's") to clear goods through customs. Brokers act as the agents of the exporter or importer in their dealings with customs authorities. It is therefore important that traders carefully instruct their brokers as to the nature of the goods and the taxes and duties they expect – and are willing – to pay. Traders may explicitly require that the broker contact them for assistance in the event of difficulties arising during clearance, because the trader will frequently be better placed to answer questions or resolve disputes concerning the technical, quality or price details of the cargo.

a. AMOUNT OF DUTY

Valuation, origin and customs classification – The amount of duty varies widely, depending on the value of the goods, tariff schedules of the importing country, customs classification of the goods and in some cases, the origin of the goods. Customs officers will strictly verify the declared value of the goods, since duty is often calculated as an ad valorem percentage. Customs valuation is covered by an international treaty, the *GATT Customs Valuation Code(1)*, which sets forth the basic rule that the customs value of the goods is the value agreed between exporter and importer in the invoice. Clearly, the invoice value will in turn depend on the amount of transport services included in the price under the chosen Incoterm; for the same goods, a CIF value will always be higher than an FOB value. In some countries duties are calculated on an FOB basis, in other countries on a CIF basis. This may generate confusion when customs officers refuse to accept values based on invoice prices calculated under other Incoterms. The easiest solution is to convert the invoice value to a customs value for the purposes of the customs declaration.

In some cases customs officers will consider that the invoice value is suspect. This may be because the transaction contains some element of fraud (as in an attempt to circumvent foreign exchange control by paying inflated prices to a co–conspiring exporter), or because the exporter is "dumping" goods into the import market at prices below the production cost in order to capture market share. In these cases, the invoice value may have to be adjusted upward to arrive at a value acceptable to the customs officials. If traders have any reason to anticipate problems in this area, they should consult with customs in advance.

In most countries, goods are classified into various categories under the *Harmonized Commodity Description and Coding System* (Harmonised System) promulgated by the World Customs Organization. Under the Harmonised System, goods are classified into more than 5000 separate categories, each of which is identified by a specific code. It is not unusual for a particular piece of merchandise to fall between two official customs designations. Understandably, the traders will wish to have applied whichever designation is assigned the lower duty. In the event of disputes, the trader will commonly have the right to appeal the customs ruling to a specialized legal tribunal.

b. COUNTRY OF ORIGIN

Generalized System of Preferences – The amount of the duty assessed will often depend on the country of origin. Thus, certain European or Mediterranean countries have customs agreements with the European Union such that imports and exports are imposed duty at preferential rates. More importantly, under the United Nations' *Generalized System of Preferences* (GSP), many developed countries have granted preferential or free entry to imports from developing countries.[2]

This leads to the important question of the *origin* of export goods. Generally, this origin is determined and documented by a *certificate of origin* which is procured from, and stamped by, a chamber of commerce or other official export agency. Origin is a simple matter in the case of agricultural products or raw commodities, or even in the case of manufactured products when their components come from the same country.

The question becomes more complex in the case of manufactured products, the components of which may not come from countries accorded preferential status. The two criteria for deciding whether a particular product meets the origin requirement for preferential status are a process criterion and a percentage criterion. Under the process criterion, the finished product will generally be accepted for preferential rates if it falls into a different product category than the components. Under the percentage criterion, a minimum of from 35% to 50% (depending on the importing country) of the content of the final product must come from the country accorded preferential status.

c. BONDED WAREHOUSES

A bonded warehouse is authorized to store imported goods without payment of duties for a given period of time. The proprietor of the warehouse must provide a bond to the customs authorities in order to cover any potential liability for duties. The utility of these warehouses is that the importer can inspect the goods, or have her customers inspect them, before paying the duty. In the event that the goods are unsatisfactory, the importer can either reject them, or if she has already purchased them, seek to have them sold or re–exported to a third party. Another advantage is that for goods assessed as having high duties (e.g., tobacco and alcohol products), payment of the duty can be delayed, thereby enabling the importer to save the interest value on the amount of the duty throughout the period of storage.

Notes

(1) For full list of signatory countries, contact the World Customs Organization in Brussels.

(2) For a full list of currently participating countries, contact the UNCTAD Secretariat in Geneva.

CHAPTER TEN

International Electronic Commerce

The basics: The Internet has transformed the practice of international trade. This transformation is likely to continue for decades as international electronic commerce evolves and becomes further integrated into legal and business frameworks. In regards to international business correspondence and communication, email provides significant advantages over telephone, fax and postal communication. In international marketing, the use of websites has allowed even small firms to reach global audiences. In international market research, the Internet has allowed traders to easily tap into large electronic databases of demographic and trade data. In large markets for corporate and government procurement, Internet B2B (business–to–business) platforms have provided the equivalent of international electronic clearinghouses or auction markets. International shipping companies now routinely provide electronic tracking of shipments for the convenience of exporters and importers. Customs authorities allow exporters and importers to submit customs documents electronically. Banks allow traders to provide payment and related documents electronically. New products and services are becoming rapidly available, although it is difficult to judge which types of electronic trading initiatives will last. Use of the Internet for business requires attention to issues such as protection of data and controlling access to computers and networks. Increased access to world markets comes with a heightened risk of fraud and a need for understanding the sensitivities of different cultures. Finally, issues of global equity and access to technology have come to the forefront. International organizations and governments must consider ways to bring economically disadvantaged areas into the Internet trading space so as to avoid a global "digital divide".

10.1 Basics of Internet use

a. GETTING CONNECTED

Virtually all large business firms are already connected to the Internet and provide some form of Internet access for their executives. Small business firms should take care to carefully analyze the options before they obtain an Internet connection or set up their first website. In many countries, small businesses and consumers can buy premium services that use connections other than the ordinary phone system, such as television cables, which allow for quicker Internet access. It is often worth the extra expense to arrange for the fastest Internet connection available as web–based research can be frustrating if the Internet connection is too slow. Companies that plan on sending photographs, designs, videos or sound–recordings over the Internet, in particular, require very fast connections.

When selecting an email service, there are a couple of service options that should be considered. The first, called "web mail", has the advantage of being accessible from any computer connected to the Internet by using a password which allows you to send and receive mails and gives you access to your personal mailbox. The disadvantage of some web mail systems is that there is a limit on how much email you can store at any given time. Sometimes, old email is automatically purged from your file, resulting in the loss of important correspondence. Another alternative, email client software, enables you to store sent and received mail on your computer so that you can access old correspondence at any time. However, some email client systems do not allow you to access your email from any computer on the Internet, requiring to use your personal workstation at your office. Fortunately, there are systems available which offer the universal access of web mail along with the storage capacity of email client software systems.

b. WHY IS EMAIL USEFUL FOR INTERNATIONAL TRADE?

Occasionally one still hears of executives who refuse to use email, but such reticence is rapidly disappearing. Email offers particular advantages in the international trade sphere. As compared to telephone communication, email does not face the problem of trying to bridge the schedules of people in different time zones: you send an email message to your contact while he or she sleeps and when you arrive at the office the next morning, the reply is there. As opposed to telephone communications, emails preserve a written record of proposals and negotiations, which can eliminate misunderstandings and can help resolve disputes. Email surpasses the fax in many respects: emails can easily incorporate colour photographs and sound recordings, can be easily sent to numerous correspondents, and can be written and read without the need to print the message out on paper.

Email can also be a very powerful marketing tool. Email client software enables you to build "address books" in which you can store the email addresses of customers and others who you wish to approach with information about your company. But beware, not everyone appreciates receiving unsolicited email and a careless email campaign can also do a lot of damage to your company. In addition, there are laws ("data protection laws") in most countries that make it illegal to gather information without an individual's prior consent and/or to send people unsolicited commercial emails (so–called "spamming"). More will be said about these legal and ethical issues later in this chapter.

10.2 Using the Web for international trade

a. AS A SUPER–LIBRARY AND MARKET RESEARCH TOOL

The World Wide Web is a huge global library on which one can find information regarding practically any topic. Executives preparing for international business travel, for example, can easily find information on exchange rates, climate, culture, etc., and has access to the websites of airlines, hotels or travel agents.

Finding international business information on the web is not difficult, though it may require time and persistence. Popular search engines include Google, Yahoo, AskJeeves, AOL and AltaVista, as well as the so–called "meta–search engines", MetaCrawler, DogPile, CNET, SavySearch, Mama, ProFusion, Search.com, TheBigHub and IxQuick.

As a brief sample of the sources of trade–related data available on the Internet, consider the following:

- *www.doingbusinessin.com* – Ernst & Young's Doing Business Around the World series provides country profiles on the investment climate, business forms and accounting practices in 40+ countries.
- *www.webofculture.com* – This website provides data on cultural dimensions for a number of countries.
- *www.Ciber.bus.msu.edu/busres.html* and *www.lib.berkeley.edu/busi/bbg18.html* – These are two university–based websites (University of Michigan and University of California at Berkeley) that provide a wide range of information for international business.

- *www.oecd.org* – The Organization for Economic Cooperation and Development provides data on economic policies for its approximately 30 member countries.
- *www.odci.gov/cia/publications/pubs.html* – The location of the CIA World Factbook, which provides basic introductory statistics on all major countries.
- *www.jetro.go.jp* – An excellent source of data on the Japanese market, provided by the Japan External Trade Organization.
- *www.euromonitor.com* – The website of a company which provides reports on international trade and marketing.
- *www.stat–usa.gov* – A very large database of international trade information provided by the US Department of Commerce available for a small subscription fee.
- *www.usatradeonline.gov* – Another source of US–based information on export and import statistics.
- *www.Iserve.wtca.org* – A website providing information about the services available through the World Trade Centers network.
- *www.iccwbo.org* – The official ICC website, providing the key source of information on Incoterms, the *Uniform Customs and Practice for Documentary Credits* (UCP 500), international dispute resolution and numerous other trade–related products and services.

b. LAUNCHING A WEBSITE: A KEY MARKETING CHANNEL

Most exporters or importers of any size will want to set up their own website. However, firms should devote serious preparation and research to this effort. It is surprising how many firms have set up unattractive, poorly designed, inefficient websites. A firm's website is, in effect, the public face it presents to the world; a bad website projects an unprofessional image. One initial consideration is whether the firm should rely on outside service providers or designate its own "web–master" (an employee in charge of the design and management of the website).

With a little effort, anyone can create a simple website using software such as Microsoft's Frontpage or Macromedia's Dreamweaver, but the design of an attractive, professional–looking site requires the services of a professional. Web design professionals can help you structure your website in a way that best suits your business needs. However, some web–designers specialize in the aesthetic or graphic design elements of websites and are not able to develop the complex databases that some firms will require. It is important to spend some time thinking about the potential growth and evolution of your firm's site: Will your site require frequent, or even daily, updating? Will your information be provided in several languages? Will you ask visitors to fill out a form in order to obtain access to parts of your site? Will some parts of your site be password–protected so that only employees and business partners may have access?

Depending on the type of business a firm does, it is also possible to structure the site as a direct sales channel. This will generally require a greater level of investment and most firms will need to hire experts to permanently maintain the site. There are many software products and services that enable one to set up a true e–commerce site with transactional functionality. However, one should not be too quick to assume that an e–commerce package which is suitable for domestic trade will also be suitable for international trade. As we have discussed in other chapters, international trade is more complex than domestic trade. For example, many countries place precise legal restrictions on the direct selling of consumer goods. If your firm receives an order from a particular country, you must be sure that you will not be in violation of that country's consumer protection regulations or laws if you provide your products directly to those consumers. For this reason, it may be necessary to restrict e–commerce sales to the domestic market, or to a limited range of foreign markets.

c. THE INTERNET AND INTERNATIONAL TRADE TRANSACTIONS

It is already possible to use Internet–based products and services directly in the negotiation and management of international trade transactions. These services are likely to increase dramatically in coming years. The following are just a few examples of electronic trade tools which are available today:

- *Paction*™ – A web–based application launched by ICC in 2002 to help traders negotiate international sales contracts. Paction™ enables buyers and sellers to negotiate and complete contracts for the international sale and purchase of goods, keeping track of every stage of the negotiation via the Internet and, once both parties are satisfied, sealing the deal by digital signature. The application can be found at *www.modelcontracts.com.*

- *eUCP* – ICC has developed a supplement to the UCP 500 for the electronic presentation of documents in letter of credit transactions, termed "eUCP" for short. Consisting of 12 Articles, the eUCP is a supplement to, and not a replacement of, UCP 500, intended to be used in tandem with UCP 500 where part–electronic or all–electronic presentations are made.

- *TradeCard (www.tradecard.com)* – TradeCard is a business–to–business service for international payments. It is intended to provide an electronic alternative for other international payment devices.

- *Bolero (www.bolero.net)* – Bolero provides an open Internet platform for processing trade–related documents. Bolero claims that some of its customers have estimated that with Bolero the time for processing documents related to a trade transaction can be cut from 25 days to less than 24 hours.

10.3 Security and trust concerns and solutions

The Internet is an ingenious technological solution for many day–to–day problems, but it also has downsides. Since the Internet is an unprotected system running over open networks, anyone can, with limited technical abilities, intercept and read information being sent over the Internet. Unless the information itself is protected, one should consider it to be about as secure as a postcard. Email, for instance, can therefore be used for many ordinary communications, but the moment matters of a sensitive commercial nature are communicated there is a risk that confidentiality cannot be maintained. Certain precautions are therefore necessary to manage the risk inherent in using the Internet for serious business purposes.

a. CONFIDENTIALITY

One concern is confidentiality: you want your email and other Internet communications to remain private between yourself and the person you are communicating with. A technology known as cryptography is used in various products and services that allow you to "encrypt" such communications. If someone intercepted an encrypted email from you, that person would see only a meaningless, garbled message. With proper encryption, only the intended recipient can read your communications.

There are many types of encryption software and services on the market, but for basic encryption one can also simply download "freeware" encryption software from sites such as Pretty Good Privacy (PGP). PGP was the first encryption program made freely available over the Internet and its inventors were prosecuted in the USA for doing so. Since the mid–1990s, governments have slowly started to relax restrictive encryption laws and strong encryption software is now currently commercially available for all users. In today's terms, "strong" encryption means a data scrambling strength that even the most powerful computers cannot break within a reasonable time.

The most widely used encryption method is called SSL (secure socket layer), which is briefly explained in the next section.

b. AUTHENTICATION AND DIGITAL SIGNATURES: THE ROLE OF PUBLIC KEY INFRASTRUCTURE (PKI)

Cryptography has another very important application. The Internet presents another problem because there is no globally accepted mechanism for identifying users. There is no control over names used in email addresses, nor is there reliable validation of the identity of companies using certain URLs (Uniform Resource Locators – in effect, Internet addresses). Although email addresses received from friends and business contacts are often provided through business cards, conversations or other circumstances that enable you to trust that you are dealing with the right person, as Internet use becomes more sophisticated and widespread there are and will be many opportunities for fraud. Without proper mechanisms for identifying counterparties, international traders may fall victim to unscrupulous Internet experts impersonating trusted parties in order to steal sensitive business information, credit card numbers and other private information. These problems are known as "trust" problems, and they are amongst the greatest impediments to use of the Internet as a medium for international commercial transactions.

Many of these trust problems can be solved using a form of cryptography known as "public key cryptography" in a technique called "public key infrastructure", or PKI. PKI relies on small packages of software called "public key certificates" or "digital certificates" which identify a person and/or company in a secure manner. Through automated and/or human certificate verification processes, one can fairly easily establish someone's identity. Digital certificates are issued by so–called "certification authorities", or "CAs", which provide a level of assurance by communicating through the certificate what procedures were used to identify the holder of a certificate. Most CAs will also accept a level of liability if the identification turns out to have been erroneous.

One very important use of digital certificates is the *digital signature*. The reason these certificates are also called "public key certificates" is that they are securely tied to a cryptographic "key" known as the "public key" which plays an important role in the process of verifying the "signature" of an email or other digitized data. If an email is "signed" with a user's "private key", the recipient can use the public key to establish not only the sender's identity, but also the fact that the mail or data have not been changed since they were signed by the sender. This provides a level of authentication in electronic communications that is many times more reliable than techniques used in paper–based trading methods.

The benefits of commercial use of digital signatures are not yet fully appreciated and this sector will likely continue to change and evolve in the coming years. However, certain other applications of PKI, such as "server certificates", are already very advanced and widely used. A server certificate identifies not a person, but a server (which is a special type of computer that interfaces with the Internet) on which websites and Internet applications are run. For instance, if you put up a website and wish to demonstrate your trustworthiness to visitors, a server certificate will do this for you. In addition, a server certificate enables you to establish a secure SSL connection with the computers of visitors so that personal data or credit card information can be securely communicated. This is the most successful application of digital certificates today.

c. IS AN ELECTRONIC AGREEMENT LEGALLY BINDING?

The enforceability of electronic agreements was one of the most difficult issues discussed in the legal community when Internet technologies became widely available in the early 1990s. Many national commercial laws are based on the use of concepts and terms such as "writing", "document" and "signature", which are notions derived from the long history of paper–based commerce. The United Nations therefore created a legal instrument in 1996 known as the "Model Law on Electronic Commerce", which countries can use to ensure that their laws are Internet–friendly. Many countries have implemented this model law and today the acceptability of electronic agreements is no longer an important issue. Nonetheless, there are still countries in which such agreements can cause legal problems – for a list of countries that have implemented the Model Law and to consult its text, see www.uncitral.org.

The UN has also adopted a model law on electronic signatures (including digital signatures), which provides further guidance on issues concerning authentication. Whereas the Model Law on Electronic Commerce sets forth a broad non–discrimination rule, it does not address the enforceability of electronic agreements with any detail. Such enforceability depends in turn on the enforceability of electronic signatures. Since the term "electronic signature" covers everything from a name under a simple email to a highly secure PKI–based digital signature, more rules were needed about what kind of signatures are valid in which circumstances. Prior to adoption of the UN Model Law on this subject, however, many countries (including the EU and its 15 member states) had already introduced country–specific electronic signature legislation. The result is that there will not be the same level of legal harmonization in the field of electronic signatures as there is concerning the more general legal issues addressed in the Model Law on Electronic Commerce. The result is that business cannot rely on a high degree of legal predictability on this issue. Unfortunately, therefore, traders still have to pay attention to legal issues if they wish to use electronic signatures across borders.

d. TRUSTMARKS AND SEAL PROGRAMMES

There are many different types of services available for businesses to communicate a variety of trust values to website visitors. Most of these methods can be viewed as the equivalent of certification programmes such as those based on International Organization for Standardization (ISO) standards, where a certificate, seal or "trustmark" shown on the website indicates that the company behind it has demonstrated a commitment to operate according to certain rules of good business practice. There is little standardization in this nascent sector, and indeed today one can find trustmarks with rigorous requirements as well as auto–certification schemes and fraudulent marks. Nevertheless, using a trustmark service from one of the more recognized providers (e.g., Web–Trust (www.webtrust.org), Square Trade (www.squaretrade.com), or Trust–e (www.truste.org) in different areas) may enhance the perceived trustworthiness of your website and e–commerce activity.

e. PRIVACY ISSUES

Trust–e, perhaps the best–known trustmark today, addresses the very narrow – but important – issue of privacy on the Internet. The term "privacy" within the context of the Internet is often meant to refer to the protection of personal or consumer data. In addition to various security threats, the Internet has also opened up opportunities for collecting data profiles about individuals beyond anything that was possible in the paper–based world. When applied unscrupulously, Internet technologies can be used to create extensive profiles on individuals by collecting digital traces left on different sites. Combined, these datum can be used to determine comprehensive behaviour patterns which most people would feel very uncomfortable sharing with business enterprises or governmental entities. Privacy–invading use of Internet technology has been the subject of much debate over the last ten years and today many countries have a more or less restrictive series of laws and regulations about how data may be collected, treated and shared.

Users of your website will want to know that you do not collect more information on them than they have agreed to and that once collected, you treat this information about visitors to your website appropriately. In addition, "privacy" laws that you must abide by outline pro–active steps you can take to demonstrate to visitors of your website that your practices in relation to user data are respectable. Trust–e is one such scheme, which requires you to post a compliant "privacy policy" on your website so that users can read in easily accessible language what you do and do not do with their details. For concrete help on creating a privacy policy, you can also go to the site of the Organization for Economic Co–operation and Development, www.oecd.org, which has an automated privacy policy generator.

f. THE VALUE OF INTELLECTUAL PROPERTY

Another reason for attending to Internet security is that digitized assets, including product manuals and other valuable intellectual property, are much more vulnerable when they are made available via the Internet. It is technologically difficult to ensure that legally protected works are not copied and distributed without the owner being able to exploit them financially. Not only do you have to be aware of these vulnerabilities, it is also important that you train your staff to respect the intellectual property of others. In writing product manuals, for instance, you should not copy text from related documents not owned by your company without prior permission from the owner. Violating others' intellectual property rights is a criminal offence that is taken increasingly seriously by law enforcement around the world. Finally, it is important that for each published document you clearly display the appropriate copyright, trademark and/or patent information.

g. MARKETING AND OTHER ISSUES

The moment you establish a website you become a global business, accessible to people from Alaska to Borneo. The global access provided by the Internet not only confronts firms with new commercial opportunities, but also with new responsibilities. This may force you to radically change your marketing approach to suit the tastes of a global audience. For instance, an exporter of agricultural machinery may have traditionally used photos of attractive young women in its marketing materials, but such advertising may well be shocking or even illegal in other parts of the world. Language is another factor: if you want potential customers to understand around the world, you may need to provide key messages in different languages, or change your usual marketing language. A good feedback mechanism, for example, using email forms on your site to enable users to send any comments or suggestions, can help you adapt to unforeseen issues. Finally, a good website developer will also have an understanding of how to avoid problems.

ICC has issued guidelines that serve as a basic global standard of ethical Internet marketing behaviour since 1995. These *Guidelines*, updated in 1998, are reproduced in the box below.

ICC Guidelines on Advertising and Marketing on the Internet

BASIC PRINCIPLES

Article 1

All advertising and marketing on the Internet should comply with the spirit, as well as the letter, of the principles set forth in the ICC's Codes on Advertising Practice, Sales Promotion, Direct Marketing, Environmental Advertising, and Sponsorship, as well as the ICC–ESOMAR Code on Marketing and Social Research Practice.

All advertising and marketing should be legal, decent, honest and truthful. "Legal", in the context of these guidelines, is presumed to mean that advertising and marketing messages should be legal in their country of origin.

Advertising and marketing messages should be sensitive to issues of social responsibility and should in addition conform to generally accepted principles as regards ethical marketing.

Advertising and marketing messages should not be designed or transmitted in such a way as to impair overall public confidence in the Internet as a medium and marketplace.

RULES

- **Disclosure of identity**

Article 2

Advertisers and marketers of goods and services who post commercial messages via the Internet should always disclose their own identity and that of the relevant subsidiary, if applicable, in such a way that the user can contact the advertiser advertiser or marketer without difficulty.

- **Costs and responsibilities associated with electronic sales and marketing**

Article 3

Advertisers and marketers should clearly inform users of the cost of accessing a message or a service where the cost is higher than the basic telecommunications rate. Users should be provided with such notice of cost at the time

---

they are about to access the message or service. This notice mechanism should allow users a reasonable amount of time, as set by the marketer or mandated by applicable law, to disconnect from the service without incurring the charge.

- **Respect for public groups**

Article 4

Advertisers and marketers should respect the role of particular electronic news groups, forums or bulletin boards as public meeting places which may have rules and standards as to acceptable commercial behaviour. Advertising and marketing messages posted to public sites are appropriate:

- when the forum or site receiving the message has a fundamentally commercial nature or activity; or
- when the subject or theme of the bulletin board or news group is pertinent to the content of the advertising or marketing message; or
- when the forum or site has otherwise implicitly or explicitly indicated consent to the receipt of advertising and marketing messages.

- **Users' rights**

Article 5

1. **Collection and use of data**

   Advertisers and marketers should disclose the purpose(s) for collecting and using personal data to users and should not use the data in a way incompatible with those purposes. Data files should be accurate, complete and kept up–to–date.

2. **Data privacy**

   Advertisers and marketers should take reasonable precautions to safeguard the security of their data files.

3. **Disclosure of data**

   The user should be given the opportunity to refuse the transfer of data to another advertiser or marketer. Personal data should not be disclosed when the user has objected, except by authority of law. Online mechanisms should be put in place to allow users to exercise their right to opt–out by electronic means.

4. **Correction and blocking of data**

   Advertisers and marketers should give the user the right to obtain data relating to him and, where appropriate, to have such data corrected, completed, or blocked.

5. **Privacy policy statements**

   Advertisers and marketers are encouraged to post their privacy policy statement on their online site. When such privacy policy statements exist, they should be easy to find, easy to use and comprehensible.

6.   Unsolicited commercial messages

Advertisers and marketers should not send unsolicited commercial messages online to users who have indicated that they do not wish to receive such messages. Advertisers and marketers should make an online mechanism available to users by which the users can make known to the advertisers and marketers that they do not wish to receive future online solicitations. Unsolicited online advertising or marketing commercial messages should be clearly identified as such and should identify the advertiser or marketer.

■ **Advertising to children**

Article 6

Advertisers and marketers offering goods or services to children online should:

- not exploit the natural credulity of children or the lack of experience of young people and should not strain their sense of loyalty;
- not contain any content which might result in harm to children;
- identify material intended only for adults;
- encourage parents and/or guardians to participate in and/or supervise their children's online activities;
- encourage young children to obtain their parents' and/or guardians' permission before the children provide information online, and make reasonable efforts to ensure that parental consent is given;
- provide information to parents and/or guardians about ways to protect their children's privacy online.

■ **Respect for the potential sensitivities of a global audience**

Article 7

Given the global reach of electronic networks and the variety and diversity of possible recipients of electronic messages, advertisers and marketers should be especially sensitive regarding the possibility that a particular message might be perceived as pornographic, violent, racist or sexist.

h. POTENTIAL COST BENEFITS

The Internet provides access to global markets and many other benefits, but is it cost–effective? How can a small company take advantage of technologies if standards, products and services change with ever–increasing speed? The honest answer is: with some difficulties. There are very few companies that can afford to buy new technologies for experimentation, but at the other end of the scale, today, there are very few technologies that can afford not to have a basic set–up providing Internet access at a decent speed and email addresses for external–facing staff.

10.4 Open and closed electronic trade

Beyond the specific type of technology used, there are also key business issues related to the distinction between open and closed electronic trade. Open electronic commerce refers generally to a business model in which firms are open to business from all other firms on the Internet; closed electronic commerce refers to commerce which is restricted to firms which have obtained access to a private network.

10.4.1 The open model – status report

Whereas open electronic commerce has been technologically possible and the stated objective of Internet standards and many services for several years now, it has not yet materialized. One reason is that trust and security solutions have not evolved at the same pace as basic Internet standards and services. But there are other reasons, including legal uncertainty and the very nature of most world trade, which is based on existing relationships.

Open electronic trade does exist, but it is marginal. Some organizations provide electronic bulletin boards or match–making services on the public Internet for companies to post business opportunities. Although some of these appear to generate significant business opportunities, there is very little information about how many of these postings lead to real transactions and to what extent these transactions are electronically–based. It is clear, however, that today open electronic trade is, at least value–wise, at the periphery of world trade. It is also evident that larger trading groups and sectors indulge little or not at all in open Internet–based trade. As techniques such as PKI become more standardized and available, this may change. However, it is likely that many larger traders will not feel the need to use open Internet transactions so long as more–restricted, community–based trading networks continue to provide more control, security and predictability.

10.4.2 B2B exchanges (business–to–business e–commerce)

For some time it looked as though moderated online marketplaces known as B2B exchanges were going to be the dominant model for electronic trade in many sectors. However, in recent years these marketplaces have changed in nature and at present it is hard to predict what the future shape and content of such online communities will be.

10.4.3 Specialized initiatives

Some of the more specialized types of Internet trading initiatives include Bolero (www.bolero.net) and TradeCard (www.tradecard.com) as well as an increasing range of others of a more or less open nature. As trust initiatives expand and gain more market acceptance, electronic trade will certainly change in nature. Private sectoral initiatives in the field of PKI, such as Identrus (www.identrus.com), which is driven by the world's largest banks, are likely to boost acceptance of digital signatures. This, in turn, may change some of the current parameters. All these initiatives will continue to explore and influence the appropriate mix between "open" and "closed" systems until the most successful formula has been found, after which a significant market consolidation can be expected.

10.5 Disputes and the Internet

As the number of cross–border transactions increases, so will the number of disputes between businesses engaged in international trade. Even before the arrival of the Internet, business had strong incentives to use private out–of–court dispute resolution mechanisms such as arbitration and mediation instead of litigation(see Chapter 3); these incentives will very likely increase with the expansion in electronic business.

A number of new online out–of–court dispute resolution providers have entered the market in recent years. Some of these, including the Centre de Mediation et d'Arbitrage de Paris (www.cmap.asso.fr), Squaretrade (www.squaretrade.com), NovaForum (www.novaforum.com), Cybersettle (www.cybersettle.com) and Jams (www.jamsadr.com), have been quite successful in certain narrow areas of dispute resolution or in using online tools to compliment offline dispute resolution services. While this sector has a long way to go before commercial maturity, viable alternatives to more established offline providers already exist today.

An area in which online dispute resolution has been very successful is domain names. Domain name disputes often arise due to the fact that many companies around the world use the same, or similar overall or product names for which only one second–level domain name is available in each top–level domain. The legitimacy of a domain name you buy can be challenged, under current rules established by the global regulatory body ICANN (www.icann.org), in front of a number of approved dispute resolution providers including the World Intellectual Property Organization (WIPO – www.wipo.org).

Export–Import Glossary

A

AAA – *See* American Arbitration Association.

aar – against all risks.

acceptance (also, **acc.**) – The agreement written on a draft and signed by the drawee – who becomes the acceptor – to pay the specified amount on the due date. The term is also applied to the accepted time draft itself. *See* bill of exchange.

acceptance credit – A documentary credit which requires, amongst the documents stipulated, provision of a term bill of exchange. The bill is then generally accepted by the bank on which it is drawn or discounted. The practical result is that the beneficiary is paid promptly at a discount.

act.wt. – Actual weight.

A/d – *See* After date.

ad valorem duty – A duty assessed as a percentage rate of the value of the imported merchandise. *See* customs duty.

advance payment guarantee/bond – A guarantee that advance payments will be returned if the party having received such payments does not perform its part of the contract.

advising bank – The bank that notifies the exporter of the opening of a letter of credit in his or her favour. The advising bank, usually located in the exporter's country, fully informs the exporter of the conditions of the letter of credit without itself making a payment commitment. *See* generally letter of credit.

ADR – *See* alternative dispute resolution.

after date – Payment on a negotiable instrument, such as a bank draft, becomes due a specified number of days after presentation of the draft.

agent/agency agreement – An agent is an independent person or legal entity which acts on behalf of another (the "principal"). In international transactions, generally refers to a sales representative who prospects on behalf of a foreign principal, earning commission on sales eventually concluded between the principal and the ultimate client; *see* Foreign sales agent. To be distinguished from sales through employees and subsidiaries – who are not independent, or through distributorship relations, which involve the distributor's buying and re–selling in his own name. Sales agents should also be distinguished from buying or purchasing agents, as the respective rights and obligations are quite different.

agio – The extra amount over and above the market price which is paid in countertrade transactions and results from the particular costs of counter–trade.

air waybill (airbill) (AWB) – A non–negotiable shipping document used by the airlines for air freight. It is a contract for carriage that includes carrier conditions, such as limits of liability and claims procedures. In addition, it contains shipping instructions to airlines, a description of the commodity and applicable transportation charges. It performs the functions of a bill of lading in land surface transport. *See* bill of lading.

all risks (AR) – A type of insurance coverage providing somewhat more than the minimum coverage, at a premium above the base amount paid under a particular policy. Unfortunately, "all risks" coverage does not in fact cover all risks – thus, for example, coverage of war, riots and strikes is not usually included; moreover, there is no standard nomenclature for all risks coverage. Traders should understand what exactly is covered in all risks coverage, and decide whether or not they need additional coverage, before agreeing to such a term.

alternative dispute resolution (ADR) – A general term for a variety of dispute–resolution mechanisms which may be used as alternatives to traditional litigation before governmental courts or tribunals. May be said to include such techniques as conciliation, mediation, arbitration, re–negotiation, and mini–trial.

American Arbitration Association (AAA) – Perhaps the world's largest arbitration forum and institution; the great bulk of cases handled under its rules and procedures are domestic US cases, although the AAA does have specific rules for international cases.

AN – *See* Arrival notice.

applicant – In the documentary credit process, normally the buyer or importer, who applies (thus, the applicant) for a letter of credit in favour of the beneficiary, the seller.

AQ – Any quantity.

arbitration – A process of dispute resolution in which a neutral third party (arbitrator) renders a decision after a hearing at which both parties have an opportunity to be heard. Arbitration may be voluntary or contractually required. The advantages of arbitration – compared to litigation – are neutrality, confidentiality, reduced costs, faster procedures and the arbitrator's expertise. Internationally, the main arbitration body is the International Chamber of Commerce, other arbitration institutions include the London Court of International Arbitration, the Stockholm Court of Arbitration, and the American Arbitration Association (AAA).

arrival notice (AN) – Communication from a carrier to the intended receiver that an international shipment will soon arrive.

at sight – A term used in international banking practice to indicate that payment is due immediately upon presentation of given documents.

ATA Carnet – "Admission Temporaire/Temporary Admission". An international customs document for the temporary duty–free admission of goods into a country for display, demonstration or similar purposes. ATA Carnets are issued by national chambers of commerce, which guarantee the payment of duties to local customs authorities should the goods not be ultimately re–exported.

Av. – Average

aval – A bank's guarantee to pay a bill of exchange. An irrevocable, unconditional promise to pay on the due date. The use of avals is common in the practice of forfaiting.

AWB – *See* Air waybill.

B

banker's acceptance – A bill of exchange accepted by a bank usually for the purpose of financing the sale of goods to or by the bank's customer. The bill may be drawn, for example, by an exporter on the importer's bank and be sold on the open market at a discount. *See* bill of exchange.

back–to–back credit – A commercial device under which a middleman uses a documentary credit to open a second credit in favour of a supplier. Should be distinguished from a transferable credit. *See* letters of credit and Chapter 6.

BAF – *See* Bunker adjustment factor.

bank guarantee – Contract between a bank as guarantor and a beneficiary in which the bank commits itself to pay a certain sum under certain, specified conditions. Thus, a demand guarantee is one in which the bank agrees to pay against the simple written demand of the beneficiary.

bareboat charter – The lease (charter) of an entire vessel under an agreement whereby the lessor only provides the "bare" vessel – that is, operation of the vessel is not included in the lease and the charterer must arrange to hire a ship's master and crew himself.

barter – The direct exchange of goods and/or services for other goods and/or services without the use of money and without the involvement of a third party. Bartering is an important means of trade with countries using currency that is not readily convertible. *See* countertrade.

basis points – One thousandths; 1/100 of 1%; i.e., 100 basis points is equal to 1%.

B/B – Breakbulk (cargo).

B/D – Bank draft.

beneficiary – Documentary credit context: generally, the exporter–seller; the one on whose behalf the documentary credit is opened by the applicant (the importer–buyer). Guarantee/bond context: the one who will receive payment under the bond should the specified documents or contingencies be produced.

Berne Union – International Union of Credit and Investment Insurers.

B/G – Bonded goods. *See* bonded warehouse.

bill of exchange (B/E) – A draft. An unconditional order addressed by the exporter to the importer for the payment of a specific sum. A sight draft requires immediate payment, while usance or term drafts indicate payment at a specified future date.

bill of lading (B/L) – A document issued when goods are entrusted to a shipping company for carriage. It can serve as a formal receipt for the goods by the shipowner, a memorandum of the contract of carriage, and documentary evidence of control over the goods. The holder or consignee of the bill has the right to claim delivery of the goods from the shipping company when they arrive at the port of destination. Bills of lading may be negotiable (order B/L) or non–negotiable (straight B/L). Bills of lading may also be distinguished by the mode of transport used for the shipment.
See marine bill of lading, multimodal transport bill of lading, air waybill, railway consignment note and sea waybill.

B/L terminology:

- *clean* – a B/L which contains no notation indicating that the goods have been wholly or partially lost/damaged.
- *direct* – a B/L for direct transport between loading and discharging ports.
- *dirty/foul/claused* – a B/L with a notation to the effect that the goods have been partially/wholly lost or damaged.
- *FIATA FBL (FBL)* – a standard–form B/L issued by a freight forwarder; considered under the UCP 500 – along with other forwarder bills in which the agents accept full responsibility as a carrier – as acceptable as a clean on board B/L issued by a carrier.
- *freight pre–paid* – a B/L indicating on it that the freight has been paid.
- *full set of originals* – for documentary credit or collection purposes, the buyer may require the seller to produce a full set (commonly up to three) of signed originals – that is, B/Ls which bear the original signature of the ship's master or agent.
- *house* – a B/L issued by a forwarder in its own name ("house") covering grouped consignments.
- *liner* – a B/L issued subject to the terms and conditions of a shipping line.
- *multimodal/combined transport* – a B/L issued to cover transport involving successive stages via different transport modes, e.g., road transport followed by sea followed again by road transport.
- *ocean/marine* – the classic B/L, a negotiable instrument used for goods shipped on board ocean–going vessels.
- *on board/shipped* – a B/L evidencing the loading on board of cargo in good condition.
- *order* – a negotiable B/L, issued "to the order" of a particular party, commonly the shipper.

- *received for shipment* – a B/L which only evidences that goods have been received, not that they have been loaded on board; common with container shipments delivered to port terminal; must be converted by subsequent "on board" notation if shipper needs an "on board" or "shipped" document for payment under a letter of credit.
- *short–form* – a B/L which does not contain the full terms and conditions of the contract of carriage; instead, it contains an abbreviated version of the carrier's condition, with a reference to the full set of conditions.
- *stale* – a B/L which is presented late (for documentary credit purposes, a B/L must be presented within a certain number of days after shipment).
- *straight* – a non–negotiable B/L; the consignee only needs to identify himself to pick up the goods.
- *through* – a B/L used when shipment will involve successive transport stages with different carriers.
- *waybill* – a non–negotiable transport document.

bolero (www.bolero.net) – Bolero is an open Internet platform for processing trade–related electronic documents. With Bolero, international traders can electronically manage the entire document flow related to an international trade transaction.

bonded warehouse – A warehouse authorized by customs authorities for storage of goods on which payment of duties is deferred until the goods are removed for domestic consumption. If the goods are re–exported, no duty has to be paid at all. *See* foreign trade zone.

breakbulk (BB) – Non–containerized cargo that is grouped or consolidated for shipment, and then is later broken down, sub–divided or distributed at a further destination point. Breakbulk cargo is often unitized cargo on pallets or packed in boxes; specialized breakbulk vessels tend to carry their own loading/unloading machinery.

bunker adjustment factor (also, **BAF**) – A surcharge charged by ocean carriers to account for fluctuations in the cost of shipping fuel, which is known as bunker fuel.

buy–back (compensation) – A form of countertrade under which exporters of, e.g., heavy equipment, technology, or plant facilities agree to purchase a certain percentage of the output of the new facility once it is in production. *See* countertrade.

C

CAD – Cash against documents.

call – A demand for payment under a loan or guarantee. In the case of demand guarantees, the abusive resort to the guarantee (i.e., in the absence of non-compliance by the principal) is sometimes referred to as an unfair call.

cash on delivery (COD) – a term specifying that the receiver of goods will make payment for them to the carrier upon delivery; common in domestic trade, unusual in international trade.

CBD – Cash before delivery.

certificate of inspection (also, **certificate of quality**) – A document certifying the quality, quantity and/or price of a given shipment of goods. The inspection certificate is often required by buyers, especially those paying via documentary credit, from sellers, in order to assure that the goods are of contract quality. Generally, the buyer will designate a neutral, independent inspection company.

certificate of origin – A document certifying the country of origin of specified goods. It is often required by the customs authorities of a country as part of the entry process, for instance to grant preferential tariff treatment on imports of goods originating in a particular country. Such certificates are usually obtained through a semi–official organization in the country of origin, such as a local chamber of commerce or a consular office.

c & f (C&F) – Warning: common but non–standard version of Cost and Freight – CFR *Incoterms 2000* (Cost and Freight). *See Incoterms 2000.*

CFR – Cost and Freight. *See Incoterms 2000.*

charter party – A contract under which a charterer agrees to rent/hire the use of a ship or part of a ship from a shipowner. The charterer in some cases will be empowered to issue his own bills of lading, known as charter party bills of lading, subject to the conditions of the original charter party contract. Note that the charter party itself is not a bill of lading, but rather a contract between the shipowner and charterer under which the shipowner hires out all or part of his ship for a given period to the charterer.

CIA – Cash in Advance.

CIF (also, **c.i.f.**) – Cost, Insurance and Freight. *See Incoterms 2000.*

CIF & C – Cost, insurance, freight and commission. (also, **CIF & I** – Cost, insurance, freight and interest); and **CIF & CI** (Cost, insurance, freight, commission and interest). Warning: these are variants on the standard *Incoterms 2000* term, so the additional abbreviations are not covered by international standard definitions. Traders may, therefore, wish to inquire and expressly stipulate as to the precise requirements implied by the additional "C" or "CI".

CIP – Carriage and Insurance Paid To...(named point). *See Incoterms 2000.*

claused bill of lading – A claused, or foul bill of lading contains notations or remarks as to defects in the goods and/or packaging. *See* bill of lading and clean bill of lading.

cld – Cleared (through customs).

clean bill of lading – A bill of lading indicating that the goods were received in apparent good order and condition. A clean bill is one which contains no notations of defect, damage or loss, and is signed by the carrier or its authorized representative. Note that a clean bill does not have to have any positive affirmation or mention to the effect, e.g., "clean bill" or "merchandise in good order". If a bill does contain a notation of damaged or missing merchandise, the bill of lading is called "claused", "foul" or "dirty". *See* bill of lading and claused bill of lading.

clean report of findings – A document issued by a pre–shipment inspection agency stating that a particular shipment conforms to specified criteria (usually relating to the quality, quantity or price of the goods).

CMR – International road transport convention.

collecting bank – In a documentary collection, the bank acting as an agent for the seller's bank in collecting payment or acceptance of a time draft from the buyer to be forwarded to the seller's bank (the remitting bank). *See* documentary collection.

combined transport document (CTD) – A transport document similar to a bill of lading but which is issued to cover shipments which are carried by more than one mode of transport.

commercial invoice – A document containing a record of the transaction between a seller (exporter) and a buyer (importer), containing information such as a complete listing and description of the goods including prices, discounts and quantities, and the delivery and payment terms. A commercial invoice is often used by governments to determine the true value of goods for the assessment of customs duties, and must therefore conform to the regulations of the importing country.

commission agent – A foreign sales representative who is paid a percentage of the sales he or she generates. *See* agent and foreign sales agent.

common carrier – In some jurisdictions, a legal term referring to carriers who offer transport services to the general consumer or business public. In contrast, for example, to carriers who may work as employees, sub–contractors or agents of the manufacturer/shipper.

compound duty – A combination of both a specific rate of duty and an ad valorem rate of duty. Whereas specific duties are based on factors such as weight or quantity, ad valorem duties are based on the value of the goods. *See* customs duty.

conference (also, **steamship conference**, **shipping conference**) – A group of steamship companies or shipping lines which have associated to offer regular service on specific routes at publicly announced prices. Conferences generally offer specific rebates for regular or high–volume shipments. Shipment by conference lines is sometimes referred to as liner shipping and the freight rates are referred to as liner terms. Shipping lines which are not members of a conference for a particular route are known as outsiders, independent lines, or non–conference liners. *See* liner terms.

confirmed letter of credit – A documentary credit issued by a foreign bank which has been confirmed by another bank (usually a local bank or an international leading bank), the confirmation consisting of an additional irrevocable undertaking to pay according to the terms of the credit.

confirming bank – In letter of credit transactions, the bank which adds its own irrevocable undertaking for payment in addition to that given by the issuing bank. The confirming bank is usually located in the exporter's country. *See* letter of credit.

consignee – In international export transactions: the intended receiver of a cargo shipment. The named person or legal entity having the right to claim the merchandise from the carrier at destination, and is generally recognized as the legal owner for customs purposes.

In international representation or distributorship relations (viz., consignment sales): the holder and re–seller of merchandise who receives payment in the form of commission or a discount as and when sales are made but does not have to purchase the goods in advance.

consular declaration – A description of goods to be shipped, made in official form to a consulate.

consular invoice – An invoice covering a shipment of goods certified by the consul of the country for which the merchandise is destined. The invoice is used by customs officials of the country to verify the value, quantity, and nature of the merchandise imported to determine the import duty. In addition, the export price may be examined in the light of the current market price in the exporter's country to ensure that dumping is not taking place.

contingency insurance (also, "**difference in conditions**") – Insurance coverage taken out by one party to an international transaction to complement and fill in any gaps in the coverage taken out by the counterparty. Thus, the open account exporter on FOB Incoterms does not have an obligation to insure the goods during the main international transport, but may wish in any event to take out contingency insurance so that if the goods are lost or damaged there will be no loss to the buyer (such a loss might lead to dis-agreements or disruption of commercial relations with the buyer, even if the seller was not legally at fault).

correspondent bank – A bank which performs certain operations on behalf of another bank, usually in a different country. Correspondent banks hold deposits with each other, and accept and collect items on a reciprocal basis. It is through networks of correspondent banks that trade banks are able to service and support international business transactions.

counterpurchase – The agreement of an exporter to purchase a quantity of unrelated goods or services from a country in exchange for, and approximate in value to, the goods exported.

countertrade – All foreign trade transactions resulting from exporters' commitments to take products from the importers or from their respective countries in full or part payment for their exports. Countertrade is typical of trade with developing countries, which often suffer from a lack of foreign exchange and/or credit facilities. Countertrade transactions include barter, buy–back or compensation, counterpurchase, offset requirements, and swap. *See* respective terms.

courtage (French) – Brokerage, brokerage fee.

cover note (also, **broker's cover note**) – An insurance document indicating coverage of a particular shipment under an open cover policy. To be distinguished, particularly as regards to presentation under a documentary credit, from an insurance policy or an insurance certificate.

CPT – Carriage Paid To...(named point). *See Incoterms 2000.*

credit risk insurance – An exporter's insurance against non–payment by the importer.

c/s – Case(s).

CSC – Container service charge.

currency future – A contract for the future delivery of a commodity, currency or security on a specific date. In contrast to forward contracts, futures contracts are for standard quantities and for standard periods of time and are primarily traded on an exchange. Forward transactions enable importers and exporters who will have to make, or will receive, payment in a foreign currency at a future time to protect themselves against the risk of fluctuations in the spot rate.

currency option – The contractually agreed right to buy (call option) or to sell (put option) a specific amount of a foreign currency at a predetermined price on a specific date (European option) or up to a future date (American option).

customs broker – Licensed agent or broker whose function is to handle the process of clearing goods through customs for importers.

customs duty – Tax levied by the government on goods crossing the customs border, usually a tax imposed on imports. Duties, or tariffs, are either based on the value of the goods (ad valorem duties), some other factors such as weight or quantity (specific duties), or a combination of value and other factors (compound duties).

customs union – An association between two or more countries whereby they eliminate tariffs and other import restrictions on each other's goods and establish a common tariff on the goods from all other countries. The European Community is the best known example of a customs union.

cw – Commercial weight.

CWO – Cash with order.

cwt – Hundredweight; unit of measurement.

D

date draft – A draft which matures for a specified number of days after issuance.

DAF – Delivered at Frontier. *See Incoterms 2000*.

D/D – Delivered.

ddc (also, **DDC**) – Sometimes said to be "delivered destination charges", referring to various miscellaneous charges in the port of destination; alternatively said to refer to dispatch money at discharge. *See* dispatch money.

DDP – Delivered Duty Paid. *See Incoterms 2000*.

DDU – Delivered Duty Unpaid. *See Incoterms 2000*.

deadfreight – Freight charge to be paid even when shipment was not made, owing to failure by the shipper or charterer to actually ship goods in the shipping space for which a reservation was made.

deadweight – Total carrying capacity of a vessel.

deck cargo – Goods shipped on the deck of a ship rather than in its holds. Since deck cargo is more exposed to the elements, traders may wish to stipulate that goods not be carried on deck (except in such cases as transport of hazardous materials, in which case carriage on deck may be mandatory).

deferred air freight – Air freight offered at cheaper rates for non–urgent shipments.

del credere – As relates to international commercial agency relationships: a del credere agent is one who guarantees the ability to pay prospective clients he has brought to the principal; in exchange, the del credere agent is usually accorded a higher percentage commission than is a regular agent.
As relates to risk in general: del credere risk is the risk that a party will be unable to meet its financial obligations.

del. – Delivery.

delivery order – An order, commonly addressed to a terminal superintendent or warehouse manager, directing the release of specified cargo to a particular receiver. The order may in some cases be issued by the seller, shipper or consignee, while in other contexts the order will be issued by the shipping line or carrier. Commonly, a delivery order directs delivery of part of a larger consignment, which is itself covered by a single bill of lading; i.e., the issuance of several delivery orders "splits up" the cargo covered by the bill of lading. In any event, delivery orders should be clearly distinguished from bills of lading: the delivery order is not a negotiable document, nor does it evidence receipt of goods, nor docs it contain the provisions of the transport contract under which the goods were shipped.

demand guarantee – A guarantee usually issued by a bank, under which the beneficiary is only required to make a demand in order to receive payment. In contrast to the conditional or suretyship guarantee – which require the beneficiary to provide proof of the principal's default, a demand guarantee only requires that the beneficiary make a simple demand, and therefore th latter guarantee is relatively risky in terms of exposure to an unjustified demand on the part of the beneficiary. Some protection against such an unfair demand can be obtained by making the guarantee subject to the *ICC Uniform Rules for Demand Guarantees* (URDG, ICC Publication 458).

demurrage – The extra charges paid to a shipowner or carrier when a specified period for loading/unloading is exceeded. The demurrage may, depending on the context, be paid by the charterer or shipper.

DEQ – Delivered Ex Quai. *See Incoterms 2000.*

DES – Delivered Ex Ship. *See Incoterms 2000.*

destuffing (also, **stripping**) – Unloading goods from a container.

devanning (also, **stripping**) – Unloading goods from a container.

discrepancy – In the context of documentary credits: a discrepancy arises when documents presented under a documentary credit do not conform to the terms of the credit; generally, an error, contradiction or omission related to the documents constitutes the discrepancy. The bank will refuse to pay against the documents unless the applicant (buyer) agrees to amend the credit or otherwise waive objections to payment under the credit.

discount – The purchase by a bank or finance house of a bill of exchange at face value less interest. It is used as a financing tool should the holder of an accepted bill of exchange require the money before the bill matures. *See* bill of exchange.

dispatch money (also, **despatch**)– An incentive payment offered by a shipowner to a charterer in exchange for completing loading or unloading in less time than is specified in the charter party contract (this time is often calculated as a number of "lay days"). *See* charter party and demurrage.

distributor – An independent person or legal entity which sells goods locally on behalf of a foreign principal. Distributors can be distinguished from agents as distributors buy the goods in their own name, then re–sell them at prices which they have some liberty to set. Distributorship is frequently based on a contract which grants the distributor exclusivity for a specific territory. *See* for comparison, foreign sales agent.

Dk. – Dock.

D/O – *See* delivery order.

dock receipt – A document certifying receipt of goods by the international carrier at the port of departure.

documentary collection – A method of payment under which the shipping documents relating to a particular cargo are released to the importer on payment (documents against payment: "D/P") or acceptance (documents against acceptance: "D/A") of a documentary draft drawn on him by the exporter. Under collections, the exporter presents a draft together with shipping documents to a bank (the remitting bank) in his country, which then forwards the documents and draft to the collecting bank in the buyer's country. The documents enabling the buyer to take possession of the goods will only be released by the collecting bank when the buyer either pays or accepts the draft.

documentary credit (D/C) – *See* letter of credit.

documents against acceptance (D/A) – The documents transferring title to goods are delivered to the buyer (drawee) only upon the buyer's acceptance of the attached draft guaranteeing payment at a later date. *See* documentary collection.

documents against payment (D/P) – In the case of a sight draft, the documents transferring title to goods are released to the buyer/importer only against cash payment. *See* documentary collection.

door to door – A transport service covering carriage from the seller's premises to the buyer's premises. Note that this term refers to a freight charge in a carriage contract between a carrier and a shipper and thus is distinct from the issue of the Incoterm chosen in the contract of sale (an agreement between seller and buyer). Depending on the circumstances of the transaction, it could be possible to quote prices on either EXW, FCA, CPT, CIP, DDU, or DDP Incoterms in conjunction with so–called "house to house" transport services. Attention should be given to the inclusion of loading/unloading charges in the "house to house" rate, especially in comparison with the responsibility under the respective Incoterm for loading or unloading. The shipper should make sure that the transport service corresponds to the contractual obligations under Incoterms. It is sometimes said that "door to door" services imply that loading and unloading are not included in the freight charge, but this is not a standard rule and traders should inquire in each particular case. Door to door is sometimes used synonymously with house to house, but it is claimed by some that there is a distinction between the two, namely that "house to house" only refers to rental rates for containers from container yard to container yard. *See* house to house.

draft– An unconditional order in writing, signed by a person (drawer) such as a buyer, and addressed to another person (drawee), typically a bank, ordering the drawee to pay a stated sum of money to yet another person (payee), often a seller. A draft, also called a bill of exchange, may be payable to a named person or his order (order draft), or to bearer (bearer draft).
The most common versions of a draft are the sight draft, which is payable on presentation or demand, and the time (or usance) draft, which is payable at a future fixed (specific) or determinable (30, 60, 90 days etc.) date. Should the beneficiary under a time draft require the money before the bill matures, he may discount his claim for immediate payment with his bank. *See* bill of exchange.

drawee – The individual or firm on whom a draft is drawn. The drawee is instructed by the drawer to pay a specified sum of money to, or to the order of, the payee, or to bearer. In a documentary collection, the drawee is generally the buyer. *See* bill of exchange.

drawer – The individual or firm that issues or signs a draft, instructing the drawee to pay a specified sum of money to, or to the order of, a named person (payee), or to bearer. In the case of a draft to one's own order, the drawer is also the payee. Like the endorser(s), the drawer is secondarily liable on the draft. In a documentary collection, the drawer is the seller. *See* bill of exchange.

D/S – Days after sight (payment term often used in conjunction with bank drafts and documentary credits).

dumping – The practice of selling a product in a foreign market at an unfairly low price (a price which is lower than the cost in the home market, or which is lower than the cost of production) in order to gain a competitive advantage over other suppliers. Dumping is considered an unfair trade practice under the GATT and World Trade Organisation agreements; it is regulated by national governments through the imposition of anti–dumping duties, in some cases calculated to equal the difference between the product's price in the importing and the exporting country.

E

EDI (also, **edi**) – *See* Electronic data interchange.

Electronic data interchange (EDI) – The computer–to–computer transmission of business messages (such as purchase orders, invoices, booking instructions, etc.) using standard, industry accepted, message formats.

EMC – *See* export management company.

est. – Estimated.

ETA – Estimated time of arrival.

ETD – Estimated time of departure.

ETS – Estimated time of sailing.

EU – European Union.

Eurocurrency – A currency being used or traded outside the country which issued the currency. The most widely used Eurocurrency is the Eurodollar.

export broker – An individual or firm that brings together buyers and sellers for a fee without taking part in actual sales transactions.

export credit insurance – Special insurance coverage for exporters to protect against non–payment by the importer (coverage may extend to certain other risks, depending on the policy. Export credit insurance is available from private insurance underwriters as well as from government agencies. Examples of well–known public export credit agencies include the US Eximbank, the UK Export Credits Guarantee Department and France's COFACE.

export licence – A government document granting the "licensee" the right to export a specified quantity of a commodity to a specified country. This licence may be required in some countries for most or all exports and in other countries only under special circumstances.

export management company (EMC) – A private firm serving as the export department for several manufacturers, soliciting and transacting export business on behalf of its clients in return for a commission, salary, or retainer plus commission.

E&OE – Errors and Omissions Excepted: when appended to a signature on a shipping document, indicates a disclaimer of responsibility for spelling, typographical or clerical errors.

Ex factory – Warning: this is a non–standard trade term, a variation of the preferred formulation: EXW *Incoterms 2000*.

EXW –Ex Works. *See Incoterms 2000*.

F

factoring – In the context of export trade: the financial service consisting of the granting of a cash advance against accounts receivable from foreign customers. More generally, a range of financing and risk management services offered by specialized firms, called factors, to sellers/exporters, particularly those who deal with a stream of low–value, short–term foreign accounts receivable. The exporter transfers title to its foreign accounts receivable to a factoring house in exchange for cash at a discount from the face value. Other basic services offered by factors include: foreign credit risk assessment, collection of overdue foreign accounts and administration of accounting ledgers.

FAK – *See* Freight all kinds.

FAS – Free Alongside Ship. *See Incoterms 2000*.

FB – Freight bill.

FCA – Free Carrier. *See Incoterms 2000*.

FCL – Full container load.

F&D – Freight and demurrage.

FI – Free in. *See* Free in and out.

FO – Free out. *See* Free in and out.

FOB – Free on Board. *See Incoterms 2000*.

fob airport – Warning: no longer a valid Incoterm, *see* FCA, *Incoterms 2000*. Free on board airport: a trade or delivery term used when delivery is effected at an airport. It was withdrawn from use as a valid Incoterm because it was felt that the term was the source of much potential disagreement, especially as regards to allocation of customs clearance and export handling charges.

foc. – Free of charge.

fod. – Free of damage.

FOI – *See* free in and out.

FOR – Free on rail. Warning: no longer a valid Incoterm, but still used by some traders. The problem is that there is on occasion confusion as to whether it only applies to rail shipments. The suitable term from *Incoterms 2000* is FCA; *see Incoterms 2000*.

force majeure – A clause that protects the parties to a contract in the event that a part of the contract cannot be performed due to causes which are outside the control of the parties and could not be avoided by exercise of due care. These causes may be earthquakes, floods, storms or war.

foreign sales agent – An individual or firm that serves as the foreign representative of a domestic supplier and seeks sales abroad for the supplier.

foreign trade zone (FTZ) – Special commercial and industrial areas in or near ports of entry where foreign and domestic merchandise may be brought in without being subject to payment of customs duties. Merchandise, including raw materials, components and finished goods, may be stored, sold, exhibited, repacked, assembled, sorted, graded, cleaned or otherwise manipulated prior to re–export or entry into the national customs authority. Duties are imposed on the merchandise (or items manufactured from the merchandise) only when the goods pass from the zone into an area of the country subject to the Customs Authority. Foreign trade zones are also called free trade zones, free zones, free ports or bonded warehouses.

forfaiting – The purchase by the forfaiter of an exporter's accounts receivable which are based on negotiable instruments such as bills of exchange and promissory notes. In contrast to factoring, forfaiting involves a series of independent, medium– to longer–term obligations of higher value. Since the forfaiter purchases the bills on a non–recourse basis, he assumes both commercial and political risk.

forward rate – The price of a foreign currency that is bought or sold for delivery and payment at a fixed future time, usually 30, 60 or 90 days. Forward transactions enable importers and exporters who will have to make, or will receive, payment in a foreign currency at a future time to protect themselves against the risk of fluctuations in the spot rate.

foul transport document (also, **"dirty"** or "**claused" transport document**) – A transport document (such as a bill of lading) which indicates that the goods to be shipped have been received in a damaged condition or in a lesser quantity than expected. Documents that are not foul are termed "clean".

FOT – Free on truck. Warning: no longer a valid Incoterm, but still used by some traders. The problem is that there is on occasion confusion as to whether it applies to motor vehicle or to rail shipments. The suitable term from *Incoterms 2000* is FCA. *See Incoterms 2000.*

franchising – A system based on the licensing of the right to duplicate a successful business format or industrial process. The franchisor (licensor) permits the franchisee (licensee) to employ its business processes, trademarks, trade secrets and know–how in a contractuallyspecified manner for the marketing of goods or services. The franchisor usually supports the operation of the franchisee's business through the provision of advertising, accounting, training and related services and in many instances also supplies products required by the franchisee for the operation of the franchise. The franchisee, in return, pays certain moneys to the franchisor (in terms of fees and percentage commissions) and agrees to respect contractual provisions dealing, inter alia, with quality of performance. The two principal kinds of franchise contracts are master franchise agreements, under which the franchisor grants another party the right to sub–franchise within a given territory, and direct or unit franchise agreements, which are direct contracts between the franchisor or sub–franchisor and the operator of the franchise unit.

Franco (French, European shipping) – "Free delivered": the shipper pays all charges to a particular point. Warning: non–standard term; for preferred formulation, *see Incoterms 2000.*

free of particular average ("FPA") – A type of marine cargo insurance providing minimal coverage; it corresponds to the Institute of London Underwriters "C" clauses.

Free in and out ("FIO") – A transport or freight term which indicates that loading/discharging costs are not included in the freight. In the charter party context this means that loading/discharging are not the shipowner's responsibility – the charterer is responsible for loading/discharging. Also possible to use either Free in ("FI") or Free out ("FO") independently. May be used with the addition of stowed and/or trimmed: e.g., "FIOS", or "FIOST".

free trade area – A group of countries that agree to eliminate tariffs and other import restrictions on each other's goods, while each participating country applies its own independent schedule of tariffs to imports from countries that are not members. Well–known examples are the North American Free Trade Association (NAFTA), the European Free Trade Association (EFTA) and Mercosur.

freight all kinds (FAK) – Freight rate applicable to all types of goods.

freight forwarder – Assembles and consolidates small shipments into a single lot and assumes, in some cases, full responsibility for transportation of such property from point of receipt to point of destination.

FTZ – *See* foreign trade zone.

G

general average – When cargo is jettisoned to help save a ship in distress, all other cargo owners must compensate the party whose cargo was lost.

gross weight – Total weight of a shipment including packing.

H

Hague Rules – International Convention for the Unification of Certain Rules relating to Bills of Lading – Brussels Convention of 1924. A set of rules for international transport contained in an international treaty first published in 1924 and subsequently implemented by the greater part of world trading nations. The Hague Rules were revised and updated in the so–called Hague Visby Rules, published in 1968, which have not received so universal an implementation as their predecessors.

Hague–Visby Rules – Set of rules amending the Hague rules, published in 1968, which have not been implemented by as many countries as the predecessor Hague Rules.

Harmonized System (HS) – An international standard system for classifying goods for customs purposes, developed by the World Customs Organization.

hazardous materials (HAZMAT) – Shipped materials which may be dangerous, such as explosives or toxic chemicals.

house air waybill (house AWB or, HAWB) – A transport document issued by an air freight consolidator.

house bill of lading (house B/L) – A bill of lading issued by a freight forwarder. Often covers a consignment of parcels from various shippers that has been grouped or consolidated by the forwarder. The forwarder may, for example, receive a single groupage bill of lading from the carrier, then issue a series of house B/Ls to the respective shippers.

house to house – This term generally refers to a container yard to container yard (CY/CY) shipment (in which case it may be used merely to quote the rental rate for the container itself), but is also used in some cases synonymously with "door to door", a term which more generally refers to overall transport services from seller's premises to buyer's premises. *See* door to door.

IATA (International Air Transport Association) – Air transport industry association and issuer of standard air waybill form.

ICC (International Chamber of Commerce) – The world business organization, headquartered in Paris, with approximately 7000 members in more than 140 countries.

ICC Arbitration – Refers either to *ICC Rules of Arbitration* or the process of submitting an arbitral complaint to the ICC Court of International Arbitration.

ICPO (Irrevocable Corporate Purchase Order) – An offer to buy stated goods under specified terms and conditions; for example, for misuse.

Incoterms 2000 – A set of 13 international standard trade terms (also known as delivery terms). *Incoterms 2000* allows the parties to designate a point at which the costs and risks of transport are precisely divided between the seller and the buyer. Incoterms also allocate responsibility for customs clearance/duties between the parties. Since Incoterms are not law but are contractual standard terms, they do not apply to a given transaction unless the parties specifically incorporate them by referring to Incoterms, e.g.: "100£/tonne Liverpool *Incoterms 2000*" (in exceptional cases, Incoterms apply regardless of explicit mention in the contract, if there is a custom of trade or prior course of dealing which indicates reliance on Incoterms, or if the local jurisprudence creates a presumption in favour of applicability of Incoterms). Incoterms are elements of the contract of sale, which may be derived from the seller's tender or pro forma invoice. Thus, Incoterms only apply to the seller and buyer, one of whom will assume the role of shipper and enter into a contract of carriage. The contract of carriage should dovetail with the Incoterm in terms of allocation of transport costs and risks, but this will depend on the shipper giving precise directions to the carrier to ship according to the constraints of the given Incoterm. For a definition of the 13 currently valid Incoterms, their standard abbreviations, *see* Chapter 4.

inland clearance depot (inland dry port) – A combination transport terminal and customs clearance centre.

institute clauses – Standard international transport insurance clauses, published by the Institute of London Underwriters. The Institute Cargo Clauses are three sets of clauses providing different levels of protection: the "A" Clauses correspond to the general notion that is commonly referred to in trade as "all risks" coverage, while clauses "B" and "C" indicate a lower level of coverage and a greater number of exclusions.

integrated carrier – A carrier which can provide shipment by air, road and sea, facilitating control of "door to door" shipments.

inv. – Invoice.

ISO 9000 – International production quality standards established by ISO (International Standards Organization). Certification that an exporter meets ISO 9000 manufacturing standards, for example, may be a minimum requirement for competing in certain markets or for certain tenders.

issuing bank – The buyer's bank which establishes a letter of credit at the request of the buyer, in favour of the beneficiary (seller/exporter). It is also called the buyer's bank or opening bank. *See* letter of credit.

L

laydays/laytime – The time allowed by the shipowner to the charterer or shipper in which to load or discharge the cargo. May be expressed in days or hours, or tonnes per day. Laydays may be set in running days (every calendar day), working days (excludes Sundays and holidays observed by the port), or weather working days (excludes in addition days where operations are prevented by bad weather). It may be contractually provided that if the charterer or shipper loads/unloads more quickly than is necessary, he will be eligible for payment of an incentive called dispatch money; if the loading/ unloading time is excessive however, the charterer or shipper may have to pay a penalty known as demurrage.

LCL (Less than container load) – Refers to shipments of goods which will have to be packed together with other consignments in order to fill up a container.

LCL/FCL – A way of quoting container freight rates in which the carrier agrees to pack the container at the outset (LCL) but the unpacking at destination must be carried out by the receiver or consignee. It is a common approach for buyers who wish to consolidate small purchases from multiple suppliers in a foreign market into container shipments.

LCL/LCL – A way of quoting container freight rates in which the carrier agrees to pack the container on departure as well as unpack the container at destination.

ldg – Loading.

letter of credit (L/C; also, **documentary credit**, D/C) – A document issued by the importer's bank stating its commitment to honour a draft, or otherwise pay, on presentation of specific documents by the exporter within a stated period of time. The documents the importer requires in the credit usually include, at a minimum, a commercial invoice and clean bill of lading, but may also include a certificate of origin, consular invoice, inspection certificate, and other documents. The most widely used type of credit in international trade is the irrevocable credit, which cannot be changed or cancelled without the consent of both the importer and the exporter. In a confirmed irrevocable credit, the confirming bank adds its irrevocable commitment to pay the beneficiary (the confirmation is an additional guarantee of payment).

Types of L/C:

- *advised* – a credit the opening of which the beneficiary has been informed by a local bank.
- *back–to–back* – a system utilized by middlemen/intermediaries to finance a single transaction through the use of two L/Cs opened in succession (e.g., "back–to–back") in order to permit the middleman/broker to use the proceeds from the first credit to pay off his supplier under the second credit.
- *confirmed* – a credit which has received an additional guarantee of payment by a local or highly reputable bank.
- *deferred* – an L/C under which payment by the importer is to take place at a specified time after his receipt of the shipping documents.
- *import* – an L/C used to finance importation of goods.
- *irrevocable* – a credit which cannot be retracted or revoked once the beneficiary has been notified; there is a presumption under the UCP 500 that a credit is irrevocable.
- *red clause* – an L/C allowing payments of advances to the beneficiary (originating in the wool trade in Australia, these clauses used to be printed in red ink).
- *revolving* – a credit which can be drawn against repeatedly by the beneficiary; it can take a variety of different forms depending on whether the credit is limited in terms of time, number of possible drafts, maximum quantity per draft, or maximum total quantity.
- *cumulative revolving L/C* – revolving L/C under which unused amounts can be carried forward and become available under the next draft.
- *sight* – an L/C under which the beneficiary is entitled to present a sight draft or sight bill of exchange, which is a call for immediate payment upon acceptance of shipping documents.
- *standby* – akin to a demand guarantee or bank guarantee, the standby L/C is generally used to assure performance or payment by the counterparty.
- *transferable* – an L/C which allows the beneficiary to make part or all of his credit payable to another supplier; used in middleman/brokerage contexts; distinguishable from back–to–back L/Cs as the transferable credit requires the knowledge and authorization of the importer (applicant/principal).

letter of indemnity (LOI) – A document commonly used in international trade to allow a carrier to release goods to a receiver who is not yet in possession of the bill of lading (exceedingly common in the oil trade, for example). The letter of indemnity is, in essence, a guarantee that the receiver provides to the carrier, assuring the carrier that he will not suffer any financial loss by having released the goods in the absence of a bill of lading. Also referred to as a steamer guarantee.

lex mercatoria – Internationally accepted general trade practices; the international, informal law of merchants.

licensing – A contractual arrangement in which the licensor's patents, trademarks, service marks, copyrights, or know–how may be sold or otherwise made available to a licensee for compensation negotiated in advance between the parties. Such compensation may consist of a lump sum royalty, a "running" royalty (based on volume of production), or a combination of both. Licensing enables a firm to enter a foreign market quickly and poses fewer risks than setting up a foreign manufacturing facility. Furthermore, it allows parties to overcome tariff and non–tariff barriers of trade.

LIFO – In international trade: liner in free out; referring to a freight charge which includes the cost of loading in the port of departure but does not include unloading costs in the port of destination. In accounting practice: last in first out.

lighters – Barges used for unloading sea vessels when normal harbour facilities are non–existent or unavailable.

liner shipping – Services provided by a steamship company or shipping line, under which cargo vessels operate according to a fixed schedule and publicly advertised freight rates.

liner terms – Freight rates that include loading/unloading charges according to the custom of the respective ports – which unfortunately widely varies. "Liner terms" is, thus, not yet a standard designation, and may or may not include cargo handling charges or the costs of moving cargo between the ship's hold and the quay; traders are therefore well advised to require full details in advance from carriers.

Lkg. & Bkg. – Leakage and breakage.

LOI – *See* Letter of indemnity.

LTL – Less than truck load.

M

marine bill of lading (also, **ocean bill of lading**) – The classic document of the traditional export trade, it plays three potential roles: 1) as a receipt for the cargo and evidence that the goods have been received in apparent good order; 2) as evidence of the terms of the contract of carriage between the shipper and the ocean carrier; and 3) as an instrument enabling transfer of control over delivery of the goods ("negotiability"), which allows the holder of the bill to trade the goods in transit by simple endorsement and physical transfer of the bill. *See* bill of lading, B/L.

marine insurance – Generic term for insurance covering international transport of export transactions; used even in cases where ocean transport is not a predominant leg in the transport chain. Marine insurance can be provided either in terms of a specific policy or certificate (exporters should pay attention to which of the two is required under a documentary credit), or by open cover, under which the insurer covers an indefinite number of future shipments; the shipper declares each shipment to the insurer as they are made.

Policy terms:
- *Average* – loss or damage.
- *General Average* – loss occurring when extraordinary measures are taken to preserve the safety of the vessel.
- *Particular Average* – partial loss or damage; loss to an individual cargo interest rather than entire vessel.
- *With Average* (WA) or *With Particular Average* (WPA) – coverage of partial loss provided the claim amounts to at least 3% of the cargo's insured value.
- *Free of Particular Average* (FPA) – coverage does not include partial loss; a very restrictive form of policy.
- *Free of Particular Average American Conditions* (FPAAC) – coverage only of losses resulting from vessel's sinking, collision, stranding or fire.
- *Free of Particular Average English Conditions* (FPAEC) – coverage only of losses resulting from or connected to a vessel's sinking, collision, stranding or fire.

master document/form – Central document in export administrative systems under which all necessary information is entered into a single master document or computer file, which is then used to generate all shipping and export documents. *See* also Chapter 10 on export software systems. Also known as aligned export documentation systems.

mate's receipt – A document issued by the carrier to the shipper, indicating receipt of the goods, but not loading on board. Like a B/L, a mate's receipt can be either clean or claused/dirty/foul, depending on whether or not the goods have been received in apparent good condition. The mate's receipt can later be exchanged for the bill of lading.

MO – Money order.

MTO – *See* multimodal transport operator.

multimodal transport bill of lading – Bill of lading used for carriage whenever there are at least two different forms of transport, such as shipping by rail and by sea. *See* bill of lading.

multimodal transport operator (MTO) – A carrier who concludes multimodal transport contracts; i.e., contracts involving transport by more than one mode of carriage, and for which the MTO accepts liability as a carrier.

M/V – motor vessel

N

N/A – Not applicable.

Non–circumvention non–disclosure agreement (**NCND**) – A type of contract frequently requested by brokers or middlemen under which buyers agree to refrain from going around the broker to deal directly with suppliers. Warning: these agreements sometimes refer erroneously to"ICC Rules for Non-Circumvention Non-Disclosure Agreements; which do not exist. ICC has issued a Model Contract for Occasional Intermediaries, *see* Chapter 5.

NCV – No commercial value.

NE (ne) – Not exceeding.

negotiable instrument – A written document that can be used to transfer the rights embodied in it by mere delivery (in the case of instruments made out to bearer) or by endorsement and delivery (in the case of instruments made out to order). Some instruments, such as the bill of exchange and the cheque, are negotiable unless their negotiability is explicitly excluded, while the bill of lading is negotiable only if made negotiable by the shipper.

N/F – No funds

non–circumvention non–disclosure agreements (NCNDs) – A type of contract frequently requested by international brokers or middlemen in order to prevent buyers from trying to go around the broker to deal directly with suppliers. Warning: these agreements are sometimes ERRONEOUSLY said to be issued pursuant to ICC Rules – such ICC Rules are NON–EXISTENT: there is no connection between ICC and these documents. While ICC is in fact studying the possibility of issuing a model international brokerage agreement, it will certainly not include the term "non–circumvention non–disclosure" in its title.

non–vessel–operating common carrier (NVOCC) – A company providing point–to–point international transport of goods although it does not necessarily operate or own transport vehicles or equipment. NVOCCs will commonly contract with a shipper to move goods from the exporter's premises to the importer's premises and will issue their own door–to–door transport document, although they will in fact sub–contract the different stages of the transport chain to various road hauliers and ocean carriers.

nostro account – A bank account held by a bank with its foreign correspondent bank, in the currency of that foreign country.

N/S/F – Not sufficient funds.

NVOCC – *See* non–vessel–operating common carrier.

O

ocean bill of lading – *See* marine bill of lading.

offset – A type of countertrade transaction. In an offset contract, which may be required by importers' governments as a condition for approval of major sales agreements, the exporter makes an additional agreement to buy goods and services from the importer's country. In a "direct offset" transaction, an exporter may be required to establish manufacturing facilities in the importing country or to use a specified percentage of the components in the product sold from the importer's country. In an indirect offset, an exporter may be obliged to buy goods or services from the importing country without any link to the product sold. *See* countertrade.

O/N – Order notify.

O/o – Order of.

OP – *See* Open policy.

open account trading – The exporter allows the buyer to pay within a specified time after receiving the shipment.

open policy (OP) – A type of insurance policy intended to cover an indefinite number of future individual shipments. The insurance contract remains in force until cancelled. Under the open policy, individual successive shipments are periodically reported or declared to the insurer and automatically covered on or after the inception date. Open policies can provide efficiency and savings for all parties concerned, especially when the insured conducts a significant volume of highlysimilar transactions.

order bill of lading – A negotiable bill of lading, which is made out to, or to the order of, a particular person and can be transferred by endorsement and delivery of the bill. In practice, the bill is made out either to the shipper's order or to that of the consignee or to his order. *See* bill of lading.

Owner's risk (OR)– Also: ORB. – Owner's risk of breakage; ORF – Owner's risk of fire; ORL. – Owner's risk of loss (or leakage).

P

P/A – Power of attorney.

PA – Particular average.

pallet – Flat support of wood or steel on which goods can be stacked and which can be easily moved by forklift trucks.

paramount clause – The clause in a bill of lading or charter party invoking coverage by the Hague Rules, Hague–Visby Rules, or by the particular enactment of these rules in the country with jurisdiction over the contract.

PD – Port dues.

performance bond (guarantee) – A bond or guarantee which has been issued as security for one party's performance: if that party (the principal) fails to perform, the beneficiary under the bond/guarantee may obtain payment. A performance bond may be of either the demand or conditional variety, which means that the beneficiary may or may not be required to prove default by the principal in order to obtain payment.

P & I Club (Protection and Indemnity Club) – A shipowners' insurance association.

pick up and delivery (PU & D) – Freight quote includes service of picking cargo up at shipper's premises and delivering it at consignee's premises.

pier–to–pier (quay–to–quay) – Freight quote which only covers from export pier to import pier (that is, which excludes handling charges to bring cargo to and from piers).

P/N – *See* promissory note.

POD – Pay on delivery.

ppd (or PP) – Pre–paid.

pre–shipment inspection (PSI) – An inspection of contract goods prior to shipment so as to ascertain their quality, quantity or price. Importers may insist on PSI, requiring the exporter to furnish a certificate of inspection (commonly issued by neutral, internationally respected firms such as SGS or Bureau Veritas), so that the importer is assured of receiving goods of contract quality/quantity. Government agencies may require inspection certificates as regards price, so as to prevent parties from under– or over–invoicing in an attempt to pay lower customs duties or evade foreign–exchange restrictions.

pro forma invoice – A sample invoice provided by an exporter prior to a sale or shipment of merchandise, informing the buyer of the price, kinds and quantities of goods to be sent, and important specifications (weight, size, and similar characteristics). The pro forma invoice not only acts as the contractual offer (which may be accepted by the importer's transmission of a purchase order), it is intended to be exactly replicated in the final commercial invoice, so that the buyer receives no surprises as regards either the goods or the price. Importers may need a pro forma invoice to be able to apply for an import licence or a foreign exchange permit. In the case of a letter of credit, the pro forma invoice is frequently used to inform the importer of the amount for which the letter of credit has to be opened.

promissory note – An unconditional written promise to pay a specified sum of money on demand or at a specified date to, or to the order of, a specified person, or to the bearer. Promissory notes are negotiable instruments and perform more or less the same function as an accepted bill of exchange.

PSI – *See* pre–shipment inspection.

PSV – Post–shipment verification. *See* pre–shipment inspection.

PU & D – *See* pick up and delivery.

purchasing agent – An agent who purchases goods on behalf of foreign buyers.

R

railway consignment note – A freight document indicating that goods have been received for shipment by rail. *See* bill of lading.

r & cc – Insurance clause: riots and civil commotion; also: srcc – strikes, riots and civil commotion.

red clause L/C – A letter of credit provision allowing the beneficiary to draw partial advance payments under the credit. This provision used to be set out in red ink, therefore the "red clause" designation. Generally, the beneficiary is only required, in order to receive payment of the authorized advances, to present drafts along with a statement that shipping documents will be provided in due time.

reefer box/container/ship – A refrigerated container or ship. Refrigeration may either be mechanical, which means involving an external power supply, or by expendable refrigerant (dry ice, liquefied gases, etc.), which requires no external power supply.

remitting bank – In a documentary collection, the bank forwarding the exporter's documents and the draft to, and receiving payments from, the buyer's bank (collecting bank). *See* documentary collection.

retention of title (reservation of title) clause – A contract clause whereby a seller declares his intention to retain title or ownership over the contract goods until payment by the buyer is complete.

roll–on/roll–off (RoRo) – A combination of road and sea transport, where loaded road vehicles are driven on to a ferry or ship (roll–on/roll–off ship) and off at the port of destination. Major benefits of RoRo are reduced handling of the actual goods and packages, competitive costs for unit loads and scheduled services.

ROT – *See* retention of title.

S

S.A. – abbreviation after names of corporations in French and Spanish–speaking countries: Société Anonyme (Fr.); Sociedad Anonima (Sp.).

SAD – Single Administrative Document; European administrative document for intra–European trade.

S & C – *See* shipper's load and count.

SD – *See* short delivery.

sea waybill – A transport document for maritime shipment which serves as evidence of the contract of carriage and as a receipt for the goods, but is not a document of title. To take delivery of the goods, presentation of the sea waybill is not required; generally, the receiver is only required to identify himself, which can speed up processing at the port of destination. *See* bill of lading.

shipper – In the export trade: the party (as between exporter and importer) who enters into a contract of carriage for the international transport of goods. The party receiving the goods (the importer or buyer) may be called the receiver or the consignee. Depending on the Incoterm chosen, either the exporter or importer (or a middleman) can be the shipper.

shipper's load and count (S & C) – A carrier's notation disclaiming responsibility for the quantity of the cargo's contents; the quantity declared is thus purely the shipper's statement. If there is a dispute because less than contract quantity is delivered, the carrier wishes to be free from liability and the receiver will have to claim directly against the shipper or insurer.

short delivery (SD) also, **short–landed cargo** – Non–delivery of cargo at the intended port. When reported, it will result in the ship's agent sending a cargo tracer to see if the cargo has been mis–delivered to another port.

short–form bill of lading (B/L) – A simplified B/L which contains a reference to or an abbreviation of the carrier's full B/L or carriage conditions.

sight draft (also, sight bill) – A financial instrument payable upon presentation or demand. It must be presented for payment by its holder (payee, endorsee, or bearer) within reasonable time. *See* draft.

specific duty – A duty based on some measure of quantity, such as weight, length, or number of units. *See* customs duty.

spot rate – Rate of exchange quoted for purchases and sales of a foreign currency for immediate delivery and payment.

S & T – Shipper's load and tally. *See* shipper's load and count.

standby credit (also, **standby letter of credit**, **standby L/C**) – A form of guarantee, usually indistinguishable from the demand guarantee. Origin lies in the fact that US legislation prevented US banks from directly issuing guarantees, so they resorted to the device of the "standby credit". In function the standby is usually used more as a security device, like a bank guarantee, rather than as a payment device, like a documentary credit. Under a standby credit the beneficiary usually obtains payment by presentation to a bank of a draft and some form of written demand, which may include a statement that the principal is in breach of his contractual obligations. Standby credits may be issued so as to be governed by either the UCP 500 or the URDG 458 (to the extent permitted by national law). A standby credit can be used to back up a payment commitment – therefore, an exporter may agree to sell on open account terms granting the importer 90–day credit terms on the condition that the importer open a standby credit in the exporter's favour.If the importer fails to honour the exporter's invoices, the exporter simply draws against the standby.

STC (said to contain) / **STW** (said to weigh) – Notations on transport documents by which carriers give notice that they do not wish to accept responsibility for the accuracy of a shipper's declarations as to the content, weight or quantity of a particular shipment. *See* shipper's load and count.

steamer guarantee – *See* letter of indemnity.

stowage – The placing of cargo in a ship's hold in such a fashion so as to assure safe and stable transport.

straight bill of lading – A non–negotiable bill of lading which specifies the consignee to whom the goods are to be delivered. The carrier is contractually obliged to deliver the goods to that person only. It is often used when payment for the goods has been made in advance. *See* bill of lading.

stripping – Unloading goods from a container. *See* devanning and destuffing.

stuffing – Loading goods inside a container.

surcharge – Charges added to ocean freight, variously, for bunker (fuel), currency fluctuation, congestion, port detention or extra risk insurance.

surety/surety–ship bond/guarantee – A surety bond is a guarantee, usually issued by an insurance or surety company, that a particular company will perform according to a contract. In order to collect payment under such a bond, the beneficiary normally must prove actual default on the part of the counterparty, as by furnishing a court judgement, arbitral award or official certificate. Suretyship bonds may be issued subject to the *ICC Uniform Rules for Contract Bonds.*

swap – The trading of almost identical products (such as oil) from different locations to save transportation costs. *See* countertrade.

SWIFT payment – International electronic funds transfer via the system known as SWIFT (Society for Worldwide Inter–bank Financial Telecommunications), offered by most major banks.

T

tare – Weight of packaging/container, without merchandise.

tender bond/guarantee – A guarantee provided by a company responding to an international invitation to submit bids or tenders (as for a large construction project). The tender bond is submitted along with the tender and is required with the purpose of discouraging frivolous bids and ensuring that the winning bidder will actually sign and execute the contract.

terminal handling charge (THC) – Handling charges assessed for services rendered within container terminals or with respect to containers which will be processed through terminals. When delivery or pickup of the goods is expected to be at a container terminal, traders are well advised to stipulate precisely which party will pay for all or part of the terminal handling charges.

TEU – Twenty–foot equivalent units; a means of measuring the carrying capacity of container ships; e.g., a ship can be said to be capable of 3000 TEUs, which is roughly equivalent to saying it could carry 3000 standard containers.

THC – *See* terminal handling charge.

through bill of lading – A B/L issued to cover transport by at least two successive modes of transport.

time draft (**time bill**) – A financial instrument demanding payment at a future fixed date, or a specified period of time after sight (30, 60, 90 days etc.), or after the date of issue. It is also called a usance draft (usance bill). *See* draft.

TIR – TIR Carnets are transport documents used to cover international transport shipments on road vehicles such as trucks/lorries. TIR Carnets, issued pursuant to the 1949 TIR Convention, allow the truck or other vehicle to pass through all TIR–member countries without having to go through customs inspection until reaching the country of destination.

T/L – Total loss.

trade acceptance – A bill of exchange drawn by the seller/exporter on the purchaser/importer of goods sold, and accepted by such purchaser. *See* bill of exchange.

tramp vessel – A "freelance" seagoing cargo vessel, available on a contract basis to carry cargoes to any given port. To be distinguished from liner ships, operating according to advertised routes, schedules and rates.

trimming – The operation of shovelling and spreading, within the ship's hold, dry bulk cargoes such as cement, ore or grains, so as to avoid weight imbalances which might hinder the ship's handling or unloading.

U

UCC – (US) Uniform Commercial Code, the codification of American commercial law, followed in substantially uniform fashion by the US states. Article 5 of the UCC deals with letters of credit.

UCP 500 – *Uniform Customs and Practice for Documentary Credits*, ICC Publication 500, the set of rules which govern international documentary credit practice. UCP 500 are generally considered contractually incorporated into the documentary credit transaction by virtue of a mention in the credit application form; the UCP 500 may also have additional force as a trade custom, and in some countries UCP are even recognized as having legal effect generally. In other countries, the UCP 500 is complementary to national law and jurisprudence on documentary credits.

UNCITRAL (United Nations Commission on International Trade Law) – UN Agency based in Vienna, specializing in the development of model legal instruments and conventions in the area of international trade law. Most notable success is perhaps the so–called 1980 Vienna Convention, the Convention on the International Sale of Goods (CISG). Also, UNCITRAL Rules for Arbitration, which provide a procedural framework for international commercial arbitration but which, unlike the ICC Rules, do not provide direct administrative supervision of the arbitral process.

UNCTAD (United Nations Commission for Trade and Development) – UN Agency based in Geneva, which has developed numerous international instruments as regards trade with developing or transition economies. Notably, UNCTAD houses the ITC (International Trade Centre), a developer of useful guides and manuals for small – to medium–sized exporters.

undercarrier – a carrier which has been subcontracted to carry out part of the transport operation.

unfair calling insurance – Insurance coverage to protect principals who have issued demand guarantees or bonds against an unfair or abusive call of the bond/guarantee (i.e., one which is not truly based on non–performance by the principal).

UNIDROIT (Institute for the Unification of Private Law) – International governmental organization headquartered in Rome. Administrative organization of treaties, conventions, model instruments, legal guides and research.

usance draft (**usance bill**) – Time draft; a written demand for payment which comes due at a specified future date.

V

VAT – Value–added tax.

Vienna Convention – 1980 Vienna Convention on the International Sale of Goods. International treaty signed by approximately 45 nations, including most leading trading nations. Amounts to a virtual commercial code for international sales transactions, but excludes contracts for services, securities, electricity, and some others; parties may be able to "opt out" of coverage by the Vienna Convention by explicitly stating so in the contract of sale.

vostro account – An account held by a bank with its foreign correspondent bank, in the currency of the bank's domestic country.

W

W – tonne of one thousand kilogrammes.

WA – *See* with average.

warehouse receipt (WR) – A document issued by a warehouse operator acknowledging receipt of goods; also referred to as a dock warrant or shed receipt. A warehouse warrant, in contrast, generally connotes a document of ownership/control over goods stored in a particular warehouse.

warehouse–to–warehouse clause – Insurance coverage of international cargo from export warehouse to import warehouse; coverage may also be substantially extended or limited according to time.

waybill (WB) – A non–negotiable transport document, issued for either ocean transport (sea waybill) or air transport (air waybill).

wharfage (WFG) – Charge for the use of docks.

wharfinger – (also Wharf inspector, Wharf superintendent, Dock super–intendent) Personnel in charge of receiving and registering goods in a port on behalf of the carrier. The wharfinger's signature of the shipping note assures the shipper that it can proceed to draw up bills of lading pursuant to the terms of the note.

With Average (WA) – Marine insurance term meaning that coverage includes partial loss (and not just total loss) of the cargo. *See* marine insurance.

World Chambers Federation (WCF) – ICC's specialized division for its chamber of commerce members worldwide. WCF has taken over from the International Bureau of Chambers of Commerce (IBCC). WCF also manages the ATA Carnet System and its guarantee chain for temporary duty–free imports.

World Chambers Network (WCN) – A global internet platform run by the WCF, fostering a comprehensive exchange of business information between chambers and their member companies throughout the world.

World Wide Web (WWW; the web) – A graphics standard that has become a virtual subset of the Internet; organizations, universities and companies maintain presence on the web via "home pages", which are much like animated telephone–book advertisements; the information on the home page may be highlighted (hypertext) in which case the viewer may click on the particular text to obtain access to another data base, home page, or further information.

Worldscale – A scale for quoting freight rates for oil tankers.

WP (w/o p) – Without prejudice.

WPA – With particular average. *See* marine insurance.

WTDR – A US government credit report on a foreign firm.

Index

A

B

C

D

E

F

G

H

I

R

S

T

U

V

W

References and bibliography

General / introductory

■ AXTELL, ROGER E. (1991). *The Do's and Taboos of International Trade: Small Business Primer.* Colorado Springs, CO, USA: John Wiley & Sons.

■ HINKELMAN, EDWARD G. (1994). *Dictionary of International Trade: 4,071 International Trade, Economic, Banking, Legal & Shipping Terms.* San Rafael, CA, USA: World Trade Press.

■ JOHNSON, THOMAS E (2002). *Export/Import: Procedures and Documentation, 4th edition.* New York, NY, USA: AMACOM.

■ LONDON CHAMBER OF COMMERCE & INDUSTRY (1993). *The Export Handbook, A Complete Guide & Reference Source for International Traders.* London, UK: Kogan Page Ltd.

■ MORRIS, MAG (1991). *Importing for the Small Business, 2nd edition.* London, UK: Kogan Page Ltd.

■ NELSON, CARL A. (2001). *Import/Export: How to Get Started in International Trade, 3rd edition.* New York, NY, USA: McGraw Hill, Inc.

■ REYNOLDS, FRANK (2002). *A to Z of International Trade.* New York and Paris: ICC Publishing.

■ REYNOLDS, FRANK (1996). *Export Documentation, Procedures and Terms of Sale, 2nd edition.* New Providence, NJ, USA: Unz & Co.

■ UNITED NATIONS (1994). *Recommendations and Guidelines for Trade Efficiency.* New York & Geneva: United Nations.

■ UNITED NATIONS (1993). *Small– and Medium-sized Transnational Corporations: Role, Impact and Policy Implications.* New York, NY, USA: United Nations.

■ US DEPARTMENT OF COMMERCE (1998). *A Basic Guide to Exporting.* Lincolnwood, Illinois, US: NTC Business Books.

■ WILSON, DONALD, ET AL. (2000). *International Business Transactions in a Nutshell, 6th edition.* St Paul, Minnesota, USA: West Publishing Company.

■ WRIGHT, MAURICE (1995). *Build Up Your Exports.* Milton Keynes, UK: Tate Publishing Ltd.

French

■ NICOLE FERRY (1988). *Comment Négocier les Achats et les Ventes à l'Etranger 2ème edition.* Editions du Moniteur, Paris, France.

■ ANDRÉ GUYOMAR & ETIENNE MORIN (1995). *Commerce International, 2nd edition*. Editions Dalloz, 11, rue Soufflot, 75240 Paris Cedex 05, France.

■ BARRELIER, DUBOIN, DUPHIL, CONTAL, GRATALOUP, KUHN, LEVY, PAVEAU, SARHAN (1992). *Exporter, Pratique du Commerce International, 9th edition*. Editions Foucher, France.

Marketing and management

■ INTERNATIONAL TRADE CENTRE UNCTAD/GATT (1992). *Export Marketing Strategies and Plans, A Case Book for Trainers*. Geneva, Switzerland.

Spanish

■ OEA, CICOM (1993). *Proyectos de Exportacion y Estrategias de Marketing Internacional*. Buenos Aires, Argentina: Ediciones MACCHI.

Legal aspects

■ AUGUST, RAY (2000). *International Business Law – Text, Cases, and Readings, 3rd edition*. New Jersey, USA: Prentice Hall.

■ DEBATTISTA, CHARLES (1998). *Sale of Goods Carried by Sea, 2nd edition*. London, UK: Butterworths.

■ FOX, WILLIAM F. (1992). *International Commercial Agreements: A Primer on Drafting, Negotiating and Resolving Disputes, 2nd Edition*. The Hague, Netherlands: Kluwer Law International.

■ GOODE, ROY (1995). *Commercial Law, 2nd Edition*. London, UK: Penguin Books.

■ INTERNATIONAL INSTITUTE FOR THE UNIFICATION OF PRIVATE LAW (UNIDROIT) (1994). *Principles of International Commercial Contracts*. Rome, Italy: International Institute for the Unification of Private Law.

■ SCHMITTHOFF, CLIVE M. (2000). *Schmitthoff's Export Trade, 10th edition*. London, UK: Sweet & Maxwell.

■ VAN HOUTTE, HANS (2001). *The Law of International Trade, 2nd edition*. London, UK: Sweet & Maxwell.

French

■ PUTZEYS, JACQUES (1992). *Les Ventes internationales et les transports – les nouveaux Incoterms*. Louvain, France: Bruylant (PEDASUP).

Spanish

■ COLAIACOVO, JUAN LUIS, OEA, CICOM (1992). *Negociacion y Contratacion Internacional*. Buenos Aires, Argentina: Ediciones Macchi.

Arbitration

- CRAIG, LAURENCE W., PARK, WILLIAM AND PAULSSON, JAN (2000). *International Chamber of Commerce Arbitration,3rd edition*. New York and London: Oceana Publications; New York and Paris: ICC Publishing.

Agency, distributorship, franchising, licensing

- BOGAERT, GEERT AND LOHMANN, ULRICH (2000). *Commercial Agency and Distribution Agreements: Law and Practice of the Member States of the European Union*, 3rd *edition*. The Hague, Netherlands: Kluwer Law International.
- BORTOLOTTI, F, ET AL. (1993). *The ICC Agency Model Contract, A Commentary*. The Hague, Netherlands: Kluwer Law International.
- CAMPBELL, DENNIS AND GRAMATIDIS, YANOS, EDS (1991). *International Franchising: an In-depth Treatment of Business and Legal Techniques*. The Hague, Netherlands: Kluwer Law International.
- CHRISTOU, RICHARD (1996). *International Agency, Distribution and Licensing Agreements, 3rd edition*. London, UK: Sweet & Maxwell.
- WHITE, EDWARD P. (1990). *Licensing, a Strategy for Profits*. Chapel Hill, USA: KEW Licensing Press.

Trade finance / documentary credits

- DOLAN, JOHN F. (1996). *The Law of Letters of Credit, Commercial and Standby Credits, Revised Edition*. Washington D.C., USA: A.S. Pratt & Sons.
- DUNFORD, CAMPBELL, ED. (1991). *The Handbook of International Trade Finance*. Cambridge, UK: Woodhead-Faulkner Ltd.
- JAHN, UWE (1999). Bills *of Exchange: A Guide to Legislation in European Countries, Asia and Oceana, 3rd edition*. New York and Paris: ICC Publishing.
- TODD, PAUL (1998). *Bills of Lading and Bankers' Documentary Credits, 3rd Edition*. Colchester, UK: LLP Professional Publishing.
- WATSON, ALASDAIR (1997). *Finance of International Trade, 6th Edition*. London, UK: Financial World Publishing.
- WEST MERCHANT BANK (1995). *Project and Trade Finance 1995 Handbook*. London, UK: Euromoney Publications.

Understanding documentary bills and credits: a practical Guide for

French

- CHEVALIER, DENIS (1990). *Le Crédit documentaire et autres sécurités de paiement*. Paris, France: Editions Foucher.
- LARDINOIS, JACQUES (1993). *Gestion du crédit commercial à l'exportation*. Paris, France: Lavoisier.

Guarantees, bonds and standby credits

- BERTRAMS, R (1996). *Bank Guarantees in International Trade, 2nd edition*. The Hague, Netherlands: Kluwer Law International; Paris, France: ICC Publishing.
- PIERCE, ANTHONY (1993). *Demand Guarantees in International Trade*. London, UK: Sweet & Maxwell.

Incoterms

- LUTTMER, GERHARD AND WINKLER , KLAUS (1991). *Trade Terms and Marine Cargo Insurance, 2nd edition*. Germany: Gerling-Konzern.
- REYNOLDS, FRANK (2000). *Incoterms for Americans*, 2nd Edition. Ohio, US: International Projects, Inc.
- SASSOON, DAVID M. (1995). *C.I.F. & F.O.B. Contracts, 4th Edition*. London, UK: Sweet & Maxwell.

Shipping and transport

- FIATA. *Customs Clearance Manual (FCCM)*. Zurich, Switzerland: International Federation of Freight Forwarders Associations (FIATA).
- HARDY IVAMY, E.R. (1989). *Carriage of Goods by Sea, 13th edition*. London, UK: Butterworths.
- INTERNATIONAL TRADE CENTRE UNCTAD (1998). *Manual on the Physical Distribution of Export Goods Volume II*. Geneva, Switzerland: International Trade Centre UNCTAD/GATT.
- JONES, PETER (1993). *Legal Handbook on Forwarding, 2nd edition*. Zurich, Switzerland: International Federation of Freight Forwarders Associations (FIATA).
- RAMBERG , JAN (1992). *The Law of Freight Forwarding and the 1992 FIATA Multimodal Transport Bill of Lading*. Zurich, Switzerland: International Federation of Freight Forwarders Association (FIATA).

French

- CHEVALIER, D. AND DUPHIL, F. (2000). *Le transport, 2ᵉᵐᵉ* édition. Paris, France: Editions Foucher.

Export forms

- SITPRO. *Export Forms*. London, UK: SITPRO.
- UNZ & CO. *Export Forms*. New Jersey, USA: Unz & Co.

Electronic commerce

- FINGAR, PETER (2000). *Enterprise E-Commerce: The Software Component Breakthrough for Business-to-Business Commerce.* Tampa, FLA, USA: Meghan-Kiffer Press.
- KALAKOTA, DR. RAVI (1999). *e-Business: Roadmap for Success.* Reading, MA, USA: Addison Wesley Longman, Inc.
- ROCKWELL, BROWNING (1998). *Using the Web to Compete in a Global Marketplace.* New York, NY, USA: John Wiley & Sons.
- SILVERSTEIN, BARRY (1998). *Business-to-Business Internet Marketing.* Gulf Breeze, FLA, USA: Maximum Press.

International organizations

Organizations	Web sites
International Container Bureau (BIC)	www.bic-code.org
Baltic and International Maritime Council (BIMCO)	www.bimco.dk
Hague Conference on Private International Law	www.hcch.net
Institute of International Container Lessors (ICL)	www.iicl.org
International Air Transport Association (IATA)	www.iata.org
International Association of Ports and Harbours (IAPH)	www.iaphworldports.org
International Bar Association (IBA)	www.ibanet.org
International Cargo Handling Coordination Association (ICHA)	www.ichca.org.uk
International Chamber of Commerce (ICC)	www.iccwbo.org
International Chamber of Shipping (ICS)	www.marisec.org
International Civil Aviation Organization (ICAO)	www.icao.org
International Federation of Freight Forwarders Associations (FIATA)	www.fiata.com
International Financial Statistics	lwww.imf.org/external/map.htm
International Institute for the Unification of Private Law (UNIDROIT)	www.unidroit.org
International Maritime Organization (IMO)	www.imo.org
International Road Transport Union (IRU)	www.iru.org

Organizations	Web sites
International Ship Suppliers Association (ISSA)	www.shipsupply.org
International Trade Centre	www.intracen.org
Internet Society	www.isoc.org
Society for Worldwide Interbank Financial Telecommunications (SWIFT)	www.swift.com
United Nations Commission on International Trade Law (UNCITRAL)	www.uncitral.org
World Customs Organization (WCO)	www.wcoomd.org
World Trade Organization (WTO)	www.wto.org

ICC at a glance

ICC is the world business organization. It is the only representative body that speaks with authority on behalf of enterprises from all sectors in every part of the world.

ICC's purpose is to promote an open international trade and investment system and the market economy worldwide. It makes rules that govern the conduct of business across borders. It provides essential services, foremost among them the ICC International Court of Arbitration, the world's leading institution of its kind.

Within a year of the creation of the United Nations, ICC was granted consultative status at the highest level with the UN and its specialized agencies. Today ICC is the preferred partner of international and regional organizations whenever decisions have to be made on global issues of importance to business.

Business leaders and experts drawn from ICC membership establish the business stance on broad issues of trade and investment policy as well as on vital technical or sectoral subjects. These include financial services, information technologies, telecommunications, marketing ethics, the environment, transportation, competition law and intellectual property, among others.

ICC was founded in 1919 by a handful of far-sighted business leaders. Today it groups thousands of member companies and associations from over 130 countries. National committees in all major capitals coordinate with their membership to address the concerns of the business community and to put across to their governments the business views formulated by ICC.

Some ICC Services

- The ICC International Court of Arbitration (Paris)
- The ICC International Centre for Expertise (Paris)
- The ICC World Chambers Federation (Paris)
- The ICC Institute of World Business Law (Paris)
- The ICC Centre for Maritime Co-operation (London)

- ICC Commercial Crime Services (London), grouping:
  - The ICC Counterfeiting Intelligence Bureau
  - The ICC Commercial Crime Bureau
  - The ICC International Maritime Bureau

ICC Publishing

ICC Publishing, the publishing subsidiary of ICC, produces and sells the works of ICC commissions and experts as well as guides and corporate handbooks on a range of business topics. Some 100 titles – designed for anyone interested in international trade – are available from ICC Publishing.

> For more detailed information on ICC publications and on the above-listed activities, and to receive the programme of ICC events, please contact ICC Headquarters in Paris or the ICC national committee in your country.

How to become member of ICC

There are two possible ways of becoming a member of the International Chamber of Commerce: either through (1) affiliation with an ICC national committee or group or through (2) direct membership where no national committee or group exists.

HOW TO OBTAIN ICC PUBLICATIONS

ICC Publications are available from ICC national committees or councils which exist in some 60 countries or from:

ICC PUBLISHING S.A.
38, Cours Albert 1er
75008 Paris – France
Customer Service:
Tel: +33 1.49.53.29.23/28.89
Fax: +33 1.49.53.29.02
e-mail: pub@iccwbo.org

ICC PUBLISHING, INC.
156 Fifth Avenue, Suite 417
New York, NY 10010
USA
Tel: +1 (212) 206 1150
Fax: +1 (212) 633 6025
e-mail: info@iccpub.net

Visit **www.iccbooksusa.com**

NOTES

NOTES

NOTES

NOTES

NOTES

NOTES